Political Peda

Series Editors
Jamie Frueh
Bridgewater College
Bridgewater, VA, USA

David J. Hornsby
The Norman Paterson School of International Affairs
Carleton University
Ottawa, Canada

The purpose of the series is to create a new space for conversations between scholars of political pedagogy, and between such scholars and those looking for guidance on their teaching, and become the main recognizable authority/series/conversational space in this field. The proliferation of journals, conferences, and workshops devoted to teaching attest to the accelerating interest in the pedagogy of Political Science and International Relations over the past two decades. While research scholarship remains the dominant criterion for hiring and promotion at top tier institutions, almost all academics in these disciplines spend most of their energy teaching, and more than two-thirds do so at institutions where effective teaching is the primary factor in career success (Ishiyama et al 2010). Even those at research-intensive positions benefit from more effective classroom environments, and institutions across the world are building centers devoted to improving teaching and learning. The challenges of teaching span sub-disciplines and connect disparate scholars in a common conversation. Indeed, teaching may be the only focus that academics in these disciplines truly share. Currently, most writing about teaching politics is published in journals, and is therefore dispersed and restricted in length. This series will provide a much needed platform for longer, more engaged contributions on Political Pedagogies, as well as serve to bring teaching and research in conversation with each other.

More information about this series at
http://www.palgrave.com/gp/series/16526

Jamie Frueh
Editor

Pedagogical Journeys through World Politics

palgrave
macmillan

Editor
Jamie Frueh
Center for Engaged Learning
Bridgewater College
Bridgewater, VA, USA

ISSN 2662-7809   ISSN 2662-7817   (electronic)
Political Pedagogies
ISBN 978-3-030-20304-7   ISBN 978-3-030-20305-4   (eBook)
https://doi.org/10.1007/978-3-030-20305-4

Cover design by eStudio Calamar

This Palgrave Macmillan imprint is published by the registered company Springer Nature Switzerland AG
The registered company address is: Gewerbestrasse 11, 6330 Cham, Switzerland

*For my parents, who taught me that I am an agent
who can make a difference,
for Eileen, my co-agent,
and for Wren and Gavin, who inspired me to keep at it.*

FOREWORD: (UN)INTENTIONAL PEDAGOGY

Most college teachers of my generation, and perhaps many since, were offered no formal instruction and little guidance about how to teach. From my vantage point, I think the assumption was that you have a bunch of really smart people in graduate school and that they'll figure it out when the time comes. Let's face it: studying for a PhD in pretty much any field of study is primarily focused on research training. You first learn the basic arguments and structuring theories of your field, spend time in seminars critiquing them, and then end up in research seminars or working with your mentors to move toward publishable research. That's the basic path to advancement in graduate school and, presumably, through much of an academic career.

The reality, though, is that the vast majority of people who seek a PhD will end up working at a college or university where teaching undergraduates is the primary focus of the faculty position. So why don't graduate programs do a better job (or in some cases any job at all) of training PhD students to teach? The cynic in me argues that this is because most PhD programs (or perhaps PhD advisors) don't want to admit that most of their brilliant students at their august universities are not going to end up with top-tier research university faculty positions. Even when I'm not being cynical, I think there's a fair amount of truth there. I also believe that the lack of attention to pedagogical training stems from the fact that my generation of mentors didn't have any either. Graduate programs are conservative institutions that don't adapt easily or willingly. The same can be said for the large share of faculty who populate program faculties.

For whatever reason, this lack of attention to pedagogical training began to change in the 1980s and 1990s, but not primarily at the program level. Rather, universities started creating institutional teaching and learning centers, and some foundations, like the Pew Charitable Trusts, made significant investments to create programs for faculty to learn and hone their pedagogical approaches in structured, innovative ways. We now find teaching centers across most of higher education.

Despite these resources, most of us still have to figure out on our own how to teach. To provide some inspiration on your own adventure, the essays in this volume describe personal journeys through pedagogical development. They reflect the extraordinary creativity that so many of our colleagues express in the ways they interact (and struggle) with the students in their classrooms. As you would expect from essays about creativity, there are striking differences between the journeys. And yet some bear similarities to my own (un)intentional path to becoming an intentional teacher.

I had the enormous good fortune of arriving at the University of Maryland for graduate work in August 1983, just as Jon Wilkenfeld was getting Project ICONS off the ground. ICONS was the first large-scale, global use of communications technologies to teach international negotiation and diplomacy across multiple universities using a computer-assisted simulation approach. I was assigned to Jon as a graduate assistant and was immediately immersed in helping to run ICONS at the college level (in its first iteration). I led a country-team comprised of undergraduates in the simulation environment each of my first few semesters at Maryland. So right from the start of my academic career, I had the opportunity to observe innovative pedagogy in action, even if I had little clue how innovative ICONS really was or how one might define innovative pedagogy.

Prior to Maryland, I also had the privilege of watching several terrific scholar-teachers in action as an undergrad at Wittenberg University. Dick Flickinger, Gerry Hudson, and others drew me into how they engaged their students, challenged them, and made the classroom a place of excitement and exploration. Little did I know as an undergrad or during my first year at Maryland just how challenging and complex teaching is.

I experienced it intimately my first summer in Maryland. Early in my second semester at Maryland, my office mate told me that she had heard that the department was having trouble finding someone to teach American foreign policy for the upcoming summer session. She suggested (perhaps jokingly) that maybe I should ask to teach it. So I went somewhat gingerly to see Kay Kline, the department's main administrator and the person who controlled pretty much everything of importance in the department, to plead my case for teaching the summer course. By then she knew me well enough at a personal level (we had bonded over how to brew good tea), but knew little about my intellectual credentials, except that I was in my first year and all of 22 years old. So she asked me if I could teach American foreign policy and I immediately answered with "Of course. That's the only thing I would feel comfortable teaching right now." She said she'd think about it (I'm sure she checked with Jon, Dave Bobrow, and some others) and about a week later told me that the course was mine. Wow! That was easy!

I then went back to look at Dick Flickinger's syllabus from Wittenberg, got ahold of the one Dave Bobrow was using at Maryland, and set about to develop a course of my own (sort of). I ordered the same books that Dick had used at Wittenberg (Nathan & Oliver, as I recall) and added in many of the Dave's selected conceptual readings about the philosophical framework of American foreign policy. The course was scheduled for two evenings per week for three hours each night across six weeks in June and July.

So I was more than ready when I arrived at the first-class session. We talked about frameworks, themes, and philosophy: isolationism, exceptionalism, the Monroe Doctrine, and a good deal more during those first three hours. I was feeling *really* good when I got home that night and told my wife how great that first class had gone. This was easy! The next day, I set about preparing for the second session. I prepared for a similar class— a fair amount of lecture, a little bit of discussion, copious notes for the lectern—pretty standard stuff in those days.

The second-class session arrived and I got going with the material I had prepared. But this time, with only 45 minutes gone in the three-hour session, I was completely done with ALL that material I had prepared for that evening. I was stunned. I took a moment to get my bearings and told the students that we had gotten through all the planned material for the day and that I would see them next week. I was embarrassed and quite worried that someone would report me for doing a lousy job (even though nobody did). What I didn't realize at the time was that these students were almost entirely non-traditional students, who had already spent a long day at a job and were likely exhausted and happy to get home early anyway. But at the time, that recognition wouldn't have helped me much.

Obviously, 35 years in hindsight, this was a seminal experience in my life as a scholar-teacher. I had been baptized by the fire of classroom silence. I learned quickly and indelibly that I not only had to worry about *what* I was teaching, but perhaps more importantly, *how* I was teaching it. I spent the next few days talking to my grad school friends about how to structure the class so my 45-minute debacle would not happen again. (I don't recall talking with those who I now consider my mentors, as I was far too embarrassed about my second session failure.) From those discussions, it was clear that I had to start thinking about how best to engage students in their learning. Fortunately, I had had some really great examples to watch at both the undergrad and graduate levels, and that's where I started.

Over that weekend, I started very consciously building discussion questions into the plan for each evening. Luckily for me, it was a talkative group. And I also integrated into a decision-making exercise that Dick Flickinger had run at Wittenberg and some other exercises (what I now know as role-playing simulations or problem-based learning exercises) to vary the instructional styles across the three hours each night. I also found out that doing things right meant devoting most of a day to prepare for a single evening session to go well. And the rest of the course did go rather well, or at least a lot better than the second session did.

As my graduate career progressed, I also had the opportunity to teach introduction to IR and comparative foreign policy (the course where ICONS was embedded in the University of Maryland's curriculum), which gave me a few more opportunities to refine my repertoire of courses prior to entering the job market in 1987. But that first course truly shaped my classroom experience and has kept me mindful of substance, structure, and method ever since.

This is not to say that I have not grown and learned from other experiences, but this one certainly shaped the foundations of what I do. Along these lines, when I entered the job market, my experience with ICONS was a point of recurring discussion on campus interviews. Jon had developed a cutting edge instructional project and lots of schools were interested in my ability to bring them into this new digital age (remember that I was first on the job market in 1987, so we were really cutting edge in the pre-internet instructional landscape).

I was able to adapt ICONS a few years later and used it to help me gain a Pew Faculty Fellowship in International Affairs at Harvard. I was a member of the third of the five Pew classes that the fellowship conducted.

Through the Harvard-Pew training and the ever-kind, though sometimes quite pointed, tutelage of John Boehrer, I learned the case method, integrated it into several of classes (including my ICONS-focused class on negotiation and bargaining), and started to become much more conscious of the nuances of good teaching. How do you shape a classroom discussion? How do you give up overt control, let students drive a discussion and the analysis, without really giving up classroom control? Through the Pew training and many hours of practice (by "doing" in the classroom, of course), I became more attuned to patterns of participation amongst students (focusing on gender dynamics, personality types, diversity issues, and much more). I became rather adept at thinking on my feet, especially when a class wasn't going as I had planned. I became more self-reflective about my strengths and weaknesses as a scholar-teacher. And for those who know me at all, being self-reflective is not one of my innate strengths. So that was real growth!

That reflective, growth-oriented attitude has continued to serve me well throughout my career. For example, I have never been a nuanced theoretical teacher. Unlike my friend Jennifer Sterling-Folker, who excels at such approaches, I have always struggled with getting students to grapple with theory in fundamental ways. But in the late 1990s, I began to recognize that I was rather skilled at taking concrete applications of theory and helping students understand the nexus of theory and practice. In this way, I could show my students how theory manifests itself the real world, even if I wasn't as strong at teasing out the differences between neoclassical realism and neorealism (and frankly, I didn't care all that much about those distinctions...sorry Jennifer). Little did I know at first that what I was doing was problem-based learning until a long-time friend from our school of education told me so. The point to take away from this is that by confronting my shortcomings as a teacher of theory, I eventually found a way to do theory with my students that engaged them and played to my own strengths. I'm sure that most of us have adapted to such challenges in our own settings and it's crucial to do so for effective classroom engagement.

In the end, I suspect that my own story of (un)intentional pedagogy is likely more the rule than the exception amongst college teachers outside of schools of education in the United States, or for that matter throughout most of the academic world. As you'll see in the essays in this volume, every scholar-teacher struggles: to find some sort of balance between telling students what they should know and letting them learn on their own;

to engage students in the stories and the puzzles that drew the teachers into academics in the first place; to generate enthusiasm (and perhaps activism) about the burning questions of the day. In the essays that follow, you will hear how teachers like you have struggled with intellectual content and the challenge of getting past one's own political beliefs while helping students critically understand what they are observing in the world. But you will also see the fundamental creativity we bring to the adventure of teaching.

That urge for creativity brings me to my last point for this foreword. Over the past 20 years, our field has witnessed the legitimization of the scholarship of pedagogy as a valid form of professional development and achievement. Journals like *PS* have been around for many years, but since 2000, *International Studies Perspectives*, the *Journal of Political Science Education*, and others have emerged as rigorous peer-reviewed forums for the dissemination of our creativity as scholar-teachers. Their development has also shown the growth of attention to other facets of our educational endeavors—assessment, curriculum development, and much more. And of course, these forums have allowed us to more easily capitalize on the good, creative work of our peers to engage an ever-changing cohort of college students. My involvement in cutting edge technological applications in the international studies classroom with Jon Wilkenfeld in the 1980s looks rather archaic now, but it taught me that I have to evolve in this (often too) fast-paced informational landscape within which my students operate so effortlessly.

Reading these essays was a wonderfully uplifting exercise for me and showed me how many gifted colleagues we have in our field. I encourage you to read each one, learn from it, and think about how you might be able to take something away that will further enrich the educational experience that you provide for your students. I challenge you to ponder your creative edge in the classroom. And when you've done that, please consider taking your creativity and putting that work out there for review so that we can all enjoy and learn from the best classroom practices being used today. I also urge you to consider how you might actually have the greatest impact on our field. Will that impact come from writing the next treatise on realism, causes of war or UN voting patterns? Or might it come from something you've done in the classroom to challenge the next generation of citizens and decision-makers as they look at the world around them and seek to affect positive change in the world? I would argue strongly that it is much more likely to be the latter. If only every student at every university were required to take a challenging and creative introductory international studies course, maybe we wouldn't be in as many global messes as we are in today. Enjoy the essays that follow. I know I did and want to thank Jamie Frueh most heartily for shepherding this project to publication.

University of Connecticut   Mark A. Boyer
Storrs, CT, USA

PREFACE

If you have picked up this volume, you are almost certainly a nerd, like us. As nerds, we spend a good deal of time reading, thinking, and negotiating about arcane details that most people find trivial, incomprehensible, and/or tedious. We traffic in the claim that we know important things that others don't, that we will continue to uncover important things at least somebody should know, and that such services are rare and valuable enough to be worthy of significant compensation. But the transactional value of what most of us know and discover is fairly marginal. Indeed, most of us keep the lights on not by unraveling knotty truths or solving practical problems, but by selling explanations of our knowledge, and often to people who have to be convinced of its value. For a price, we are willing to explain what we know and why listeners will be better off if they know it too. Among nerds, getting paid to explain things to non-nerds is not quite as prestigious as selling books that excite other nerds, but it is a pretty good way to make a living.

Even if we possess a certain natural predilection toward knowledge and explanations, most of us who find our way into academia can point to a particular teacher who is responsible for making us think of professing as a viable profession. Mine is Otto Hentz. I took Otto's "Problem of God" course during my junior year of college. I took the course at exactly the right moment in my life, but that in no way diminishes the brilliance of Otto's teaching or what it did for me. His teaching challenged me to think both systematically and creatively, and demanded that I respectfully attend to a wide variety of thinkers who had done the same. He showed me why their questions might interest me, and how their answers were so much more than just different from the ones I thought I knew. He taught me to use "How could anybody think that?" as a question of genuine curiosity rather than as a statement of derision. Every day Otto came into class excited, open to both questions and unexpected rabbit holes, passionate about the subject, and genuinely interested in what I might have to say. He was empowering and respectful, and he convinced me to chase my ideas with both confidence and skepticism. In his class, I remember not just experiencing, but labeling and deciding I was addicted to the rush that comes when an idea comes together. I didn't just have ideas; I created and owned them. In the years since, I have become a connoisseur of that rush. Otto made college about ideas, and I haven't been able to see a college course any other way since.

And Otto did this all without making the experience about him, although clearly, I have given him credit for it, so much so that the previous paragraph sounds less like I took his class and more like I imprinted upon him. I'm OK with that. Otto is a nerd's nerd—he knows and loves his stuff. But I got so much more than knowledge from the experience. I caught nerdiness. Anyone who knew me in high school knows that I was predisposed to nerdiness from a young age, and if I wasn't yet a nerd, I sure played the role well enough to fool a lot of people. But as I look back now, I think I was just practicing, and that my proto-nerdness didn't really mature until it was an informed choice. I credit Otto with teaching me not just the joys of being a nerd, but that teachers can inspire students to choose nerdness. I have decided that spreading nerdness is a great way to pay that forward.

The best way to create nerds of all types is to engage students the way Otto engaged me—with passion, respect, curiosity, confidence, and skepticism. For some students, the subject matter will inspire engagement. Others can be motivated by connections to past experiences or future lives and careers. Some just want to be entertained or to make sense of some event they heard about. Some will be immune to everything we try. But all of us (teachers included) seek engagement, the feeling that comes from being present and invested in a task, not in spite of, but because it is challenging. Engagement generates attentive curiosity, creativity, ownership, surprise, and even confusion. Undergraduate courses should maximize engagement by creating environments in which students can choose to become agents of their own understanding. Every fall, high schools send us people who have been taught that education is about simplifying the world so it fits into one of those little ovals on an answer sheet. Our job is to help them experience the rush of engaging with complexity, and expose them to nerdness. The project of creating learning environments has all of the elements of a good challenge, and thus of engagement.

This volume exists because these authors were willing to narrate their identities, in public, for the purpose of helping others make sense of what it means to be a teacher of global politics. As you will see, in many cases, their commitment to that mission (ultimately to you, dear reader) comes at the cost of sharing descriptions of themselves (past/present) that would normally not come up in a conference panel or cocktail reception. They invested their selves in these chapters in a way that "the discipline" usually considers "unprofessional." They did so in hopes that their stories could help others find shortcuts, that recalling the confusion, frustration, and self-doubt of stepping in to lead a class without training or sometimes even without any good advice would help readers feel both less alone and more empowered. The project originated in sympathy, and in a belief that the discipline's neglect of pedagogical training perpetuates unnecessary suffering by academics and the students they teach. Those of us involved in the project think we are serving both global politics as a field of knowledge and the societies into which our students will graduate, hopefully, more thoughtful and prepared as a result of encounters with global political nerdness. We think you can do that too.

Bridgewater, VA, USA   Jamie Frueh

ACKNOWLEDGMENTS

Acknowledgments are like Oscar speeches; unless the comments are outrageously political, or the acknowledger seems drunk, or there is a wardrobe malfunction, they do not usually make much news. But they are important to acknowledgers, who want everyone to know that the accomplishments are not really theirs alone, and to the people thanked, who get to hear in a public way that they contributed to a celebrated feat. Despite knowing that everything is outrageously political, despite being sober and fully clothed, and despite the lack of an orchestra to let me know when my 45 seconds are up, there are people I'd like to thank.

The first thanks go to the authors who bought into this idea and whose stories are this book. Each of you 22 courageously agreed to share what amounts to pieces of yourselves to make this project real. As readers encounter what you have shared, and ponder what their reactions might mean for their own teaching, it will be obvious to everyone that it is an honor for me to be associated with the journeys of such fine colleagues. Your narratives have repeatedly sparked cascades of thoughts for me, and my interactions with you over the two years (!) it took for this to come together have been among the most fulfilling of my IR career. I have changed my teaching because of my encounters with your narratives. My students thank you too.

In academia, we are lucky enough not to have bosses, per se. Oh, there are people who can fire us, and people who make us do things we otherwise wouldn't. But academics (especially academics with tenure) are generally entrusted with autonomy that other employees covet. I have been lucky to work for some great administrators who build environments at

Bridgewater College conducive to teaching, and who invited me to contribute to that mission: my first BC president, Phil Stone; my current president, David Bushman; Dean Art Hessler; Dean Carol Scheppard; and (after a title change) Provost Leona Sevick. All of you have supported me over the decade and a half I have been working on my teaching here at Bridgewater. You have empowered my creative impulses and made me feel like I could make a difference. Your approach has given me the confidence to take that same approach with my students.

My fellow Division Heads—Betsy Hayes, Barbara Long, Jeff Pierson, and Phil Spickler—and I moved into administration together, and I can't imagine a better way to do it. It is a genuine luxury to have you to make stuff up with. We have built a space in which it is OK to try ideas on for size because I can be wrong and you will not only tell me before I do something stupid, but help me figure out a much better way. I especially want to thank Betsy, who is mostly responsible for the fact that the projects that continue to come out of Academic Citizenship have actually changed Bridgewater's culture. Our work together has made a difference.

This project grew out of insecurity—never feeling like I had enough time to come up with something important to say at ISA conferences, or more accurately, enough time to frame ideas the way they needed to be framed to make a dent. But I have been lucky to find a group of friends who would listen to me anyway, even when I was shouting. Some of those people contributed essays in the book, but I also want to thank Harry Gould (who was on the panel when I presented my first conference paper in Roanoke, VA twenty-three years ago), Jack Amoureux and Mauro Caraccioli. You guys keep acting as if I have something to say, and so I thought I must. Extra special thanks to my fellow Iowans Jeremy Youde and Brent J. Steele for exploring the pedagogical insights of constructivism with me. It was a panel presentation for Brent and Harry's Tactical Constructivism project in 2015 that led to a book chapter written with Jeremy and a compliment from Melody Herr that made me think it was high time for people to recognize the pedagogical power inherent in IR. And I wouldn't have had much to say unless Harry, Jessica Auchter, Daniel Levine, Jennifer Lobasz, and the rest of the ISA Northeast Governing Council hadn't decided to give me the reins of a new pedagogy workshop. Thanks to you all for the opportunity.

Thanks also to Anca Pusca. You listened to an unscheduled, discombobulated, distracted, half-pitch for this book in November 2016, and didn't toss me out on my ear. Your honest encouragement throughout the process made this book possible. Thanks for taking a chance.

This book is dedicated to my family. Mom and Dad, I have always felt your love, even though I can't seem to get a job in Iowa. Eileen, my partner and my love, you know me. You chide and plan and handle the important stuff and call me on working too hard. Thanks for more than three decades of ironwood tree love. Wren, you made me a dad, a persona I love as much as your independence, courage, and strength. Gavin, you are a lot like me, only smarter, better looking, and more balanced. Who doesn't love you? Thank you all for your love, the foundations upon which creative enterprises are built.

Oh, and I'd like to thank the real academy.

CONTENTS

IDENTIFYING KEYWORDS FOR AUTHORS AND THEIR INSTITUTIONS

In addition to a biographical sketch, keywords are provided so that readers can chart their own way through the chapters.

J. Samuel Barkin, University of Massachusetts Boston, USA
Chapter 20: Strategies of a Boring Teacher
J. Samuel Barkin is a professor in the Global Governance and Human Security program at the University of Massachusetts Boston. His research is in the areas of international relations theory and epistemology, international organization and sovereignty, and global environmental politics.
Current institution: large public research university
Typical classroom setting: classes ranging from 6 to 300
Typical pedagogical approach: pedagogical approaches vary with class sizes, levels, and topics
Disciplinary identity: International Relations Theory, International Organization, Environmental Politics

David L. Blaney, Macalister College, USA
Chapter 8: Teaching in Capitalist Ruins
David L. Blaney, Professor of Political Science, Macalester College, works on colonialism and political economic thought. With Naeem Inayatullah, he has written *International Relations and the Problem of Difference* (Routledge, 2004) and *Savage Economics: Wealth, Poverty, and the Temporal Walls of Capitalism* (Routledge, 2010). Currently, he works on neoclassical economics.

Current institution: private liberal arts college
Typical classroom setting: small classes, never larger than 20 students
Typical pedagogical approach: reading, writing, discussion
Disciplinary identity: international relations and political theory

Mark A. Boyer, University of Connecticut, USA
Foreword: (Un)Intentional Pedagogy
Dr. Boyer is a Board of Trustees Distinguished Professor at the University of Connecticut and serves as Executive Director of the International Studies Association (www.isanet.org). As a scholar-teacher, he has actively sought the integration of teaching, research, and service in all his professional activities.

Jacqui de Matos-Ala, University of the Witswatersrand, South Africa
Chapter 15: My Metamorphoses as an International Relations Teacher
Jacqui de Matos-Ala is currently a senior lecturer in International Relations at the University of the Witwatersrand, South Africa. Her primary research interest is IR pedagogy, specifically investigating the incorporation of indigenous knowledge within IR theory curricula in the global South. Jacqui was a recipient of the Wits 2001 Vice-Chancellors Team Teaching Award.
Current institution: partially government-subsidized university
Typical classroom setting: large classes and seminar groups
Typical pedagogical approach: facilitating deep learning approaches; peer learning; reading and writing rich environments and critical engagement
Disciplinary identity: joint academic qualifications in IR and Higher Education pedagogy. Interests in the decolonization of knowledge in IR in general and IR pedagogy in particular; gender and race perspectives for the Global South and teaching and learning practices in IR

Paul F. Diehl, University of Texas-Dallas, USA
Chapter 17: An Individual Odyssey in Teaching International Relations
Paul F. Diehl is Associate Provost, Ashbel Smith Professor of Political Science, and Director of the Center for Teaching and Learning at the University of Texas-Dallas. Previously, he was Henning Larsen Professor of Political Science at the University of Illinois at Urbana-Champaign. He is past President of the Peace Science Society (International) and past President of the International Studies Association.

Current institution: large public Research I university

Typical classroom setting: small (10–20) seminars, medium (25) lecture discussion, large (100) lecture

Typical pedagogical approach: lecture with a wide variety of active learning strategies

Disciplinary identity: War and Peace

Kevin C. Dunn, Hobart and William Smith Colleges, USA

Chapter 5: Things I've Learned from Failure and Friends

Kevin C. Dunn is Professor in the Department of Political Science at Hobart and William Smith Colleges in Geneva, NY. He regularly teaches courses on International Relations, US foreign policy, and African politics. His publications include *Global Punk: Resistance and Rebellion in Everyday Life* (2016) and the textbook *Inside African Politics* (with Pierre Englebert; 2013 and 2019).

Current institution: small private liberal arts college

Typical classroom setting: seminar, large class lecture

Typical pedagogical approach: lecture, discussion

Disciplinary identity: IR Theory, introduction to IR, American foreign policy

Jamie Frueh, Bridgewater College, USA

Chapter 1: Introduction

Chapter 6: Teaching as Service: Losing and Finding My Identity in Global Classrooms

Jamie Frueh is Professor of History and Political Science at Bridgewater College. As a Director of the Center for Engaged Learning, he oversees Bridgewater's interdisciplinary academic programs and four endowed institutes. He runs pedagogy workshops at home and abroad, and is the 2019 recipient of the International Studies Association's Deborah Gerner Innovative Teaching Award.

Current institution: private liberal arts college

Typical classroom setting: interactive classes of 18–35 students

Typical pedagogical approach: collaborative learning, with lecture

Disciplinary identity: IR pedagogy, political identity

Gigi Gokcek, Dominican University of California, USA
Chapter 19: Swimming, Not Sinking: Pedagogical Creativity and the Road to Becoming an Effective IR Teacher
Gigi Gokcek is a professor of political science at the Dominican University of California. She researches and teaches in the areas of international relations and comparative politics. Her publications, which are featured in a variety of journal articles and books, focus on security and development issues, and engaged learning in international studies.
Current institution: small private comprehensive university
Typical classroom setting: small lecture classes (25–30 students), with some smaller seminars of 10 or fewer
Typical pedagogical approach: combination of lecture and interactive learning (discussion, activities, and other engaged learning techniques).
Disciplinary identity: primarily IR, with some comparative politics, but very interdisciplinary/international studies

Axel Heck, University of Kiel, Germany
Chapter 23: "Love's Labor's Lost": Teaching IR in Germany
Dr. Heck is Senior Lecturer in International Relations at Kiel University in Germany. He has taught more than 70 B.A. and M.A. courses at four universities on theories of International Relations, qualitative methods and research designs, as well as on representations of wars and violent conflicts in media, culture, and society.
Current institution: large public research university
Typical classroom setting: seminars of 10–30 students
Typical pedagogical approach: PowerPoint-based presentation and Q&A, regularly followed by group discussions
Disciplinary identity: Peace and Conflict, International Security

Naeem Inayatullah, Ithaca College, USA
Chapter 2: Teaching Is Impossible: A Polemic
Naeem Inayatullah is a professor at Ithaca College. With David Blaney, he is the author of *Savage Economics* (2010) and *International Relations and the Problem of Difference* (2004). He is an editor of *Autobiographical International Relations* (2011), and co-editor of *Narrative Global Politics* (2016). He is an Associate Editor for the *Journal of Narrative Politics*.

Current institution: private liberal arts college
Typical classroom setting: large lecture courses/small seminars
Typical pedagogical approach: structured collective discussions and interrogations
Disciplinary identity: Political Economy, IR theory, popular culture, writing

Patrick Thaddeus Jackson, American University, USA
Chapter 4: Time for Class
Patrick Thaddeus Jackson is Professor of International Studies in the School of International Service at American University in Washington, D.C. His award-winning book *The Conduct of Inquiry in International Relations* was published in a second edition by Routledge in 2016. In 2012, he was named the U.S. Professor of the Year for the District of Columbia by the Carnegie Council on Undergraduate Education.
Current institution: mid-sized private research II university
Typical classroom setting: small classes (<25)
Typical pedagogical approach: close reading; structured debate; simulations; open discussion
Disciplinary identity: <rant>INTERNATIONAL STUDIES IS NOT A DISCIPLINE BUT A MULTI-DISCIPLINARY FIELD<rant> international theory, introduction to world politics, research methods and methodology, philosophy of (social) science, science fiction, and international affairs

Eric K. Leonard, Shenandoah University, USA
Chapter 12: From Two-time College Dropout to Full Professor: The Non-traditional Route to Teacher and Mentor
Eric K. Leonard is Henkel Family Chair in International Affairs at Shenandoah University. He has been teaching in higher education for 20 years and recently published an edited textbook entitled, *Building Your IR Theory Toolbox: An Introduction to World Politics.*
Current institution: small private liberal education university
Typical classroom setting: seminar discussion
Typical pedagogical approach: collaborative learning with some Socratic method
Disciplinary identity: International Politics, Foreign Policy, Political Philosophy

Julie Mueller, Southern Maine Community College, USA
Chapter 16: Oh Yeah, There's Always Community College
Dr. Mueller teaches a variety of political science courses on the scenic South Portland campus of Southern Maine Community College, however, her passion is international relations. Her research interests include the International Monetary Fund and economic development, although teaching has been her primary focus in recent years.
Current institution: community college
Typical classroom setting: small lecture (<30)
Typical pedagogical approach: active learning, case studies, lectures
Disciplinary identity: all fields of political science

Marc J. O'Reilly, Heidelberg University, USA
Chapter 22: Better Than Before: My Pedagogical Journey
Marc J. O'Reilly is Professor of Political Science, Chair of the International Studies Committee, and Advisor to the Model UN Club at Heidelberg University, a liberal arts institution in Tiffin, Ohio. He teaches a variety of global politics courses. His research spotlights U.S. foreign policy vis-à-vis the Middle East.
Current institution: small private liberal arts university
Typical classroom setting: small classroom lecture/seminar
Typical pedagogical approach: Socratic method
Disciplinary identity: IR

Jennifer M. Ramos, Loyola Marymount University, USA
Chapter 14: Learning to Teach IR: An Active Learning Approach
Jennifer M. Ramos is Associate Professor at Loyola Marymount University. Prof. Ramos' books include *Preventive Force: Target Killings and Technology* (NYU Press, 2016; co-edited with Kerstin Fisk), and *Changing Norms through Actions: The Evolution of Sovereignty* (Oxford UP, 2013). Her articles have appeared in, among others, the *Journal of Politics*, *Public Opinion Quarterly*, and *Journal of Conflict Resolution*.
Current institution: private liberal arts university
Typical classroom setting: seminars, small lectures
Typical pedagogical approach: active learning, engaged learning, student-centered, immersion courses, travel courses community-based learning
Disciplinary identity: international security, international norms, peacebuilding

Felix Rösch, Coventry University, UK
Chapter 9: Pedagogies of Discomfort: Teaching International Relations as Humanitas in Times of Brexit
Felix Rösch is Senior Lecturer in International Relations at Coventry University. He works on encounters of difference in transcultural contexts. His most recent books include *Power, Knowledge, and Dissent in Morgenthau's Worldview* (2015), and *Modern Japanese Political Thought and International Relations* (2018). Felix co-edits the *Global Political Thinkers* and *Trends in European IR Theory* book series.
Current institution: large public university
Typical classroom setting: seminars
Typical pedagogical approach: community of learners
Disciplinary identity: International Relations Theory, History of International Relations

Kate Schick, Victoria University of Wellington, New Zealand
Chapter 3: Pedagogical Micro-communities: Sites of Relationality, Sites of Transformation
Kate Schick is Senior Lecturer in International Relations at Victoria University of Wellington. Her research lies at the intersection of critical theory and international ethics. She is particularly interested in the way critical theories highlight our vulnerability and interdependence, and their countercultural critique of the pursuit of invulnerability and self-sufficiency.
Current institution: large state research university
Typical classroom setting: large seminar classes (25–75)
Typical pedagogical approach: relational pedagogy, micro-communities of learning, critical self-reflection, vulnerable recognition
Disciplinary identity: international ethics, critical security studies

Carolyn M. Shaw, Wichita State University, USA
Chapter 21: The Unexpected Gift: "Oh, and You'll be Responsible for the Model UN Program"
Carolyn M. Shaw is a Professor of Political Science and Associate Vice President of Strategic Enrollment Management at Wichita State University. She has published pedagogical research in *International Studies Perspectives* and *The Journal of Political Science Education*, and serves as the faculty advisor for the Model UN program on campus.

Current institution: large public research university
Typical classroom setting: mid-sized classes, mostly upper division
Typical pedagogical approach: active learning, skills development
Disciplinary identity: International Organization, Conflict Resolution, Human Rights

Rosemary E. Shinko, American University, USA
Chapter 10: I Love Teaching: It Is Fun!
Rosemary E. Shinko is an IR theorist whose work is predominately inspired by postmodern/poststructural critique. She has published critical investigations of sovereignty, identity, peace, and power. Her teaching has included courses on IR Theory; Identity, Race, Gender and Culture; Peace Studies; Ethics in IR and World Politics.
Current institution: mid-sized private research II university
Typical classroom setting: seminars (<19), survey courses (<25)
Typical pedagogical approach: mini framing or summary lectures (no PowerPoints, no more than 10–15 minutes), discussion around textual (in the broadest sense) analysis, small group-based activities
Disciplinary identity: political theory, IR theory, theoretical approaches to peace and identity

Amy Skonieczny, San Francisco State University, USA
Chapter 13: Teaching Writing as Social Justice
Dr. Amy Skonieczny is an Associate Professor at San Francisco State University in the International Relations Department. Her research interests include Populism and Foreign Policy, Narratives, and US Trade Politics. Dr. Skonieczny is currently working on several projects on the rise of populism in the United States and its impact on US trade policy.
Current institution: large public comprehensive university
Typical classroom setting: seminar discussions, >35 students, writing and research courses, senior thesis/capstone
Typical pedagogical approach: active learning, group collaboration, mini-lectures with discussion
Disciplinary identity: US Foreign Policy

Brent J. Steele, University of Utah, USA
Chapter 24: Journey to the Unknown: Survival, Re-awakening, Renewal, and Reformation

Brent J. Steele is the Francis D. Wormuth Presidential Chair, Director of Graduate Studies, and Professor of Political Science at the University of Utah. His research focuses within International Relations on International Ethics and International Security. His most recent book is *Restraint and International Relations* (Cambridge University press).

Current institution: large state research I university
Typical classroom setting: seminars and large class lectures
Typical pedagogical approach: some lecture, but usually collaborative learning and readings discussions
Disciplinary identity: International Ethics, Foreign Policy, International Security, International Relations Theory

Jennifer Sterling-Folker, University of Connecticut, USA
Chapter 7: Confessions of a Teaching Malcontent: Learning to Like What You Do
Jennifer Sterling-Folker is the Alan R. Bennett Honors Professor and Honors Director of Political Science at the University of Connecticut. She has been a co-editor of International Studies Perspective, Review of International Studies (BISA) and an ISA Vice President. At the University of Connecticut, she has been the recipient of the Alumni Association Faculty Excellence in Teaching Award at the Graduate (2011) and Undergraduate levels (2017).

Current Institution: large state research I university
Typical classroom setting: large lecture, graduate seminar
Pedagogical approach: lecture, Socratic, active learning
Disciplinary identity: International Relations theory, research methods

Marcelo M. Valença, Brazilian Naval War College, Brazil
Chapter 18: Disciplinary Dungeon Master
Marcelo M. Valença is Assistant Professor at the Brazilian Naval War College (*Escola de Guerra Naval*, EGN). He holds a doctoral degree in International Relations and a J.D. from the Pontifical Catholic University of Rio de Janeiro (PUC-Rio).

Current institution: state military academy
Classroom settings: large classes; introductory classes
Pedagogical approach: active learning; storytelling
Disciplinary ID: Political Science, International Relations; International Politics

Jeremy Youde, University of Minnesota Duluth, USA
Chapter 11: "Come on Down!" Pedagogical Approaches from The
Price Is Right
Jeremy Youde is Dean of the College of Liberal Arts and Professor of
Political Science at the University of Minnesota Duluth. He previously
held appointments at San Diego State University, Grinnell College, and the
Australian National University. His research focuses primarily on issues of
global health governance and African politics. He received his BA from
Grinnell College and his MA and PhD from the University of Iowa.
Current institution: large public research university
Typical classroom setting: seminar discussions, lecture (30–75 students)
Pedagogical approach: collaborative/interactive
Disciplinary identity: IR/comparative, sub-Saharan Africa, global
health, international organization/global governance, international
development

Suggested Uses for the Volume

Quiet, honest reflection is almost always time well spent, and this is particularly true when the objects of reflection, say a course or teaching technique, will be repeated. It can be especially helpful to reflect in writing, to force oneself to reify amorphous feelings and scattered thoughts by articulating them with communicable precision. The narratives collected here demonstrate the value of writing to explain—of writing with a purpose of helping others understand. Academics are usually expected to do a lot of writing to explain. We write, usually addressing other academics, to articulate our conjectures, research, and knowledge claims. The narratives here are different because they are personal and about teaching, but each chapter serves as a citable reference for theory, concepts, and vocabulary that can help readers explore approaches to teaching and articulate the nuances of their pedagogical identities.

Teachers can also benefit from writing to understand—seeking precision for no audience other than one's current and future self. One of the best ways to improve a course is to break down the experience during those first hours or days after submitting final grades, to look back at notes scribbled on the syllabus, to ponder feedback from students or visiting colleagues, to revel in successes and to confront failures. Writing to understand a course as a completed whole, honestly and while the emotions and perspectives are still fresh, is work, especially when nothing would feel better than forgetting about teaching for a while. But that future self will appreciate the reminders when it comes time to reset the course for a new semester, weeks, months, or years after the last time it was taught. These insights are also useful resources when building an overarching philosophy of teaching, a network of concepts and rules that serves as a reference for daily pedagogical decisions, and as a resource available when called upon to make sense of acts of teaching.

These monologues, while valuable, should be supplemented by interactive conversations with other teachers. Articles, essays, books, and blogs provide opportunities to be provoked by others' explanations of their teaching, but because no approach will work for every teacher, course, or collection of students, such narratives are best deliberated over with others—a colleague or two, a faculty book club, or a graduate seminar. This volume can be used to provoke such conversations. Discussions could begin by having a member present a chapter to the group (like briefing a court case) and evaluate its arguments. Chapters could be approached in clusters based around the tactics endorsed or types of institutional contexts, or they could be juxtaposed to maximize creative friction. Group members or invited visitors could use the prompts to which the authors responded or questions from the list below to inspire more conversations. Because our home institutions are geographically dispersed, the authors in this volume used conference panels and file sharing to build a collaborative discourse about the themes in our essays. It is our hope that readers will find similar or creative ways to construct environments conducive to their own pedagogical conversations.

This volume is built on the assertion that such conversations are even more powerful when broad pedagogical principles are embedded in details that are concrete and personal. There is no better way to make teaching concrete and personal than to invite colleagues for classroom observations. The anxiety such observations often inspire can be mitigated by forming a team of three, making visits reciprocal, and establishing an atmosphere of collaborative improvement. Teams of three help observers couch conversations in comparative terms, and account for a range of experience and/or disciplines. All teachers can benefit from seeing their techniques through the eyes of a fellow pedagogue, and even those whose classroom experience is mostly as a student have perspectives that can spark deep conversations about teaching and learning. Team members might ask their colleagues to pay particular attention to problem areas, but observers should be looking for anything that might provoke conversation and improvement. The round robin of observations should be completed before team members get together in a casual setting (lunch, coffee, happy hour) to discuss reactions and insights. The conversation can start with positives, but specific time must be designated for problems and suggestions too. The purpose of the team is mutual improvement, and the core principle of the relationship has to be honest and constructive feedback. One side effect of these reciprocal visits is that team members get accustomed to the feeling of having non-student observers in their classrooms. Indeed, these observations can be seen as inoculations; and the more observations, the greater the immunity to the fear during the evaluative observations that are increasingly integral to hiring and tenure processes.

QUESTIONS FOR REFLECTION/DIALOGUE

The following questions are intended to provoke and could be the subject of writing to understand, writing to explain, or conversations with one, two, or a dozen interlocutors.

1. What did you learn about teaching from your best teachers? What did you learn from the worst ones?
2. In your experience, why do students become engaged in a class/course?
3. Is the answer to the previous question different for a C student than for an A student?
4. Who is responsible for student learning?
5. How should good teaching be evaluated?
6. Which author's approach seems most likely to work with your students? Which ones do you wish you could use more, but don't think they will work for you?
7. Is teaching given enough importance at your institution?
8. Do you feel constrained in your teaching strategies by your students' expectations? Do you feel constrained by your colleagues' expectations?
9. Did you find innovative or insightful approaches that you would like to know more about?
10. Have you tried something in class that didn't work? How did you know it failed? What did you do?

11. Are the purposes of your assignments clear? How can you build more goal and process transparency into your assignments? How about into your grading?

12. Are there statements or policies that you think should be added to syllabi? Are there statements that feel superfluous or overly burdensome?

13. Are there places in your courses where you can devote more attention to *PROCESSES* of a successful undergraduate education?
    - critical reading (how to read like a college student)
    - critical thinking and analysis of arguments
    - civil discourse about controversial or difficult issues
    - listening thoughtfully and with resilience to opposing opinions
    - research and information literacy
    - presenting arguments in writing with clarity and precision
    - other processes you think especially relevant to your courses

14. Should a syllabus be more like a contract between faculty and students, or more like a general guide that all parties expect to adapt and change with circumstances?

CHAPTER 1

Introduction

Jamie Frueh

In the global division of labor, academics are apportioned two broad sets of responsibilities. The first is to create and curate the information that societies designate as knowledge—descriptions, insights, and explanations that have been deemed truthful, valuable, and worthy of being preserved. Universities are repositories of societies' accumulated wisdom, and academics serve society by organizing that knowledge and generating, evaluating, and authenticating new knowledge claims. To secure a career as a knowledge worker, academics master a disciplinary canon and demonstrate a propensity to contribute to its expansion. Academics practice scholarship, the methodical search for novel insights and the collective evaluation of their knowledge value. Societies rightly reward those with expertise in the myriad complexities that undergird everyday life, although research that seems far removed from practical societal problems can inspire questions about the value of the whole enterprise. Indeed, some of academia's more arcane deliberations can feel a lot like public art—a meaningful but luxurious indulgence. Nonetheless, academics do get paid to think about stuff—to pose thoughtful questions and work to answer them—and the most successful scholars are compensated with both a very comfortable lifestyle and significant prestige. This is good work if you can get it.

J. Frueh (✉)
Center for Engaged Learning, Bridgewater College, Bridgewater, VA, USA
e-mail: jfrueh@bridgewater.edu

© The Author(s) 2020   1
J. Frueh (ed.), *Pedagogical Journeys through World Politics*,
Political Pedagogies, https://doi.org/10.1007/978-3-030-20305-4_1

This volume concerns the second broad category of academic responsibility: academics teach. They acculturate society's emerging agents into its intricate webs of knowledge and meaning. Education presents complexity so that uninitiated individuals can make sense of it and integrate it into their pre-existing worldviews. It succeeds when those individuals value both the extant complexity and the processes of sense-making. Especially in capitalist democracies (premised as they are on the participation of reasoning individual choosers), society as a whole benefits when citizens are knowledgeable, thoughtful, reflective, ethical, and wise deciders who make choices that align their behavior broadly with societal trajectories and the choices of others. Citizens in these liberal systems all benefit when individuals make good choices, and education is the social mechanism for producing good choosers. Academics serve that goal by preparing those who will participate in, lead, and improve its institutions. They do this by giving their students both resources that enable successful decision-making and practice using those resources. This is not just good work; it is important work.

One of the aphorisms that emerging academics learn as they are acculturated into the profession is that there is a tension between the scholarly responsibility and the teaching responsibility. This tension goes beyond the normal stress of allotting time and energy among the opportunities life presents. The tension is also about identity; it presents a choice between being a scholar and being a teacher. Academics in training receive messages both subtle and explicit that they should focus their time and energy on scholarship, until or unless they are forced to teach. While we do not have any tricks for magically expanding reserves of time or energy, the contributors to this volume reject both the false choice between the responsibilities of scholarship and teaching and the implicit disparagement of those who devote themselves to teaching well.

The best evidence we have for our claims is personal, and the most effective way to organize such idiosyncratic evidence is through stories. In these chapters, good teachers of global politics tell the stories of how they came to be good teachers of global politics. Unlike most of the published work on teaching and learning in Political Science and International Relations (IR), the chapters are not designed as evidence-based pedagogical recipes to be followed, but rather as empathetic encouragement that anyone can become an inspiring teacher and assurances that it is worth the effort. The volumes on which this one is modeled—Joseph Kruzel and James Rosenau's 1989 *Journeys Through World Politics* and Naeem

Inayatullah's 2011 *Autobiographical International Relations: I, IR*—are collections of autobiographical essays focused on the authors' development as researchers, theoreticians, and scholars. The editors of these volume felt the need to justify a format—autobiographical essay—that diverged widely from the traditional scholarly treatise. They did not, however, justify scholarly research and theory development as legitimate subjects for scholarly narratives. For a volume on teaching, such a justification seems prudent.

A Case for Pedagogy

As a result of the widespread perception that teaching is a sacrifice of academic opportunity, most prospective global politics academics, most programs that train them, and most institutions that hire them invest too little (time, energy, thought) preparing them for the second set of academic responsibilities. As a general rule, doctoral programs in Political Science and IR do not teach emerging academics how to teach, and when they do, they tend to provide only rudimentary instruction focused primarily on the practicalities associated with being a teaching assistant—grading rubrics, discussion topics, and preparing an occasional lecture (Ishiyama et al. 2010; Gaff et al. 2003). Trepanier has found that "[d]espite discussion and evidence that graduate students are not prepared to teach, there has been little formalized training developed in Political Science graduate programs"(2017: 141–2). A 2010 survey of 122 Political Science doctoral programs found that only 41 offered a course or guided practicum on teaching and only 28 of those required at least some students to take the course (Ishiyama et al. 2010). The general disciplinary assumption seems to be that academics, having spent so much of their lives in classrooms, have simply absorbed effective pedagogy by osmosis. Deep exploration of the purpose and meaning behind teaching is too often left up to chance, and to supervising professors, who, given the dominant incentive structure at doctorate-granting universities and the dearth of opportunities for professional development in this area, are likely to have neglected such exploration in their own careers. This lack of attention is also evident at a disciplinary level: of the 97 professional awards listed on the International Studies Association (ISA) website, teaching is only recognized by two, which together have only been presented five times (ISA 2018). It seems unlikely that this neglect is unique to IR, but the stakes of undergraduate teaching are higher for our discipline and in this century.

Partly as a cause, partly as a result, many academics see teaching as a burden, a distraction that costs energy that would be better spent (and rewarded) doing disciplinary knowledge work. Given the benefits earned by those who excel at the profession's creative/curatorial responsibilities, paying attention to pedagogical skills can seem actively harmful to one's career prospects. Axel Heck's chapter in this volume describing his pedagogical efforts in the research-centric German higher educational system is evidence that it sometimes is. But even for most moderately successful scholars, teaching well provides a better chance to make a lasting impact on the world than disciplinary knowledge work. Helping undergraduates become engaged observers, empowered choosers, and persuasive leaders creates multiplier effects that are almost always subtle and untraceable, but which are real and can have significant impacts as students actualize their agency.

The discipline's disproportionate emphasis on academia's knowledge responsibilities not only colors how academics spend their time and the identities to which they aspire, it also influences what they think teaching is. The responsibility to create and curate knowledge and the responsibility to acculturate undergraduate students into those regimes of knowledge pull academics toward different pedagogies. Appropriating Robert Cox's (1981) precept, teaching is always for someone and for some purpose. If the discipline emphasizes academics' creative/curatorial responsibilities, if academic see their societal value as based on information (hard-earned and rare) that they own, being a teacher becomes primarily about transferring that valuable knowledge to students. Knowledge is power, and an academic's identity as a teacher (and students' identities as students) is reduced to the students' abilities to master a certain field of knowledge, or at least the portion of it allotted to a particular course.

For academics who instead prioritize the responsibility to acculturate, professional focus shifts from the structural power of knowledge to the agency of students. Agency is the rhetorical core of liberal individualism and thus late-modern capitalist democracies. If the purpose of education is to prepare emerging citizens to contribute to those societies, teachers/students are valued not as containers of pre-existing knowledge, but as unique, creative minds who can participate in the continuous, collective sorting through of competing claims of all sorts. The focus of education shifts from the transferring particular knowledge to the nurturing of processes and attitudes that make liberal individuals successful. Education and educators serve society not just by ensuring that future generations know the right stuff, but also by empowering students as citizens who analyze and appreciate complexity, communicate ideas effectively, work with others to solve problems, and approach challenges with confidence in their own creativity. Effective teaching is evaluated not just by how much the teacher/students know, but by how they think and what they do with their knowledge.

A Case for IR Pedagogy

Even with an acknowledgment that a college education should mobilize the social agency of emerging citizens, the case must still be made that teachers of global politics should help carry this burden, instead of leaving the task to areas of the curriculum more directly focused on students' selves (perhaps humanities courses or first-year seminars). The most basic argument in favor of this proposition is that *all* teaching should be designed to nurture agents by helping students appreciate and work with the complexities, paradigms, and methods of exploration particular to the instructor's area of expertise. But global politics has distinct pedagogical advantages over other disciplines when it comes to creative, engaging, and empowering teaching and learning. Most obviously, global politics courses provide opportunities for emerging agents to practice wrestling with the kinds of complexities they will confront in an increasingly globalized world, and drawing attention to global political issues unfolding in real time provides evidence of the practical value of our courses. But beyond content, other characteristics of IR make it possible for the discipline to become a model of student-centered undergraduate teaching.

The subjects of global political studies span the entire scope of contemporary human experience, which encourages students to connect their identities to the issues, ideas, interests, and communities of distant others. Handled with care, this global scale alone can challenge assumptions and provoke genuine surprise and curiosity. Weighing one's immediate normality against the vast diversity of practices and beliefs that human societies treat as normal can be uncomfortable, but it can also inspire the kind of sincere questions that are the foundation of student engagement. Analyzing global interactions and relationships can lead students to discover ways they are similar to those we have long considered to be different and to create new understandings of what it means to be different. By providing the opportunity to question contemporary assumptions, values, and patterns of behavior, the study of global politics can not only help students navigate these complex relationships more successfully, it can also encourage them to invent ways to make these global interactions more constructive and more peaceful.

In addition, we teach politics—the processes communities go through to decide what is important and what to do about it. Global politics classrooms can be sites of negotiation over issues that have yet to be settled, and instructors and students can enter those spaces as participants in a continuous and challenging set of public and private deliberations. This opens up pedagogical opportunities unavailable to instructors using knowledge-based pedagogies to teach "the facts" of geology, anatomy, or accounting. Global politics classrooms are spaces where students can engage the complexity of modern, liberal citizenship by bringing in their own unique perspectives and creative ideas. Here, they can be authorized to practice agency, to sort through thorny issues about which smart people disagree and author their own views on those subjects. Students will disagree with each other and with the instructor, but such frictions can be empowering of collaborative deliberation and should be presented as such. Students can learn to attend critically to the arguments of others, to break arguments down into their component pieces and put them back together again, to work with others to explore ideas and policy proposals, and to contribute their own analysis and assertions to these deliberations. They can learn to build arguments and support their conclusions with evidence and rationales. Participation in global political negotiations offers special pedagogical opportunities to nurture the agency of students.

At the same time, the subject matter teaches humility. General education students often are convinced that they hate politics because it involves conflict and seems to reject straight answers they can memorize. Of course, the discipline does have some settled knowledge, and students must be provided some context, common vocabulary, and guidance if their deliberations are to be productive rather than merely frustrating. While not all of the authors in the volume agree, I believe teaching global politics should involve lecturing to model analysis and demonstrate methods for sorting nuances that deserve attention from those most likely to be smokescreens or noise. But global politics also presents plenty of opportunities for students to hear their professors say honestly, "I don't know." Smart people disagree about complex issues like North Korean nuclear weapons, the causes of economic inequality, and solutions to the Syrian civil war, and the smartest people approach these global political topics with a healthy dose of intellectual humility. More than many other subjects, studying global politics makes one suspicious of simplicity. Our courses can be opportunities for students to build analytical agility and practice (on their own and with others) finding patterns in the complex flow of contemporaneous events.

The disciplines of Political Science and International Relations maintain healthy conversations about how to translate these advantages into tactics and techniques that teach global politics well. Starting in 1968, the American Political Science Association's (APSA) quarterly, *PS: Political Science and Politics* began publishing research and informative articles about teaching and learning in the discipline (although pedagogy is just one of the journal's numerous and broad areas of interest). Craig (2014) documents a significant increase in published articles on teaching and learning over the past two decades. In 2000, The International Studies Association launched *International Studies Perspectives (ISP)*, which included pedagogical analysis as one of the four types of articles it publishes. In 2005, APSA launched the *Journal of Political Science Education (JPSE)* to deal exclusively with research related to pedagogy in Political Science. As the value of Scholarship of Teaching and Learning (SoTL) has increased in academia generally, the prestige and audience for work on the pedagogy of IR have also grown (see the comprehensive International Political Education Database maintained by the UK's Political Science Association Teaching and Learning Network). APSA has run an independent Teaching and Learning Conference since 2004, although beginning in 2018, every other year the conference will be held in conjunction with APSA's annual convention. ISA has two sections devoted to education—the Active Learning in International Affairs Section and the International Education Section—and as part of its 2017 annual conference, ISA sponsored full-day teaching workshops (on simulations, online curriculum, and writing assignments). In 2018, ISA renamed these workshops the Innovative Pedagogy Conference and moved them to be held in conjunction with regional ISA conferences. That same year also marked the third biennial European Conference on Teaching and Learning Politics and the third annual Pedagogy Workshop at ISA's Northeast Regional Conference.

These resources have helped many of the authors in this volume throughout their pedagogical journeys, often providing powerful solutions to practical teaching problems. Owing in part to the current American academic culture of "assessment," however, most existing work on Political Science pedagogy is focused on finding and passing along evidence (often quantitative/statistical) that particular tactics and techniques promote student learning. The essays in this volume are instead devoted to the personal, philosophical, and identity-based contexts of such tactical decisions. The authors attest that pedagogical philosophies and tactical proficiencies interact continuously and iteratively over the course of a career, and that contemplation can add continuity and identity to that flow. The authors model the strategic investments of reflection and creativity required to become teachers worthy of their students' potential and contend that anyone can overcome the challenges to become a successful teacher of global politics.

ORGANIZATION OF THE CHAPTERS AND THE BOOK

While each chapter tells a personal story, authors have built their essays around a broad common structure. The best adventure stories begin in a context readers find familiar, and each chapter opens with reflections on the (often inauspicious) first steps of the author's pedagogical journey. The reflections anchor developmental stories about these teachers and their approaches to pedagogy. How did they learn to teach IR? What have they learned about teaching global politics to undergraduates that they did not know when they started? What kinds of pedagogical approaches have they come to believe in and what have they learned to avoid? What specific practices or techniques epitomize their approaches to teaching? All the authors acknowledge that their pedagogical adventures continue and that the hallmark of exemplary teachers is the ongoing process of attending to one's teaching, not any specific techniques or tactics. The adventure is in the processes of reflection, exploration, requesting help, training, trial and error, failure, evaluation, and starting the cycle all over again. What emerges from these narratives is that good teaching requires creativity, agency, and honest hard work. Lastly, the essays conclude with summarizing statements of teaching philosophy, pedagogical mission statements at this point in the authors' careers. What motivates their teaching? How do they explain teaching global politics to colleagues from other disciplines? How do they explain the purpose of the work of studying global politics to students?

As should be obvious by now, the tone and the rhythm of this volume are intentionally different from those typical of the discipline. Editors of other autobiographical and autoethnographic IR collections (Kruzel and Rosenau 1989; Inayatullah 2011; Dauphinee and Inayatullah 2016) have pointed out how difficult it can be for authors to suppress their scholarly training (detached academic arguments, foundations in the disciplinary canon, data as evidence) and just write about themselves. The authors in this volume approached the prompt's instructions and suggested structure in a variety of ways, and readers will undoubtedly find themselves drawn to some styles more than others. Some authors use citations and footnotes, for example, while others were more comfortable with a basic narrative storytelling style. As an editor, I saw my job as two-fold: to ask questions to help authors find their best pedagogical development narratives, and to help them communicate those narratives clearly. I tried not to meddle too much; the stories are often very personal, and the authenticity of each voice is critical to the message.

The chapters are loosely organized along a spectrum from the more philosophical to the more practical. There are no bright lines, and readers may prefer to choose a different path through the chapters. For example, readers may be primarily interested in experiences at a particular kind of institution, or with particular types of global politics courses. To facilitate this, authors have provided some keywords that describe both their home institutions and their own disciplinary footprints. This should help readers place texts in conversation with each other in ways that will serve their own particular needs. The point of the exercise, after all, is to build discussions and empower creativity about IR pedagogy rather than convince readers to adopt particular pedagogical outlooks or techniques. The "Suggested Uses" and "Questions for Reflection/Dialogue" sections that appear after the table of contents are intended to facilitate those discussions and that creativity.

Naeem Inayatullah opens the volume with the provocative argument that "teaching is impossible and learning unlikely." Any learning that happens in his classes, he asserts, happens not because he explains things well, but because students are provoked at a subconscious level. On the surface, students have learned how to please teachers, which is pleasing for teachers, but, he argues, does not constitute learning. It is wrong for a teacher to take credit for anything other than structuring opportunities that students-as-agents already possess—to take their own questions seriously, embrace curiosity, and follow honestly where the answers lead. To the degree that a teacher's livelihood and sense of self(worth) flow from being responsible for the learning of students, teaching, he seems to say, is a con. Teachers can truly earn their keep and social privileges if they instead help students-as-agents authorize their own learning. This is tough to do and this "radical pedagogy" is not for the faint of heart, as there is often a lot of wailing and gnashing of teeth associated with rejecting a definition of teaching/learning that has structured most students' educational work to that point. The implications of his argument are profound and important enough that the reader may need to engage them before going on.

The authors of the next three chapters embrace a version of Naeem's conclusion and their chapters provide practical examples of pedagogical structures that exemplify it. **Kate Schick's** pedagogical micro-communities both express her relationalist epistemology/ontology and help students (and especially her non-western students) learn by building relationships to both the course material and each other. Her students are learning global politics, but they are also finding their positions within its complexities. Likewise, instead of solving complexities for his students, **Patrick Thaddeus Jackson** builds classes (and as an administrator, systems of classes) that focus on arguments, and students as arguers. His learning objectives transcend disciplines, and both he and his students understand how the work they do together engages the purposes of an undergraduate education. **Kevin Dunn** maintains that students are more likely to be engaged when instructors invest in strategic construction of experiences that accommodate a variety of learning styles and especially in narratives that challenge their critical thinking. He too argues that beyond holding students accountable for the objectives of a course, instructors must build instruction and assignments that continually invite students into its deeper purposes. These chapters all accept Naeem's basic premise that, as Patrick puts it "I can't make one of my students learn, any more than I can make a seed grow into a plant; all I can do is create some favorable conditions." Ultimately, students are the agents that matter and the chapters are mostly about finding effective ways to get out of the way. **My** chapter goes quite far down this same road but argues that the strategies of student engagement can still exist side by side with lecturing and (gasp) even PowerPoint slides.

This same message about student empowerment comes through in a very personal and developmental way in chapters by **Jennifer Sterling-Folker** and **David Blaney**, both of whom found the courage to share honestly about the personal costs of teaching. Jennifer is especially good at demonstrating how difficult this student-centered approach can be to find, articulate, and implement if the only educational systems one has experienced have been premised on a knowledge-based model of education and infused with gendered thinking. Seeing students as a threat to professorial authority makes it almost impossible to see them as collaborators in a joint project. But seeing them as collaborators does not suddenly make teaching easy. In fact, as David points out, teaching in this way can be significantly more draining, even when students are looking for engaged learning and willing to meet the instructor halfway. Creating a truly collaborative relationship requires not just knowing thyself, but caring for yourself as well, and that involves balancing the incentives of the job against who you are and who you have the capacity to be.

As the reader moves further into the volume, authors begin to mix more tactical details into their explorations of theoretical context. Indeed, the next few chapters somewhat resemble statements of teaching philosophy in applications for employment or tenure/promotion. The narratives demonstrate the author's pedagogical flexibility and sincere dedication to student learning needs, backed up with evidence that the authors see students in four dimensions, as possessing unique, creative minds that can stretch and grow, rather than as merely backdrops for instructors' performances. The blend of personal philosophical principles and particular techniques in these essays is evidence that the authors are likely to sustain the investment in pedagogical development over the long haul.

Like Kate's essay, **Felix Rösch's** chapter exemplifies how to ground pedagogical innovation in a theoretical commitment, in his case to the concept of *humanitas* as articulated by Hannah Arendt, Karl Jaspers, and others. In a stroke of real pedagogical courage, Felix had his students participate in a form of modern dance to understand the mutual dependence, vulnerability, and ambiguity inherent in contemporary global power. Encounters with postmodern political theory inspired **Rose Shinko** to shift from a Socratic method, which she criticizes for running all classroom interactions through the professor, to a more student-centered approach. In addition to some very practical advice about how to pull off a student-centered classroom, Rose also reminds us that it is important to empathize with students as humans and build fun into courses. This theme is continued in **Jeremy Youde's** pedagogical allegory of the television game show *The Price Is Right*. Jeremy does an excellent job of centering very specific and practical advice within a larger philosophical/theoretical context and demonstrating in a very entertaining essay how to explain a thoughtfully personalized pedagogical approach to others.

While all the essays rely on personal stories to frame the narratives, the authors of the next five chapters particularly emphasize the connections between their teaching and their own identities. The story of **Eric Leonard's** rather unconventional path to becoming a professor highlights his rationale for choosing a career at a teaching-oriented institution. Eric combines empathy for his students, earned trust from administrators, and a heavy dose of creativity to make pedagogical transformations that serve both his students and his teaching and life goals. **Amy Skonieczny** anchors her identity as a teacher in a commitment to teaching her students to write. Amy's story of her own professorial transformation, from complaining about her students' writing to a deeply personal commitment to making them better writers, illustrates how reflection, hard work, and courage that can make IR courses into, as she says, "a way to make a difference in students' lives." Helping students make a practical investment in communities both local and global animates **Jennifer Ramos'** narrative about building active learning into IR courses, including service learning at a food bank and a travel course to study the Northern Ireland peace process. But it is choices like requiring research as part of the Northern Ireland trip that define it as a "signature course." Teaching in post-apartheid South Africa helps explain **Jacqui de Matos-Ala's** commitment to the liberation pedagogy of Paulo Freire. Not only has she built systems that nurture her students' agency into her introductory IR and gender studies courses, but she has also modeled the approach to learning by pursuing additional degrees in teaching. **Julie Mueller** found far different attitudes toward teaching and learning at her community college than she expected before she arrived. Community college faculty teach a lot, and Julie's conscious thoughtful commitment to understanding *her* students allowed her to embrace teaching fully, and to become the teacher she had always intended to be. These five essays, in particular, demonstrate the motivating power of the identity label "teacher." These authors are investing time and energy, not just in their students, but also in an image of self they find genuinely fulfilling.

The next set of chapters are written more directly to readers as teaching colleagues or those who aspire to be. Here authors focus more on practical teaching advice and hard-earned wisdom that only experience can provide. These illustrations of praxis aim to encourage pedagogical courage through examples of trial and error that have eventually paid off. In addition to modeling the demanding nature of pedagogical creativity, the autobiographical details demonstrate that IR teachers of any professional level, institutional affiliation, or sub-disciplinary/theoretical bent can find communities to both embolden their efforts and challenge them to think deeply about what it means to teach IR.

For **Paul Diehl,** the guiding principles of the evolution of his IR teaching practices over the past four decades have been a commitment to teach both an ethic of civic engagement and the skills to participate in those democratic deliberations. Contrary to Naeem, Paul argues that evidence and experience show that instructors' interventions can produce student learning, in part because some techniques produce more than others. Similarly, **Marcelo Valença** focuses on the power of the instructor to influence learning. If classes are adventures and students are adventurers, Marcelo says instructors should create the narratives that lead them through, like dungeon masters in a Dungeons and Dragons game. This conceptual framework of teaching as creating useful narratives that help students form connections between the material and practical experiences is related to Kevin's focus on teaching as performance. Rather than creating those narratives, **Gigi Gokcek** imports them in the form of popular films and asks students to find connections to course themes. Gigi explains how the development of a film-based system for teaching IR theories transformed her teaching philosophy and her chapter is a reminder that investing in one's teaching can pay off throughout a career.

Sammy Barkin's chapter is a tight and compelling summary of student engagement techniques from a self-described "boring" teacher, including small group work in numerous forms, assigning specific "expert" roles for class discussions, and an intricate simulation based on water rights. The latter was developed in collaboration with a colleague, a practice Sammy advocates wholeheartedly. Those collaborators can be found in other disciplines or institutions. In her chapter, **Carolyn Shaw** explores the joys of advising her campus's Model UN chapter and gaining a new perspective on teaching by investing in the network of advisors from other institutions. Hers is a story of working through the complications of an unsought assignment, and the satisfaction of making a difference for her students. **Marc O'Reilly's** chapter also discusses his involvement with Model UN, as well as other off-campus excursions. The practical pedagogical advice in Marc's chapter is embedded in the process of finding and managing a career at a teaching-oriented institution.

The volume concludes with one chapter that emphasizes the costs of an academic system in which teaching is discounted, and one chapter that proposes concrete changes to pedagogical training. **Axel Heck's** journey through the German academic system demonstrates the power of structural constraints that measure worth in scholarship alone. Axel's choices to invest in improving teaching/learning are similar in many ways to the other authors, but have left him in a very vulnerable career position. On a more pedagogically hopeful note, **Brent Steele's** chapter presents an alternate vision in which IR doctoral programs and the discipline as a whole place a greater emphasis on the structures and incentives that will be required to produce better teachers of global politics. Having served as director of such a doctoral program, Brent makes a strong case for the importance of teaching future teachers to teach, and embeds four recommendations for reforming the discipline's approach to teaching pedagogy in reflections about his own evolving approach to teaching. While they conclude this book (much more eloquently than I could), his suggestions are a concrete starting point for the disciplinary conversations all the authors advocate. They are, therefore, a perfect transition to the discussions we hope the project inspires.

Engaged Teaching/Learning and IR

Learning to teach global politics should not be a trial by fire, or the deep end into which one is thrown, or a lonely bumbling walk in the dark. The discipline knows a lot about how to teach global politics well, and smart, passionate people should not be sent into teaching positions with little more than some faith that they will figure it out on their own. Learning the basics of how to teach should be a requirement for the certification that nominally tells the world an individual is an academic ready to perform academic functions. We should not reduce this responsibility to training teaching assistants about grading and rubrics, or to the voluntary monthly teas I had as part of my doctoral program. For lots of reasons—fairness to those doctoral students and to the undergraduate students they will teach, simple efficiency of outcomes, and not least because democracies need more citizens invested in global perspectives—Political Science and IR doctoral programs should require a semester course on teaching. The disciplines know how to help undergraduate students appreciate, analyze, and formulate explanations of global political complexities, and even those scholars who do not teach often should be good at it when they do.

The volume provides guidance from teachers who have embraced the challenge of undergraduate education. Its objective is to spark reflection and conversations about why and how to be a teacher of global politics and to argue that such reflection and conversations are not just valuable, but important for the discipline. It will be a success to the degree that it catalyzes conversations about what it should mean to be a teacher of global politics and how to represent that identity to students, colleagues, and administrators. The narratives in this volume are not going to change the incentive structures of the discipline or academia. But they might help teachers of global politics maximize the payoffs for investments in their teaching, which might, in turn, help them find personal and career fulfillment. Perhaps the rest will follow.

REFERENCES

Cox, Robert W. 1981. Social Forces, States and World Orders: Beyond International Relations Theory. *Millennium: Journal of International Studies* 10 (2): 126–155. https://doi.org/10.1177/03058298810100020501.

Craig, John. 2014. What Have We Been Writing About?: Patterns and Trends in the Scholarship of Teaching and Learning in Political Science. *Journal of Political Science Education* 10 (1): 23–36. https://doi.org/10.1080/15512169.2013.859086.

Dauphinee, Elizabeth, and Naeem Inayatullah, eds. 2016. *Narrative Global Politics: Theory, History and the Personal in International Relations.* London/New York: Routledge.

Gaff, Jerry G., Anne S. Pruitt-Logan, Leslie B. Sims, and Daniel D. Denecke. 2003. *Preparing Future Faculty in the Social Sciences and Humanities.* Washington, DC: Council of Graduate Schools and Association of American Colleges and Universities.

Inayatullah, Naeem, ed. 2011. *Autobiographical International Relations: I, IR, Interventions.* Milton Park/New York: Routledge.

International Studies Association (ISA). http://www.isanet.org. Accessed 16 Sept 2018.

Ishiyama, John, Tom Miles, and Christine Balarezo. 2010. Training the Next Generation of Teaching Professors: A Comparative Study of Ph.D. Programs in Political Science. *PS: Political Science & Politics* 43 (03): 515–522. https://doi.org/10.1017/S1049096510000752.

Kruzel, Joseph, and James N. Rosenau, eds. 1989. *Journeys Through World Politics: Autobiographical Reflections of Thirty-Four Academic Travelers,* Issues in World Politics Series. Lexington: Lexington Books.

Political Science Association, International Political Education Database (IPED). https://sites.google.com/site/psatlg/resources/journal-articles?authuser=0. Accessed 16 June 2018.

Trepanier, Lee. 2017. SoTL as a Subfield for Political Science Graduate Programs. *Journal of Political Science Education* 13 (2): 138–151. https://doi.org/10.1080/15512169.2016.1227264.

Teaching Is Impossible: A Polemic

Naeem Inayatullah

Current institution: private liberal arts college
Typical classroom setting: large lecture courses/small seminars
Typical pedagogical approach: structured collective discussions and
   interrogations
Disciplinary identity: Political Economy, IR theory, popular culture, writing

PROLOGUE

Dear reader, first and foremost, I ask your forgiveness for what I am about
to do. Please know that I oppose polemics. I have enjoyed a few, for example, that one by Emma Goldman and that one by Marx and Engels.
Manifestos have their uses, of course. Still, most of my career, I have
moved toward confessional and autobiographical writing styles. There is a
politics to that decision: as the fiction writer Moshin Hamid says, "The
confession that implicates its audience—as we say in cricket—is a devilishly
difficult ball to play. Reject and you slight the confessor; accept it and you
admit your own guilt" (Hamid 2008: 70).

I have published three autobiographical pieces on pedagogy. I meant
this one to be the fourth. But when I drafted the first page, it came out as

N. Inayatullah (✉)
Ithaca College, Ithaca, NY, USA
e-mail: naeem@ithaca.edu

© The Author(s) 2020
J. Frueh (ed.), *Pedagogical Journeys through World Politics*,
Political Pedagogies, https://doi.org/10.1007/978-3-030-20305-4_2

a polemic. Wrong, I thought. A second try still found my tone strident. A week later, the result was the same. I vowed to sleep on it and ask my subconscious to help me solve this problem. Its command: get out of the way and embrace the polemic.

The five pages of notes I have (with the help of Akta Kaushal and a set of attentive friends one night at Vassar College) contain lists of ideas and principles. Later on, I added to these notes the names of scores of students from my teaching career. The names denote biographical vignettes. It was my plan to sketch those stories. But such a form, I now realize, requires 40,000 words and not the 4000 authorized by our editor. I am still hoping to write that short book—in the confessional and autobiographical mode, of course.

But there is also an urgency that comes with going past six decades of age and realizing that, now more than ever, we plan our lives with a fictional certainty that is exposed when winter winds blow. And then one wants to say it all—suddenly, forcefully, and with the aim of jarring the reader into a different dimension of possibility.

POLEMIC

Teaching is impossible. Learning is unlikely. Why then enter the classroom? This is the question that is left. If we pose it non-rhetorically, it creates thinking space. My answer: we enter the classroom to encounter others. With them, we can meditate on the possibility of our own learning. All else is posing.

How did I get here?

By two means: constant experimentation with pedagogical forms and the application of theoretical questions to our everyday work as teachers.

First, experimental forms: I have sat on a table wearing blue jeans while teaching. I have worn tweed jackets and beige ties. I have lectured with microphones while running up and down the stairs of lecture halls. I have removed all furniture and sat on the floor in a circle. I have said less than five words for weeks on end. I have experienced a coup and accepted that three of my students would run the class for the remaining weeks of the semester. I have read short answers, essays, journals, diaries, research papers, poems, and even a song or two. The question is why so much experimenting? I'll come to that soon.

Second, theoretical application: Do societies learn? The philosophers of tragedy think not. At least not in time to make a difference. If we learn, it is always too late. Why then should I think that individuals—the microsystems that constitute societies—can learn? That students learn is a premise (but also a fantasy) without which we cannot do our jobs in the classroom. We busy ourselves creating syllabi, assignments, and practices to support this fantasy. The purpose of this busy work is to leave undisturbed the deepest of our sleeping suspicions: that we cannot teach, that they do not learn.

Does my tone need to be so assertive? No, it needn't be; you are right dear reader. Because I can more likely bypass your repressive energy with hints instead of with declarations. Would you prefer if I asked: "Can we teach? Can they learn?" Better?

Teaching's impossibility began to hover early in my career. I wished to defeat that doubt. Hence my constant experimenting.

I worked at being a good teacher. My students liked me fine (check). I received favorable evaluations (check). I connected—even when I yelled at them. And perhaps especially then (check and check). But were they learning what I was trying to convey? (I am still waiting on that check.)

At first, I could not tell. Ten years later, I knew. No, they were not. Even as my classroom was filled with seemingly good things, they were not acquiring what I was trying to impart. A few more years and I became convinced they never would learn what I was trying to teach. I wanted them to confront the structural economic inequalities of global capitalism. They wanted to express their joy at being in my classroom. I didn't reject their implicit affection but nor, somehow, was I fool enough to believe that my positive indicators spelled success. (Did I mention I have never won a teaching award? Smiley emoticon here.)

Today I know. Teaching is impossible. Learning is unlikely. Encounter is the remainder. What is left is accepting these conclusions, these assertions, these hypotheses. Only this acceptance sharpens my skill and hones my encountering travels. You too, dear comrade, have only this option. Because this story is not mine alone. It is also yours. "No, no, no" you say. "Yes, yes, yes" I counter.

Principles *(at this point, still randomly listed)*

- *The classroom must be a living space.* At all costs. It breathes only if there is something at stake for you the teacher, it lives if you aim to learn something. You need not know what it is. But absent that searching, the space is barren. They recognize vacated space. All of them.

This is the prime directive; all other principles bow to this one. It does not matter if you lecture, stage opposing dramatic persona, use PowerPoint (God forbid and common sense prohibit), deploy collective Socratic interrogation, sit quietly in the shadows only to pounce once or twice, or invite your students to silently meditate with you. Only the teacher's desire matters. It evokes, awakens, and spurs student desire. Like you, they may not know their desire's nature. The classroom frames and explores these not-yet-formulations—yours and theirs.

Why are you teaching the course? The income? The imagined reputation? Yes, of course. But so too for chefs and masseurs. They are paid, their status develops. I ask again: why do you teach? Is it not because you wish to learn something? You cannot but let them see this even as your training veils your intrinsic curiosity. They see it even through their incomprehension.

When you are brave enough you may show them that you are learning from them. Careful though not to upset their expectations. Approach the inversion indirectly, as if you were complimenting someone who shrivels at their own positive appearance. If you do this well, their collective intelligence adds to your own. I go into a classroom well-read and well prepared but unsure of my position. Their articulations serve as my chorus. They stake out and enunciate various positions. I hear them within me. I smile and share by saying, "somedays, I can't believe I get paid to have you teach me." Then I quickly move on.

- *Students do not want to learn.* If you know this and you know nothing else about what we call teaching, you still know more than someone who knows everything else but does not know this. Of course, this negation opposes their natural curiosity, the ready to be unfolded desire of every human. It is this curiosity, this desire that the student may model after the teacher's self-learning in the classroom.

Nevertheless, student desire does not unfold in free, frictionless space. It moves slowly, stickily, and bumpily. It is cathected. It binds itself to bodily investments in family, in culture, and in nation. Against these investments, we teachers stand no chance. Hence the impossibility of teaching. Because to learn, to unfold desire is also to squander the potential love of family members, to risk losing the cultural embrace, and to turn one's back to the nation's endorsement. Learning is a kind of social death that produces loss, grief, and mourning. Hence the impossibility of teaching.

Students lie. Students lie when they provide the appearance of wanting to learn. No one is ready (until suddenly, unexpectedly, unintentionally, and miraculously they are) to risk social death, loss, grief, and mourning. Hence the impossibility of teaching.

- This is why, as teachers, *we must align ourselves with their subconscious*. We address ourselves only to their unconscious, to their long-term bodily investments. Not to their ego. Not to that part of them that longs to produce seamlessly worded, thoroughly organized, and perfectly executed papers. Not to that part of them that performs in search of accolades. Not to the part of them that strums the professor's ego.

  There is some curiosity alive in them despite the preening and pruning. We play to expose that curiosity—whether in the tones of Coleman Hawkins, Dexter Gordon, or Pharaoh Sanders. We must play to their subconscious even at the cost of losing student affection, of receiving their approbation, of garnering poor evaluations. Because only their subconscious is open to possibilities.

  Find the student's boundary and cross it. Then cross back into the range of their acceptability. Apologize when you step too far and hurt feelings. Apologize privately but also publicly in front of the class. Learn to say sorry. Without this skill, encounters are not possible.

- *Friction is encounter's lubricant.* Let them yell. Let them scream. Let them cry. Let them laugh. Let them wail, bemoan, and complain. They will look to you to know how to react. If you stand your ground, letting it go through you, then they will be fine. More likely, you will panic. I did. But when I could anticipate the waves of emotion, coming, I found my sea-legs. All emotions are welcome: we cry together, laugh together, rage together.
- They do not come to class. They do not read. Don't protest. People like me read those complaints and laugh (so as to not cry and scream). *They do not read, they do not come to class. These are your problems.* Indeed, they are foundational to our craft. If you have not "confronted" these theoretically, you have not managed the ABCs of our profession.

Attendance: students rise to the level of expectations. If you patron-ize them with attendance policies, they will act like children; if you envisage maturity, then expect them to manage their time as adults. This is by no means a small thing. Attendance policy is the true litmus test of democratic politics.

Requiring attendance admits defeat before your encounter begins. You announce to them: "I lack the ability to have the course serve your needs well enough for you to attend voluntarily. Therefore, I will punish you for my inadequacy."

I have lived and died by the "come if my class serves your needs" attendance policy. Lived because they bring their best selves when they come. Died because I am aggrieved. Thirty years later, I am still pained. I declare out loud: "It hurts my feelings when you don't come. Come only if you want, but please know that I want you to attend. And that I hurt when you don't." To paraphrase Marvin Gaye: "I want you, I want you, I want you. But I want you to want me too."

Eliminate the *participation* grade. Quiet students are doing the best work. Do not punish them for listening well and deliberating with a judicious pace. Loud students allow you to escape your fear of silence. But at what cost?

Reading: give them a motive to read. If you summarize the assign-ment, they have no reason to read. But if the discussion proceeds on the assumption that they have read then they will figure out that, unless they read, they cannot follow the discussion. It need not be this impetus. But provide them a motivation.

If you cannot get them to read, you are failing in your responsibili-ties. If then you complain about your students on social media, here is what you are actually confessing: "Help me, dear God, for I don't know how to be a teacher." Getting them to read is the true litmus test of motivating human beings. This is by no means a small thing.

They do not know how to articulate their feelings and thoughts. Your job is to translate their half-baked utterings. Encourage them to say anything, even perhaps especially those things we find most hurtful—sexist, racist, classist things. Judge not. Their prejudice expressed is an *achievement*. It means trust is building. Wait for them to critique each other. Help them to articulate those cri-tiques. Do not take sides. Doing so collapses trust's fabric. Articulate to them their own position. What they say will sound different to them when they hear it brought back in translation. They may well disavow their own articulation. This happens every day in my classes.

Resist the temptation to answer questions, to deploy your own expertise. Remain the amateur. We know answers, we teachers are rehearsed in them. Instead of the answer, look for the deeper, barely hidden question. What are they *really* asking when they ask a question? Even their deepest convictions expressed as assertions are really questions. What need are they trying to fulfill? It is likely that the question is about their own uncertainty, their own lack of confidence in the work that their question provokes in them. Bring them back to a better version of their own question and leave them with it. Sustain and deepen the tension; don't resolve it.

Don't teach. But also: don't let anyone else teach. When students observe a teacher vacate the teaching imperative, many will volunteer to command the space. They say to themselves, "S/he is not teaching, so I will." Don't allow this. You have relinquished the space so that they can be still with their own questions. Use your power and authority to sustain the emptied space. Disallow students from teaching.

- If the course is failing, *do not rescue it.* Only the possibility of failure can produce collective success. They expect the rescue. Make them believe you will not save the day. This is an everyday principle. If the conversation is going badly, let it go badly. We are not performing brain surgery. There is always another day. Think of the long term.
- Some love you. Some hate you. Some love and hate you. Some are aggressively indifferent. Some bully you. Some flirt. Some expect emotional cultivation. None of it is about you. They are projecting. They project. They place you in a relationship they have with a parent object. Transference it is called. There is also counter-transference. There is *projection, transference, counter-transference.* No way around it. It happens always. This is the screen within which encounters occur. You can ignore this. Or you can become aware of it.

A student is screaming at me. But I know it is not me. A student is showering me with praises. But I know it is about someone else. I love this student, I avoid that one. I know this is just counter-transference. None of it is about me, my classes, or my teaching. But all of it is mine to administer.

- *Identity is subterfuge.* Do not trust a seeming identity. Students are always more than they appear. Wait, wait, wait for them to disclose, to self-identify. Remember the disclosure but don't fall for its momentary reification. They will change their minds, find other sources of the self. Identity is fluid. Swim in its stream.
- *Radical pedagogy is not for the faint of heart.* Expect massive resistance. From students. But even more from colleagues, from deans, from the institution itself. They really do not want a serious engagement. Doing so exposes their illusions. What they need is the appearance of it all. Prepare to be alone. Get comfortable with accusations and insinuations.
- Recognize, above all, that *we are not the good guys*—the ultimate delusion. Educational Institutions are designed to kill curiosity. From kindergarten onward we teachers deliver this structural violence. Students are the victims, teachers the executioners. There are no good soldiers in this bad war, no good agents in this rigid structure. Only the willing and the compromised. We will never be the good guys. Deal with it or suffer the illusion. Red pill, blue pill.

Epilogue

We can talk more if you like. Nothing here is set in stone tablets. And, despite all the imperatives, I have learned to whisper. Because only a whisper drives a nail into the wall.

*   *   *

Questions from Jamie Frueh

Jamie: Here are some questions. You don't have to answer them.

Jamie: *Have you learned why some overcome the barriers to learning? Can you predict who will succeed? What is evidence that learning has happened?*

I have not been able to predict much about what students might do. At least five times over the years, I have had students who I might have written-off as "middling" come to my office and say "You are not taking me seriously enough. I need you to push me. I need you to assess my work with more rigor." These are truly miraculous moments.

"Success" is not a semester thing. It needs a longer time span. A lifetime maybe. Some currently excellent students will, in their thirties and forties, sag and fall asleep in suburbia. Someone who never spoke a word will, ten years later, write you a long letter with breathtaking insights from an island in Indonesia. You never really know. But such moments alert me to the force by which students enfold the teacher's body into their own lives.

The evidence for learning is the usual: insightful work, confidence in the search, grounding in uncertainty, an awareness of one's self-deception, and a security in long-term goals. But the evidence is also in the little stuff: a gleam in the eye, a playfulness in tone, a shift in the relationship between mentor and mentee in which the latter wanders into hikes uncharted, a rigor in student habits, a belief that it is cool to vie for smartness, and a sense of having merged seriousness with fun.

Jamie: *I know it did when you began, but now does the content matter? Another way to say this might be, what is it that most do not learn? Is it to trust curiosity? Is it a process for approaching the world? Is it an orientation/attitude? Or is part of it still the structural economic inequalities of global capitalism?*

Content *never* matters to students, even if when they think it does. That is the biggest takeaway of all. But it does matter in two smaller ways. First, it matters to the teacher. What we as teachers are trying to learn in the classroom is not abstract, there is something specific that moves our curiosity. Second, if what we are trying to accomplish is to create learning communities that, eventually might run autonomously, then those learning communities need a particular focus. We might say that no particular content matters, but content still has to be present and specified for the larger meta-goals to emerge.

What they/we most do *not* want to learn is that it might be impossible to be good in a world structured by tragedy. None of us wants to apprehend our constitutive role in the very problems we are trying to solve.

In the living space of the classroom, how do you know if encounters are alive for students?

The first and best answer is: I don't know. But there are indicators: alert body posture, good eye-contact, a willingness to listen, side-chatter about the material that cannot be contained in the main conversation, interruptions that cannot wait their turn, multiple conversations after class as they walk out, a willingness to meet me after class or in the office to continue a conversation, a look that suggests some inner conversation is at play, the desire to bring back an idea from a previous session, bringing friends and parents to class, and ultimately a pleasure in the company of their classmates—even those with whom they disagree fervently.

When these elements are absent and the space seems to have died, I try to stop and ask myself: "This is not working. What do I need instead?"

Also, when they come to the office, I simply ask them, "Are you getting anything out of this class?" I listen for tone, not necessarily the words. Sometimes they are able to say "I am getting nothing."

Do you find it fulfilling? Does it make you happy?

I find it fulfilling, energizing, and fun. I suspect it is a dream compared to anticipating armed drones, the aftermath of bombings, and the desperation of hunger.

Acknowledgments I have received thoughtful, playful, and precise comments from Hannah Gignoux, Narendran Kumarakulasingam, Kaela Bamberger, Rick Miller, and Paulo Chamon. I am very grateful for their engagement. Alas, I am unable to respond even partially to their insights and provocations without undoing the compressed nature of my presentation. No doubt we can take up the conversation when next we meet face to face.

REFERENCE

Hamid, Moshin. 2008. *Reluctant Fundamentalist*. New York: Harvest books.

CHAPTER 3

Pedagogical Micro-communities: Sites of Relationality, Sites of Transformation

Kate Schick

Current institution: large state research university
Typical classroom setting: large seminar classes (25–75)
Typical pedagogical approach: relational pedagogy, micro-communities of learning, critical self-reflection, vulnerable recognition
Disciplinary identity: international ethics, critical security studies

My journey in teaching world politics has taken me from a traditional lecture model, where I imparted knowledge from a distance, to a relational model where I facilitate student learning in the context of 'micro-communities'. This shift toward a more relational pedagogy has been, in part, a journey of increasing congruence between my academic research and my teaching practice. I now support my students on relational journeys of coming-to-know in the context of trusting micro-communities within the classroom. Supported by communities of learning, I invite them to reflect deeply on their own assumptions about themselves and their location in global political norms and structures. I have found that students are more willing to be vulnerable in small group structures and

K. Schick (✉)
Victoria University of Wellington, Wellington, Aotearoa New Zealand
e-mail: kate.schick@vuw.ac.nz

© The Author(s) 2020
J. Frueh (ed.), *Pedagogical Journeys through World Politics*,
Political Pedagogies, https://doi.org/10.1007/978-3-030-20305-4_3

that this facilitates transformation; more mundanely, students are empowered to participate more actively in class and the groups provide networks of support for increasingly stressed and isolated students.

My postgraduate study was in the United Kingdom, where graduate students are not required to teach. I was encouraged to teach 'enough': enough so that I could put some experience of teaching global politics on my curriculum vitae, but not so much that I was distracted from the main task of completing my thesis. As a newly minted PhD graduate applying for jobs, then, I had tutored one class (Introduction to International Relations) twice during two semesters and had never lectured. I applied for jobs at research universities in the United Kingdom and Aotearoa New Zealand, none of which required a teaching statement. I arrived at my first permanent lecturing job with minimal teaching experience, no formal training beyond a research PhD and lacking even a rudimentary teaching philosophy.

A major challenge I faced, then, as an early career academic, was that I was flying blind, particularly with undergraduate teaching. Apart from some hurried teaching observations at the end of my postdoctoral fellowship, it had been 11 years since I had been in an undergraduate International Relations lecture hall. My new colleagues told me that Victoria undergraduates expected visually interesting PowerPoint slides and YouTube clips; I subsequently spent hours searching for arresting images and pithy video clips to accompany my lectures. I felt required to inform, engage and entertain my students and felt woefully inadequate. I found small group tutorials and seminars more familiar and comfortable teaching environments; however, the techniques I used were drawn from my experience of teaching English as a second language, not intentionally focused on teaching global politics. I knew that I wanted to challenge my students to think differently about global politics but I didn't know how.

My journey toward identifying strongly as a relationally oriented educator of global politics has been multilayered. It has evolved in part through reflection on the pedagogical missteps I made in those early classes and from my desire for a deeper connection with my students. It has emerged through closely observing student interaction and listening to students' learning stories, communicated through formal teaching evaluations, self-reflection essays and informal conversations in my office or via email. Perhaps most significantly, it has emerged as I have brought my teaching practice more in line with my academic research. As the congruence between my theoretical commitments and my teaching has increased, so too has my identification as an educator.

In what follows, I discuss three related pedagogical missteps that I made on my journey toward intentional teaching: dissemination of knowledge from a distance, 'serendipitous' group work, and transformation by stealth. I then discuss my journey toward more intentional pedagogy, outlining the technique of building 'micro-communities' that is now central to my teaching practice and highlighting the theoretical commitments that underline my (still-evolving) teaching philosophy.

PEDAGOGICAL MISSTEPS

A fundamental mistake I made in early lecture courses was to assume my role was primarily to impart knowledge: I would communicate and students would absorb. This was multiply problematic. I soon realized that I could not bear the mantle of expert-knower, imparting knowledge from a distance: the experience felt cold and inauthentic and at odds with my identity as a critical international theorist. I began to explore ways of engaging students more in their own learning, posing questions for them to discuss in small groups, roaming the lecture theater during discussions to check in with a small subset of students, and getting students to report back to the whole class so that multiple voices were heard, not just mine. Although I embedded small group discussions into my large lecture classes partly to increase my own comfort and congruence, students reported that they felt they were learning more and that they found the chance to connect with other students valuable.

Using informal discussion groups during class was the beginning of my journey toward more relational teaching. However, these early attempts at group work in undergraduate teaching were content-focused rather than relational: this was my second misstep. My early experiments in enacting more relational pedagogy stemmed from my desire to connect with my students and to see them relate to each other; however, in practice they were less about relationship building and more about deepening students' engagement with course content. This was the case both for my large lecture and smaller seminar classes: the composition of the smaller discussion groups changed weekly depending on where people sat. The haphazard nature of these groups means that some students got 'lost', particularly in large lecture classes. It also meant that groups tended to be imbalanced—for example, in one smaller seminar class the parliamentary interns (a select group) tended to sit together, have in-group conversations, and failed to get to know other students. Even in the second or third year of my teaching, then, relationship building was shallow or serendipitous rather than carefully thought through and intentionally fostered.

A third pedagogical misstep relates closely to the first misstep of taking on the mantle of 'expert-knower' imparting knowledge from a distance. I hoped that by presenting alternative lenses through which to view the world I might enable the transformation of students' worldviews: a sort of transformation by stealth, if you will. I hoped to encourage and provoke students to 'think otherwise' by presenting alternative, persuasive or provocative ideas from the lectern and/or in core readings. This did not always go well: I was berated by an irate student at the end of a lecture in my first year of teaching who felt his closely held beliefs about the world had been trampled on; I was asked to 'tone down the feminism' by another. Nor, I now realize, does it reflect what we know about how people change their minds: increasing access to contrary or persuasive information does not reduce ignorance.[1]

In the years that have followed, I have come to adopt a self-consciously relational pedagogy that avoids my initial missteps in part by removing myself from the position of expert-knower and facilitating student learning from the side. As I discuss in more detail below, I now carefully structure my classes to facilitate student co-learning and critical self-reflection. Students learn with and beside one another in preconstructed 'micro-communities' where their relationships grow and deepen over time. In the context of community, I have found, students are more willing to be vulnerable and to challenge their preconceived ideas about global politics. In what follows, I briefly outline my theoretical commitments before describing how these are outworked in practice in pedagogical micro-communities.

Vulnerable Recognition (A Theoretical Digression)

My journey toward identifying strongly as an educator has been one of realigning my teaching practice to reduce the early dissonance between theory and practice. International ethics is dominated by moral rationalism, which prioritizes the accumulation of 'useful knowledge'[2] that can be

---

[1] See, for example, the discussion of research on listening in Emily Beausoleil, 'Listening to Claims of Structural Injustice', paper presented at American Political Science Association Conference, 2017.

[2] Raymond Geuss, *Outside Ethics* (Princeton, NJ: Princeton University Press, 2005), 3.

wielded to mitigate global problems. Moral rationalism assumes that amassing expert knowledge enables more efficient and effective solutions and that a failure to understand is primarily a failure to know enough.[3] These rationalist assumptions are writ large in contemporary political theory, too, where scholars maintain that conferring 'more recognition'[4]— whether through increasing respect or understanding for the misrecognized or by removing barriers to active participation—mitigates inequality and injustice. International ethics and contemporary political theory have become 'hyperrationalist'[5] theory that promotes technical solutions to produce a more stable and secure global politics. Robert Cox famously terms this response to global challenges 'problem solving theory',[6] claiming that formulating solutions to particular global problems leaves deeper political and economic structures intact and fails to address the fractures of the global order that underlie observable manifestations of dysfunction. (Hyper)rationalist theorists perceive themselves as 'competent moral agent[s]',[7] confident in the judgments they make at little risk to their sense of selves. They are self-certain subjects who 'make mistakes' but 'can never be fundamentally wrong'.[8] Captured by a fantasy of the independent, invulnerable subject, these knower-theorists face outwards, too often focused on what *we* (as competent moral agents) can do for *them* (those deemed vulnerable, incompetent or incapable).[9]

My research seeks to unsettle the confident epistemology of rationalist international ethics and political theory, inviting in its place a relational ontology that tarries with ambiguity and vulnerability. I posit a fundamentally different way of knowing that is indebted to contemporary (radical)

[3] Hans Morgenthau, *Scientific Man* Versus *Power Politics* (Chicago, IL: University of Chicago Press, 1946), vi.

[4] Patchen Markell, *Bound by Recognition* (Princeton, N.J: Princeton University Press, 2003), 180.

[5] Nicholas Rengger, "Political Theory and International Relations: Promised Land or Exit from Eden?," *International Affairs* 76, no. 4 (2000): 769.

[6] Robert W. Cox, "Social Forces, States and World Orders: Beyond International Relations Theory," *Millennium – Journal of International Studies* 10, no. 2 (June 1, 1981): 126–55, https://doi.org/10.1177/03058298810100020501

[7] Kimberley Hutchings, "A Place of Greater Safety? Securing Judgement in International Ethics," in *The Vulnerable Subject: Beyond Rationalism in International Relations*, ed. Amanda Russell Beattie and Kate Schick (Basingstoke: Palgrave Macmillan, 2013), 32.

[8] Hutchings, 35–36.

[9] Hutchings, 35.

Hegelianism.[10] Against the rationalist fantasy of the independent, invulnerable subject, I argue that we are radically dependent, vulnerable subjects. And unlike those who take recognition to be an instrument of emancipation to be wielded with little risk to our sense of selves, I advocate vulnerable recognition—a deeply relational process of coming to know (to re-cognize) ourselves and our implication in oppressive norms and structures.

Vulnerable recognition is at the center of my approach to international political theory. It posits an ongoing and difficult journey toward comprehension that *comes to know*, which disrupts the confident accumulation of knowledge that is so central to rationalist international ethics. The concept of 'knowing again'—or re-cognizing, to use the Hegelian term—orients us to a very different way of knowing, one that is less self-certain and more open to transformation. It invites us to re-examine what we think we know about global politics as well our own relation to (and implication in) the global political. A radical theory of recognition takes for granted the need to revisit that which we think we know—who benefits, who speaks, who theorizes, who acts (and on behalf of whom)—and maintains that what we know will inevitably be mistaken or partial and require us to re-cognize, to know again. Being willing to question one's closely held assumptions necessitates a willingness to be vulnerable; it asks us not only to rethink what we know about global politics but also to interrogate our own implication in oppressive norms and structures.

Relational Pedagogy

My teaching practice is now explicitly underpinned by the construction of students and educators as always already vulnerable and relational. A relational pedagogy turns traditional pedagogy on its head: it unsettles traditional binaries of teacher and student, knower and known, and it rejects the confident accumulation and dissemination of useful knowledge that

---

[10] Note that I am engaging with a particular reading of Hegel, here, which differs significantly from conservative communitarian readings. I am particularly indebted to the philosophy of Gillian Rose and her 'radical Hegel' (Gillian Rose, *Hegel Contra Sociology* (London: [Atlantic Highlands] N.J: Athlone; Humanities Press, 1981), viii.) See also Kimberly Hutchings, *Hegel and Feminist Philosophy* (Cambridge: Polity Press, 2003). Judith Butler, *Subjects of Desire: Hegelian Reflections in Twentieth-Century France* (New York: Columbia University Press, 1987). Kate Schick, *Gillian Rose: A Good Enough Justice* (Edinburgh: Edinburgh University Press, 2012).

seeks technical 'solutions' to complex and deeply rooted problems. This *unsettling pedagogy* seeks to know differently, refusing the valorization of more and better knowledge and inviting students to re-examine their beliefs about global politics in supportive communities of learning.[11] Building micro-communities of learning is central to my practice of relational pedagogy. My hope is that these micro-communities facilitate self- and-other-recognition by providing support for the difficult process of *knowing again* in the context of a community they can trust. However, I note at the outset that these goals are only partially and imperfectly realized in practice and that there is much greater risk attached to relational pedagogy than to the traditional dissemination of knowledge.

PEDAGOGICAL MICRO-COMMUNITIES

I employ micro-communities in my teaching practice in order to facilitate self- and other-recognition in the context of supportive communities. I facilitate recognition through self-reflection and engagement with peers, giving students opportunities to come more deeply to know themselves and their place in global political norms and structures. This necessarily vulnerable and ongoing endeavor invites uncertainty and ambiguity and sits ill with visions of students as sponges absorbing expert knowledge.

To create micro-communities of learning, I carefully preconstruct mixed groups of approximately 8–10 students, paying attention to gender and ethnic balance within and between groups. Students sit together around a large table (or in clusters in lecture theaters in larger third year classes) and spend time getting to know each other in the initial class meeting. From that class onward, students' group members become their peer co-learners. Over time, they learn to trust their peers and to treat their ideas with respect and they become increasingly comfortable sharing their thoughts, their beliefs and their writing.[12] Students reflect, discuss, debate, present and peer-review in their groups (often in smaller groups of

---

[11] Kate Schick, "Unsettling Pedagogy: Recognition, Vulnerability and the International," in *Recognition and Global Politics: Critical Encounters between State and World*, ed. Patrick Hayden and Kate Schick (Manchester: Manchester University Press, 2016), 25–44.

[12] Interestingly, in their final self-reflection essays, more than one student noted that they felt more comfortable and supported having difficult discussions about international and local politics in the context of their small group in class than they did with their family or friends, where people were more likely to be affronted and to refuse to listen to another point of view.

three to four students). Where possible, I encourage students to consider meeting up with group members outside of class to write and revise together, further consolidating their learning.

The rhythm of my fourth year class on War and its Aftermath (of 25–45 students) provides a window into the way my classes are structured. The class begins with reflective writing, where students are given time to think in silence—with pen and paper, not devices—and to quietly process their reflections on course content (and/or their research essay) at the beginning of class. This deliberate pause helps students to slow down and gives them permission to connect with their own thoughts, feelings, and questions before they are invited to communicate these with one another. They then share some portion of their reflections with two or three other students in their small group, gently moving them out of themselves and toward the group. Students then present (simultaneously) in their small groups of 8–10, with one student giving an overview of the week's topic and another presenting a case study, in a deliberately non-assessed exercise designed to build student confidence. The next segment of the class is devoted to discussion and debate in their small groups and is followed by a final segment of the class that changes weekly and may focus on skills (such as freewriting), exercises to support their research essay (such as peer review of essay outlines), or exercises to support deeper reflection on content. More generally, over the course of 12 weeks of teaching, I gradually assign materials that are more challenging, not just intellectually but also to students' sense of selves, ensuring that the most unsettling material is encountered when students have had time to develop and deepen small group relationships.

As relational subjects, part of studying global politics is learning to ask how we are shaped by and implicated in global political norms and structures. This 'unpacking' of our selves is not a solitary journey but one that is facilitated and supported by community. Research on listening indicates that subjects are more likely to actively listen and to learn when they feel safe.[13] Underpinning the construction of micro-communities in the classroom, then, is a desire to provide communal spaces where students feel supported and heard as they engage in the (potentially challenging and difficult) work of coming to know themselves and their place in the world.

---

[13] Emily Beausoleil, 'Listening to Claims of Structural Injustice', paper presented at American Political Science Association Conference, San Francisco, 2017.

Over time, my hope is that relationships become more trusting, students become more vulnerable, and learning deepens.

During the more intimate discussions that follow the period of reflective writing as well as the larger group discussions that take place, students listen to what each other has to say.[14] They become more willing to 'know again'—to re-cognize—to challenge deeply held assumptions about global norms and structures and to reflect on how they are situated (and implicated) in those norms and structures. Providing space for students to sit in silence and reflect together each week gives them a valuable opportunity to pause and to process what they have learned in a deeper and more meaningful way. Some students report that these rhythmic pauses in their weeks help them to form deeper connections between course content, their lived experience and the global political—others report less transformative, though still empowering, effects including increasing their confidence with course material and helping them to later verbalize their thoughts.

Giving students time to be silent together as well as time to be verbal also caters to diverse student learning styles and personalities. Another significant consequence of enacting micro-communities in the classroom has been the positive feedback I have received from students who have never before felt comfortable debating or presenting in class but were able to do so for the first time in the context of structured micro-communities. These more introverted students find it immensely helpful to have scheduled quiet time during which they can process their thoughts and begin to articulate their responses in writing before sharing them aloud with their small group. This empowers students who have previously felt paralyzed or silenced in large group discussions to author their own views and to verbalize them in class, some of them for the first time in their three or four years of undergraduate education. For these students, the small group structure is transformative indeed: they find their voices in the context of a community they can trust.

A relational pedagogy also acts as a corrective to the strong cultural bias toward individualism and rationalism in Western pedagogy, which systematically disadvantages students who have more relational and holistic

---

[14] Note that for some students, listening does not come easily and students have to *learn* to listen (in part by learning to be silent and to wait before speaking). This is one of the primary challenges I have faced with this model of teaching.

worldviews and ways of being.[15] In Aotearoa New Zealand, where I teach, Māori and Pasifika students are confronted by the overwhelming predominance of rationalist Western pedagogies in the mainstream school and university systems. Adopting a more relational approach better supports their learning, giving Māori and Pasifika students space to develop meaningful and trusting connections with their classmates—to build whanaungatanga.[16] In a study of relational responsive pedagogies in a school setting, Chrisandra Itirana Joyce highlights the significant transformation that takes place for Māori students when a culturally responsive pedagogy of relations is adopted: this includes teachers establishing non-dominating and dialogic relationships with students, culturally responsive teaching, intentional learning with and from others, connectedness through relations of care (manaakitanga and mana motuhake),[17] and a 'socially just…vision of excellence'.[18] Anecdotally, at least, Māori and Pasifika students have responded well to the relational micro-community structure in my classes, with some students noting that they feel more comfortable expressing their ideas in small group discussions and one noting that she felt supported in placing her experience of colonialism in national and global political context.

This shift from unplanned, informal group discussions to carefully crafted micro-communities has transformed the way students learn in my classes. Instead of learning at a distance—where knowledge is transferred from expert-knower to student-learner—students learn alongside one another, in community. They allow themselves to become vulnerable in their small groups and, in so doing, become less self-certain and more open to transformation. Students engage in self- and other-recognition: they come to know their group members (and group members' varying perspectives on global politics) better; they also come to know *themselves* better and to question their own closely held assumptions and beliefs.

---

[15] See, for example, the discussion in Chrisandra Itirana Joyce, "Relational Responsive Pedagogy: Teachers and Māori Students Listening and Learning from Each Other" (University of Waikato, 2012).

[16] In this context, whanaungatanga refers to the sense of belonging that students build through reciprocal engagement and working together.

[17] Manaakitanga is the process of showing respect, support and care for others. Mana motuhake, in this context, refers to the articulation of "high learning and behavioural expectations". Joyce, "Relational Responsive Pedagogy: Teachers and Māori Students Listening and Learning from Each Other," 41.

[18] Joyce, 43.

Constructing the learning experience in this way addresses the pedagogical missteps I outlined earlier in this chapter: dissemination of knowledge from a distance has given way to facilitation from the side; 'serendipitous' group work has given way to preconstructed groups and actively fostered community; and transformation is left to emerge through community interaction.

Adopting a self-consciously relational pedagogy in the classroom has transformed my teaching and students' learning. As an educator and co-learner, I have had to become more willing to sit with unknowing and discomfort as I accompany students on their learning journeys. Part of my own pedagogical journey is an increasing commitment to encourage students to engage with the history and ongoing colonial practices that shape Aotearoa New Zealand, resisting the temptation to teach global politics as something that happens 'out there'. I would not by any means claim that students' worldviews have been radically transformed as a result; however, I have on multiple occasions seen (and read in self-reflection essays) evidence of some students changing their minds and reevaluating closely held beliefs and these moments of transformation are both powerful and hopeful. One of the more provocative readings that I set my fourth year students in the last third of the class is Robbie Shilliam's 'Who Will Provide the West with Therapy?',[19] which provides terms to productively unsettle students' deeply held views about indigenous-settler relations in the context of structures of global white supremacy. One of the exercises I get my groups to do in the third hour of class is to divide each small group in two and discuss quotes from the chapter, one focused on the settler history of Aotearoa New Zealand and the other focused on liberal intervention, before swapping reflections on the quotes.[20] After reading this chapter and

---

[19] Robbie Shilliam, "Who Will Provide the West with Therapy?," in *The Vulnerable Subject: Beyond Rationalism in International Relations*, ed. Amanda Russell Beattie and Kate Schick (Basingstoke: Palgrave Macmillan, 2013), 133–48.

[20] The first quote discusses anti-racism workshops for Pākehā in the church, which were guided by these rules: 'first, you must know that you are not cultureless, but carry a particular culture of individualism, a culture that is embraced and privileged in the mainstream institutions of society; second, you must know your own history, not the santitized history of the diffusion of Western civilization, but rather the history of colonial dispossession that, like it or not, you—and your culture—are implicated in and benefit from'. Shilliam, 140. The second quote relates to dominant expressions of Western liberalism in foreign policy making: 'All these argumentations tacitly or explicitly repress the memory of Western liberal violence; they displace Western culpability in the making of a 'dangerous' world for Western liberalism;

discussing it with his group members, one of my Pākehā[21] students went from strongly resisting the notion that he was in any way implicated in the ongoing systematic oppression of Māori to realizing that he has benefited (and continues to benefit) from choices and structures that privilege non-Māori New Zealanders and is complicit in upholding these structures. This was a radical shift that would not have taken place outside the context of community, where the practice of the group has grown to become one of working, learning and questioning alongside one another.

Before I close, however, I acknowledge that relational pedagogy is risky and can be disrupted by students who refuse (or are unable to) listen. It is decidedly countercultural to relinquish attachment to certainty and some students struggle to let go of their desire to 'win' arguments and to have their voice dominate others. In one class, I invited a student to my office to discuss the importance of listening in order to secure a more supportive group experience. It was difficult for this student to grasp the idea that having the loudest or most persuasive argument was not the goal of small group discussions. However, the student eventually changed the way he engaged with other group members and ended up reporting that the class had shaped him as a person, not just as a scholar—another example of transformation that was productively unsettling not just for the student concerned but also for me as an educator and for the group more generally.

My approach as an educator and co-learner of global politics builds from a relational ontology that emphasizes the ongoing process of coming to know ourselves and our location in global politics. It resists the traditional conception of students as discrete learners who absorb useful information from the lectern. Such pedagogy constructs students as rationalist subjects who reproduce and repackage useful knowledge in order to gain high marks, secure employment, and 'solve' political problems. Relational pedagogy also resists the moral rationalist accumulation of knowledge, which is underpinned by the assumption that the more (and better) information we have gathered, the more likely we will be able to solve global problems that concern us. A relational ontology invites students and educators on a deeper and more vulnerable learning journey that emphasizes

---

and they rationalize fantasies of white domination via an abstract universality given the perverse name of human rights'. Shilliam, 145.

[21] New Zealander of European descent.

the value of *knowing again* or recognition as we transform the way we understand ourselves, others and our place in the global political. Relational pedagogy seeks to know differently, refusing the valorization of more and better knowledge and inviting instead a turn to self- and other-recognition, where students learn with/from/alongside one another in supportive micro-communities.

REFERENCES

Beausoleil, Emily. 2017. Listening to Claims of Structural Injustice. Paper presented at American Political Science Association Conference, 2017. San Francisco.

Butler, Judith. 1987. *Subjects of Desire: Hegelian Reflections in Twentieth-Century France*. New York: Columbia University Press.

Cox, Robert W. 1981. Social Forces, States and World Orders: Beyond International Relations Theory. *Millennium: Journal of International Studies* 10 (2): 126–155. https://doi.org/10.1177/03058298810100020501.

Geuss, Raymond. 2005. *Outside Ethics*. Princeton: Princeton University Press.

Hutchings, Kimberly. 2003. *Hegel and Feminist Philosophy*. Cambridge, UK/Malden: Polity Press in association with Blackwell Pub/Blackwell Pub.

Joyce, Chrisandra Itirana. 2012. Relational Responsive Pedagogy: Teachers and Māori Students Listening and Learning from Each Other. Master's Thesis, University of Waikato. https://researchcommons.waikato.ac.nz/bitstream/handle/10289/7038/thesis.pdf?sequence=3

Markell, Patchen. 2003. *Bound by Recognition*. Princeton: Princeton University Press.

Morgenthau, Hans J. 1946. *Scientific Man vs. Power Politics*. Chicago: University of Chicago Press.

Rengger, Nicholas. 2000. Political Theory and International Relations: Promised Land or Exit from Eden? *International Affairs* 76 (4): 755–770. https://doi.org/10.1111/1468-2346.00163.

Rose, Gillian. 1981. *Hegel Contra Sociology*. London/Atlantic Highlands/Athlone: Humanities Press.

Schick, Kate. 2012. *Gillian Rose: A Good Enough Justice*. Edinburgh: Edinburgh University Press.

———. 2016. Unsettling Pedagogy. Recognition, Vulnerability, and the International. In *Recognition and Global Politics. Critical Encounters Between State and World*, ed. Patrick Hayden and Kate Schick, 25–44. Manchester: Manchester University Press.

Shilliam, Robbie. 2013. Who Will Provide the West with Therapy? In *The Vulnerable Subject: Beyond Rationalism in International Relations*, ed. Amanda Russell Beattie and Kate Schick, 133–148. Basingstoke: Palgrave Macmillan.

CHAPTER 4

Time for Class

Patrick Thaddeus Jackson

Current institution: mid-sized private research II university
Typical classroom setting: small classes (<25)
Typical pedagogical approach: close reading; structured debate; simulations; open discussion; bounded wandering
Disciplinary identity: <rant>INTERNATIONAL STUDIES IS NOT A DISCIPLINE BUT A MULTI-DISCIPLINARY FIELD<rant> international theory, research methods and methodology, philosophy of (social) science, science fiction and international affairs

Since 2012, the same year I was promoted to full Professor, I have been a full-time academic administrator. My daily job, I like to joke (but it's not just a joke), consists of two simple mantras: "find fire, fight fire" and "see trouble, shoot trouble." And of course the ever-popular round of meetings that could and should have been e-mails, the endless haggling over minor points of process and the wording of symbolic declarations, drafting annual reports, and setting strategic goals…it never ends.

Except at 2:30 pm on Monday afternoons this past semester (Spring 2018). I had kicked around the idea of teaching one class each year during

P. T. Jackson (✉)
American University, Washington, DC, USA
e-mail: ptjack@american.edu

© The Author(s) 2020
J. Frueh (ed.), *Pedagogical Journeys through World Politics*,
Political Pedagogies, https://doi.org/10.1007/978-3-030-20305-4_4

the last administrative reorganization, during which my office—the office of the Associate Dean for Curriculum and Learning—acquired two new Assistant Deans, one for undergraduate education, one for MA education. With the resulting redistribution of responsibilities, I could finally get back to engaging in the most fulfilling part of my academic vocation, and offer a course on "research on popular culture" as part of our sophomore-year research methodology sequence. I'd run it my usual way: put texts on the syllabus for us to discuss, oscillate between whole-group conversations and various forms of small-group in-class work, avoid lecturing at all except for the first day when I would lay out a conceptual framework, and hold office hours for students to come talk one-on-one about their individual projects as they developed. This being a popular culture class, most of the texts were pop-cultural artifacts of one kind or another: a movie, a novel, comic books (we looked at the first 12 issues of *Black Panther* written by Ta-Nehisi Coates, collectively titled *A Nation Under Their Feet*), and so on. One Monday I walked into class, a couple of minutes late as usual because the bi-weekly Senior Staff Meeting was scheduled from 1:00 to 2:30, and proceeded to turn on the classroom DVD player and lower the screen to show an episode of *Buffy the Vampire Slayer* so we could talk about the particularities of using serial television shows in one's research. The class was silent, and several students looked confused. "What?" I asked, "We're doing television today." No, they replied, the syllabus said that today was simulations and gaming, and they'd done the reading for that and were puzzled as to where the games were that I said I'd bring in so we could do a little experiential learning by playing those games and talking about rules and strategies and the formation of attitudes. And they were correct, I'd mixed up the days, probably because I hadn't looked at the syllabus in weeks. I was so busy zipping back and forth between administrative duties that even though I dearly missed teaching, I'd forgotten to *make time for class.*

Rookie mistake, perhaps. Except that when I was a much less experienced classroom instructor, I would *never* have gone for that long without looking somewhat obsessively at the semester plan, making sure that I had my notes in order, and generally taking care to control the class and the classroom. Since that time I had adopted or evolved a very different approach to teaching, one that demanded far less worrying about the minute details of each and every moment of each and every class session. But it did require—as this slightly embarrassing incident drove home to me—being "in the flow" of the class in a way that my administrative job made extremely difficult. The temporality of academic administration is like the temporality of other modes of management and bureaucratic process, segmented into discrete tasks that have to be completed somewhat in isolation from one another. The temporality of the classrooms I strive to facilitate and sustain is more holistic, more of a bounded wandering back and forth over a landscape than an efficient dash toward a clear goal. To make it work I have to be a fellow wanderer, and make time for and with my students in a way that administrative practice simply does not permit.

That realization means that it's time for a change of direction in my own academic career: it's time for me to stop being a full-time administrator, and to return to the lessons I'd learned in the classroom years before.

*   *   *

The first class I ever taught as the "instructor of record" was a U.S. foreign policy course at New York University. The scheduled instructor was a fellow Ph.D. student of mine in the Political Science Department at Columbia University, and for whatever reason he couldn't teach the class that summer. So he asked if I'd like to do it, I said sure—summer money!—and suddenly was parachuted into a syllabus I hadn't designed, with a textbook I hadn't ordered, and a roomful of students interested in learning about something I was far from an expert about. I'd been a TA before, and from having been a student for many years I had a pretty clear sense of what was expected: I needed to lecture, students would take notes, then I'd administer an exam or two and grade them. The textbook didn't really lend itself to discussions, so I set about writing a series of lectures that fleshed out some of the textbook's points, provided some additional context, and talked about things I was more comfortable sounding off about, like embedded liberalism and the post-WWII international order. In class I spoke from my notes, embellished a bit as the mood struck me, told a few jokes and got a few laughs, and generally enjoyed the almost-daily reminder that I did, in fact, know more than the undergraduates sitting in front of me. On the last day of class, I gave a lecture about the future of US foreign policy in which I laid out the case for a return to the Moon, not as an exclusively US project, but as a US contribution to the creation of an effective human-global identity; this garnered spontaneous applause, which made me feel like I had done my job well.

But what had I actually *done?* I'd talked a lot, and given my students some pieces of information that they hadn't had previously. I'd answered questions and clarified vocabulary. At best, my students would walk out of the semester with a few stories to use in illustrating their debates and discussions about stories they might read or watch on the news. I didn't really feel like anyone's mind had been changed or even that anyone's core commitments had been re-examined; given that I did most of the talking in the class sessions, and given that the exams tested the students' abilities to give the correct answers to questions about the (textbook-provided) sources of US foreign policy, there really wasn't a lot of time or space for any serious exploration by students who were just trying to keep up with the material I was rapidly dishing out. But the students were pretty happy with the class, and on the strength of my evaluations I was offered another NYU class for the fall, this time with little more than a title attached to it: "War, Peace, and World Order." My own syllabus, my own readings, my own exams. Now things would be different...except that they largely were not, as what I promptly did was to write a syllabus chock full of theoretical concepts about war and peace and world order that I wanted the students to know, wrote lectures about those concepts, and gave exams intended to ascertain whether the students had gotten the concepts. Basically the same play on a different stage, albeit with more of my own set design and dialogue. And similar results: great evaluations, generally happy students, and a lingering sense that I was somehow not actually encouraging the kind of critical reflection that I really wanted students to engage in.

After all, in undergrad, the program I had been in was one that featured much more debate and discussion, and much less lecturing. But I wasn't sure what else you could *do* with 75 students in a room *except* lecture. As a result of student pressure on the department, I was offered a third class at NYU the following spring, and this time it was a senior seminar with a topic I picked myself: "Culture and Identity in World Politics." Since this would be only 20 or so students I could do a book a week, and run class sessions as completely open-ended free-form discussions, with me only asking questions and prodding to keep the conversation moving. *That* felt like teaching—but many of the students started asking me for main points, summaries, something to take notes on, some authoritative declaration from me that one or another of the texts we were considering was *correct*, or that one or another of the interpretations of those texts offered by someone in the class was correct. It was as though what the students wanted from me was some kind of mini-lecture, even though this was a seminar. As I thought about it I realized that, in fact, almost every seminar I had ever attended as a student defaulted back to some kind of lecture in the end, when it became clear that the instructor wanted us to get something in particular out of what we were reading. And I had generally treated those moments as just another interpretation, preferring my own sense of the text as long as it was defensible, and if the instructor agreed with me, great! My favorite classes were always those in which the instructor encouraged that, so I decided to do the same—but I was at a bit of a loss trying to explain to my students *why* I was not going to give them the "right answers" they seemed so desperate for.

This was the first time I fully realized that at least some students approached their college education with a very different attitude than I'd approached mine—indeed, an attitude very different from how I had *always* approached school of any kind. I had typically either been the teacher's pet or the teacher's biggest headache, because I had always done a lot of independent reading and often came to class, whatever the class, bursting with a lot of outside information and was never at all shy about sharing it. Any authority that the teacher had over me was entirely dependent on whether she or he accepted me as independently knowledgeable. I never entered a classroom expecting the instructor to tell me something I didn't know, and even though I clearly didn't know everything, I always expected to learn whatever facts I was going to learn on my own. I mean, I could read things at least as well as the instructor could, so what I wanted from a class was something I *couldn't* get from reading a book or five on the subject. But I couldn't really say what that was, and all I had any idea how to do in front of a classroom was either gushing like a fountain of facts spouting off things that I knew, or having a conversation. And while the former didn't feel like the thing I was supposed to be doing as a teacher, the latter wasn't what many students were expecting, and to my great surprise many of them resisted it.

It wasn't until the following year, when I taught in the Contemporary Civilization Program at Columbia, that I started to figure out a way to express what I was trying to accomplish in the classroom, and to articulate clearly what it was that I myself had been looking for in previous classes I'd taken. Contemporary Civilization is the original "Plato to NATO"/"Western philosophical tradition" course and is still required of all sophomores in Columbia College. The course is taught in small sections of about 20 each, and is taught by a mix of full-time faculty, postdocs, and a small number of graduate students from across the university (we were called "preceptors," I think from the Latin for "you're graduate students so we don't have to pay you as much"). About two thirds of the syllabus is set collectively by the folks in charge of the program, and individual instructors can innovate and improvise with the rest: spend a couple more class sessions on Plato so there is time to read the *Apology*, cover both Rousseau's *Discourse On Inequality* and his *Social Contract*, add in Kierkegaard and de Beauvoir, and so on.

We also had great freedom when it came to exams, so I started giving students a list of six potential questions all of which asked for a compare-and-contrast across two or three authors on some topic, and then coming to class on exam day and rolling a die twice to determine which two questions they'd have to answer. This sort of examination mirrored what we did in class each day, which invariably involved a group discussion about what a text said and meant, along with an effort to place the text in dialogue with other texts so as to carry on a broader conversation. I never asked anyone to declare themselves personally and irrevocably part of Team Hobbes or Team Kant; I did ask everyone to become conversant with the various perspectives under consideration, and to develop *sustainable* readings of the various texts. "I don't care whether you agree with Machiavelli or with Montesquieu," I would tell my students; "I care that you have good reasons for whatever your position is." And: "you don't know what your position is on most of these issues, because you haven't had a chance the think them through before. Now you do, by trying on a variety of 'classic' arguments for size." So the focus of the class was on *argument*, and specifically, on helping students practice the art of making and evaluating arguments. I genuinely did not care if my students came away remembering anything specific about any of the authors we read. I figured that if they wanted to go more in depth with any of those authors, they'd read more, and remember things that way. What I wanted them to come away with was a lasting sensibility about what it meant to engage with philosophical issues in a textually precise way, and how they would acquire that sensibility was through practice in the classroom.

Teaching Contemporary Civilization was a profound episode in my development as a teacher. I realized that there had to be a fit between the pedagogy I was pursuing in the classroom and the evaluations I was using to determine student's grades, because the grade was the immediate motivation for their engagement in the class. I could *use* that to get them to do things that they might not otherwise do, and by setting the syllabus up so that they would be evaluated on their capacity to make textually precise arguments, I was able to provide a disincentive for the recurrent query about correct answers that could be memorized and spat back on a test. Exam questions for the lecture class I was still offering at NYU changed, as did the content of the lectures for that class; I made a deliberate effort to use my lectures as springboards for conversations, argued with the assigned readings, left more time in class for more open-ended discussions of what I'd just presented and responded to questions by pressing the questioner back into the text or by replying to their reading with a contrary, but equally well-sustained, reading of the same thing. Policy questions—"but what should state X do?"—got some version of "it depends" in response, followed by an exploration of what a number of different answers to that question might look like.

I could do this with relative ease in my NYU courses and in Contemporary Civilization, because they all were pretty philosophical by design, and because I pretty quickly got a reputation for teaching this way so those students interested in learning this way began to seek out my classes. But when I moved to American University a few months before defending my dissertation, I was dropped into two decidedly less philosophical, and already established, courses: World Politics and Introduction to International Relations Research. World Politics, an introductory IR course taught from a common textbook, was more amenable to transformation once I realized that although I had to assign the required textbook, I could assign it merely as background reading, and spend my actual class time on the "supplemental" things I assigned, like *The Prince* and the novel *Snow Crash*. That said I do distinctly remember the first question a student asked during my first class session after I had walked the class through the syllabus: "is there such a thing as 'international political theory'? Because that's what you seem to be talking about and I'm here to learn about world politics." I asked what he meant by "political theory" and how that was different from "world politics," and to my complete lack of surprise he said that political theory was all abstract opinions while world politics was concrete facts. This led me to expound on the indispensability of theory for identifying facts in the first place, using "national security" as my example and channeling Arnold Wolfers. So despite the unphilosophical character of much written on the subject—the textbooks, for sure, but also a large amount of what was published in the major disciplinary journals with which I was familiar—I relatively easily found ways to make World Politics more a course to my liking, more of an exploration of arguments and perspectives and less of an occasion to read the newspaper or the textbook and opine about it for credit. And here again, since there were many sections of World Politics offered each semester, students began to self-select into my classes because they wanted this kind of exploratory educational experience.

Introduction to IR Research presented more of a challenge. Most sections of that course were taught as introductory statistics classes, with an emphasis on how to use SPSS software to conduct elementary hypothesis tests. This I had no interest in doing, both because I didn't think one could actually teach statistics without requiring the students to have a sufficient math background, and because I did not feel that most of the questions that the students were interested in were especially amenable to statistical analysis. And I did not want to use the class as an occasion for disconnected software skills training, because that seemed to me like a waste of all of our time. If anything, what students would benefit from was an opportunity to develop their own research questions along the methodological lines appropriate for the specific question and the specific student. So when I took over that course I made it into an exploratory space where students would take a topic and tease it out through multiple methodologies, producing plans to carry out a project on their topic as a large-n or a small-n statistical-comparative project, as an ethnographic-hermeneutic project, and as a discourse-relational project, before choosing one of those three and making a good faith effort to carry it out. Along the way we spent a good deal of time talking about—what else?—the parameters and rules for a good argument in each of these different idioms. Together with a number of classroom exercises intended to allow students to practice working in various methodological traditions, the result was a course I was actually quite happy to teach, and one that produced results in the form of the research projects that many of my students undertook subsequently as Honors theses or Fulbright proposals.

Over the course of a few years I developed a pretty consistent pedagogical pattern, regardless of the topic or title of the class. "Borders and Orders." "Social/Science/Fiction." "The Conduct of Inquiry in International Relations." "Introduction to IR Theory." The classroom was invariably a space for practicing the craft of argument: reading arguments made by others, taking them apart to see what made them work, getting inside of them and driving them around, advancing one's own arguments and having them carefully considered by others. The classroom was in important ways *depersonalized*, since the focus was on ideas and arguments, and on giving students the opportunity to improve their critical capacity for producing and evaluating arguments that were held, so to speak, at arm's length, in front of the class, in the public but enclosed space of the classroom. Yes, we were contemplating arguments about the wider world, but we were relatively removed from the world while doing so. That relative removal was the boundary within which we wandered, and teaching in Washington DC—a city in which internships grow out of cracks in the pavement, and the maelstrom of partisan politics collides with the frantic hustle of the policymaking process to produce a perfect storm of opportunities to leave the contemplative life behind—I soon grew to appreciate that a not insignificant part of my role as a teacher was to sustain that boundary and give students permission to read and discuss and think without being immediately worried about the practicalities of life outside of the classroom.

In that way, over a few years, I carved out a space for myself to teach the way I felt called to teach. Did it work? Sometimes I was more successful promoting critical reflection than at other times, and with some students I was more successful than with others. Some students responded, learning took place, and despite having almost no one else in my school who really understood what I was *doing* in my classrooms, I had the freedom to keep on doing it because, on the whole, I got better-than-average teaching evaluations. More important than those end-of-semester surveys, though, were the students who came through my classes and began to self-identify—and to be identified by others on the faculty—as "PTJ students," characterized by their extremely broad sense of what constituted international affairs (novels? films? sports?), an appreciation for the meaningful and meaning-making aspects of social life, and by a general commitment to relate their specific empirical claims to broad currents in the history of political thought. One of my great delights was advising the senior capstone projects many of these students eventually did, perhaps none more memorable than the project that resulted from a student, recently returned from a year studying abroad, coming to my office and outlining a detailed project that it was clear to me her heart simply wasn't in. "This sounds great, but I don't think you really want to do it," I told her, and she broke down in tears, confessing that she was bored and frustrated with international studies and international politics and economics, and had realized while abroad that what she was really passionate about was high fashion and the everyday politics of gender representation. "So do that as your capstone," I advised. "Can I do that?" she asked. "Can I really do that?" Of course, I told her, and I'd be more than happy to be her capstone advisor. That simple act of *giving the student permission* allowed the flood-gates of her creativity to open, and before she left my office we'd sketched a completely different capstone on the global high fashion industry, one that involved the student learning to sew so that she could try her hand at actually designing clothes for women that the industry considered overweight (and the rest of us would likely consider "normal-sized"). As far as I know this was the first capstone project featuring a fashion show of student-produced clothing that the School of International Service had ever seen—and that student went on to study fashion in Paris, and now works in the industry promoting high fashion designs meant for the rest of us.

All of which is to say that I count "my" successes one student at a time, one class at a time, sometimes one class session at a time, and I put "my" in scare-quotes because what happens to and for my students in and through my classes is something that is centrally and critically dependent on their coproduction of the space of learning. "Joint action," a term I first encountered in John Shotter's utterly brilliant book *Cultural Politics of Everyday Life*, concisely captures what I work to facilitate in my classrooms:

> ...as an outcome of the joint action between them, people find themselves "in" a seemingly "given" situation, an "organized" situation such that it has a "horizon" to it and is "open" to their actions. Indeed, its "organization" is such that the constraints (and enablements) it makes available influence, that is to say, "invite" or "inhibit," people's next possible actions.[1]

Which is to say that whatever my students learn is certainly not something specific that I beamed into their brains or stamped on their foreheads. In fact, I am most delighted when my students learn things I could not possibly have had already in my mind to transmit to theirs: their own sense of vocation, their deepest commitments, and their most potent passions, the simple yet profound realization that their own perspectives are *perspectives* rather than the neutral conveyance of a view from nowhere. If they come to know better who they are and who they are in the process of becoming, in part as a result of their participation in the joint action of a discussion-oriented classroom where bounded wandering is the whole of the law, I am content.

*   *   *

[1] John Shotter, 1993. *Cultural Politics of Everyday Life*. Toronto: University of Toronto Press, p. 47.

After I got tenure, I was invited by the university's Dean of Academic Affairs to become Director of the General Education Program. I'd been on the GenEd committee before, and was known on campus as someone who would often speak up in meetings in favor of less of an emphasis on job skills and more of an emphasis on broad learning. AU's General Education program had the fairly typical baskets of curricular areas, and like many universities where departmental and school professional identities are strong, had no faculty of its own, but borrowed classes and faculty from across the university by designating particular courses "GenEd" in one of those curricular areas. But what was most intriguing about our GenEd program was that it was also home to a new experiment in residential education, a "University College" that featured first-year students living on a residence hall floor with the other students in a specific GenEd course they'd applied to be a part of. The Director of General Education also got to head that program, and I jumped at the chance. With these two responsibilities, I had the opportunity and the capacity to craft a broader space on campus for the kind of education I was interested in. Through my discussions around the university, I had identified people of a similar mindset (although almost none in my own school), and I set about recruiting them to help me build the space out. And as Director, I of course got to teach in my own program, running a section of World Politics that started off talking about soccer and baseball (including field trips to see D.C. United play soccer, and to the site where the Washington Nationals baseball park was being built) and the globalization of sport, and ended up with the film *District 9* and discussions about refugees and aliens.

If the story ended here, this would be somewhat more of a fairy tale. Unfortunately, it does not end here. Changes in higher-level university administrative priorities led to increasing resource constraints on University College, and after fighting those fights for several years, the new Dean of my home School of International Service offered me the opportunity to become Associate Dean and shape an actual undergraduate program out of the variety of classes that we offered without much overall design. Again, an opportunity to build something larger than my own classrooms and to reach more than my own students. Plus, with about two thousand undergraduate students, there were opportunities to create a number of different pathways to degree completion without having to worry overmuch about low enrollment issues, or fighting resource battles at the center of the university. So I accepted the challenge of "scaling up" my own classroom practice into a whole curriculum designed as a discernment engine, a way for students to learn about their vocation in the global world by charting their own pathway through international studies, not with a complete lack of structure but with just enough structure to ensure that their education remained broad and exploratory rather than specialized and disciplined. Students would begin with a first-year seminar taught by a faculty member on some topic of the faculty member's particular interest; regardless of the topic, the seminar would primarily be about developing and encouraging the critical habits of mind that would enable students to engage in bounded wandering later on. In the sophomore year, students spend a year on research methodology, in a massively expanded version of what I had been doing in Introduction to IR Research: the first semester was a "menu of methodological options" and opportunities for students to develop sketches of possible research projects, and the second semester was a class specifically focused on whichever topic or technique the student chose to pursue in more depth for an independent research project. At the same time, sophomores took "gateway" courses in the eight thematic areas we decided to divide international studies into, areas like "Peace, Global Security, and Conflict Resolution" and "Identity, Race, Culture, and Gender." Subsequent coursework in the student's two chosen thematic areas—they can't hyper-specialize in just one—culminates in a senior capstone project, once an option, now a requirement for *all* graduating seniors.

Designing and implementing the program took about three years, and by almost any measure— including retention, student satisfaction, and most importantly the quality of the work students produce and the discernment students undertake—it's been a resounding success. The cost of my building the program, however, was that I was unable to teach on a regular basis; Associate Dean is a full-time job, unlike Director of General Education, which was only part-time. Before this immediately past spring semester, the last full-semester class I taught was in spring 2012. So when the Interim Dean suggested that I teach a class this spring, I jumped at the opportunity, hoping it would restore some balance and remind me why I was an academic in the first place. But to be honest, the whole semester has been an exercise in cramming class in where I could, office-hours interrupted for emergency meetings, make-up meeting-times placed where they wouldn't interfere with staff meetings, and, most dramatically, the day I came to class all prepared for what the syllabus specified for the *next* class session, not the current one. When I did my grading at the end of the semester, it took me three hours to just *compile* all of the assignment grades I had given throughout the semester, because I hadn't had the time to keep track of them. No time. No time for serious contemplation, no time for reflection, no time to really *dwell with* my students as we together wrestled with something. No time for class.

At the end of June 2018, I am done being Associate Dean for the time being. I am looking forward to having more time for class.

And yet. What I taught this semester was one of those second-level research methodology classes, in which students needed to design and execute an original research project over the course of the semester. Most students entered without a clear sense of exactly what they were planning to do, or with vague and unimplementable plans for projects that could never succeed. Over the course of the semester, some—not all, but some—of them had those kind of "aha" moments in which things crystallize, and after that managed to produce very engaging projects. Despite my lack of time, despite my struggles to properly sustain the temporality of bounded wandering, some learning still took place. But the most I did was show up sort-of on time and take seriously the things that people said in our discussions, and sit with them in my office (or in the corridor walking from one meeting to another, or once on the shuttle to the metro station) and talk the project through with them. Maybe that's enough: to be committed, to be clear about how it is that I teach, and to make an effort to do as much of that as I could in the limited time I had. Maybe, in the end, teaching is about being the kind of teacher that you are, as much as you can be, and having faith that learning will take place. After all, I can't make one of my students learn, any more than I can make a seed grow into a plant; all I can do is create some favorable conditions. Being concerned about your students and their learning is perhaps the most important of those favorable conditions, more than any clever game you play in the classroom, more than any innovative assignment or radical reading. Our students are *people*, and if all we do is remind them of that by taking their thinking seriously, we've given them permission to become who they are. And that too is class time, time for thinking clearly, time for conversation and encounter and time and space for learning.

References

Shotter, John. 1993. *Cultural Politics of Everyday Life*. Toronto: University of Toronto Press.

CHAPTER 5

Things I've Learned from Failure and Friends

Kevin C. Dunn

Current institution: private liberal arts college
Typical classroom setting: seminar, large class lecture
Typical pedagogical approach: lecture, discussion
Disciplinary identity: IR Theory, introduction to IR, American foreign policy

A few days before 11 September 2001, I began teaching at the small liberal arts college that still employs me. Before I could even begin refining my pedagogical approach, the stakes within the classroom got very high. I had connections to several people in the hijacked planes, and many of my students had connections to the victims in the Towers. Suddenly our conversations about world politics and American foreign policy took on degrees of personal importance that I had never experienced before or since. The national media decided to follow one of my students for a day, callously reporting to the world his observation that my conversations about the Rwandan Genocide in our African Politics class seemed meaningless in the face of the American tragedy that he was experiencing. And as the new IR "expert," I was thrust onto public panels and forums where several of my new colleagues berated me for trying to understand the thinking of the

K. C. Dunn (✉)
Hobart and William Smith Colleges, Geneva, NY, USA
e-mail: dunn@hws.edu

© The Author(s) 2020
J. Frueh (ed.), *Pedagogical Journeys through World Politics*,
Political Pedagogies, https://doi.org/10.1007/978-3-030-20305-4_5

terrorists and for situating this epic tragedy within the broader history of the postcolonial world. At one such gathering a few weeks later, I predicted the US invasion of Iraq, missing its start date by only a week or two (when one is so successfully prophetic, it is important to constantly remind everyone that one was once so successfully prophetic).

The following year, as the reality of the Iraq invasion (and a drawn-out occupation of Afghanistan) was beginning to dawn on people, I organized a daylong conference on campus. One of the people I invited to speak was my friend Naeem Inayatullah. He gave a talk about the Afghanistan occupation and the recently released *Lord of the Rings* films. The thrust of his talk was that imperial occupation inevitably failed. To illustrate this point, he suggested that "teaching was impossible" and drew a comparison between trying to educate unmotivated students and "civilizing" an occupied people. Elsewhere in this volume, Naeem offers this position as the foundational wisdom upon which he riffs brilliantly, showering pedagogical insights upon us with deft ease. But when he unveiled that "teaching is impossible" insight, it was almost a throw-away line for him. I know because when I mentioned it a few times afterwards, he practically disavowed the statement. When I told him that I was using it as my framing motif for my third-year review Teaching Statement, he warned me against doing so, questioning both the validity of the claim and the wisdom of my telling the review committee that what we aspired to do was bullshit. In some ways it is rewarding for me to see that Naeem now fully owns this incredibly important insight about the impossibility of teaching. But I also should have listened to him at the time, because my review committee really didn't like me questioning the validity of their pedagogical craft. When I came up for tenure a few years later, I made no mention of my disbelief that teaching was possible. Naeem kindly wrote me a letter of support and I'm pretty sure he didn't say anything like that either.

I got tenure, but I didn't stop believing that teaching, as we tend to conceive of it in North American higher education—experts imparting wisdom on absorbent students—is an impossible task. This basic belief has been my touchstone for almost two decades now. As Naeem notes in his contribution, students don't want to be taught, learning is unlikely, posing is probable. All we can hope for is a productive encounter with others in which we can meditate on the possibility of our own learning. He does a far better job exploring this, so if you haven't read his contribution yet, go read it now. I can wait. Sorry, but now the rest of this chapter is going to pale in comparison to what you just read.

Naeem has not been the only invaluable sage in my two-decade career of "teaching." Undoubtedly I have learned most from my own failures. But I've also been fortunate to have highly skilled teachers as friends and I've stolen ideas and practices from them without reservation. In the chapter that follows, I talk about some of my failures and what I have learned from friends much more skilled than I. (While I will credit these friends, I must offer my apologies to each for my clumsy distillation of their own ideas and practices.)

Performance and the Art of Good Story Telling

In graduate school, I was a teaching assistant (TA) for the university's massive Introduction to International Relations course. I eventually scored a few adjunct positions in the area, teaching a variety of political science courses. As a starving graduate student, I would teach anything from Public Policy to Comparative Political Theories. At first, my default practice was simply teaching from the book—structuring the course around a lecture that summarized the basic material from the readings. I am sure it must have been deadly boring for the poor students. I was focused on imparting what I thought was *really important* information and I certainly failed miserably at that because I was not putting much passion into what I was doing.

But I had the good fortune to be a teaching assistant for Michael Corgan, who took over the Intro to IR course after his predecessor (who I was also a TA for) failed miserably. Turns out, peppering your lectures with racist, off-color jokes is a really bad idea. The course was offered every semester and drew around two to three hundred students. After a few semesters, I became Mike's unofficial "head" TA and would occasionally stand in for him if he was unable to make a lecture. I had to attend each of Mike's lectures (offered early in the morning in the vain attempt to keep enrollment down) in order to take attendance for my sections. After the first semester or two, I pretty much knew the content of all of Mike's lectures. Very rarely would he surprise me with the introduction of new material. But I was always riveted by Mike's performance.

Because that is what it was, a performance. There were several hundred bleary-eyed 18-year-olds packed into a cavernous lecture hall for over an hour several mornings a week. Mike is a decent scholar, but more importantly he is a great performer and he would utilize his physical expressions and booming voice to great effect. This was one of the most important pedagogical lessons I learned in graduate school: *performance matters*. Of course, this works well for me personally. At 6′3″, I take up a lot of space in front of the classroom. I also have a good bit of energy, and I use a lot of it while prowling around the classroom, gesturing passionately, occasionally jumping up on a chair. Occasionally students will complain about my constant movement (I recall someone once asserting that I made them seasick), but more often, students will talk about my "passion." But really, what they are witnessing is a "passionate performance."

From Mike, I realized that what I was doing—"teaching"—was a craft. The craft involves more than just performing, but I think it is a significant part of it. I realized fairly early on that a significant part of perfecting one's performance was memorizing the lines. Not that there is a strict script to follow. Much of my lecturing style, like Mike's, has become improvisational. If I recall correctly, Mike only used a page or two of notes for each lecture. These were basically cues to remind him of the important concepts that he needed to include in that day's lecture. The point is that he would only occasionally glance at his notes in order to make sure he wasn't forgetting anything significant. I've tried to follow that lead in my Intro to IR courses. Before walking into the classroom, I review my page or two of notes to make sure I can remember all of the key points I want to cover. I'm pretty sure exactly how the first five to ten minutes are going to go. After that, I try to only casually refer to my notes to ensure that I am on track or, more often, to make sure I have a name or date correct.

In addition to his performance skills, Mike's genius was also in his storytelling. Mike would weave together these concepts in a delivery that was often quite captivating. By the time I finished graduate school, I had heard most of the stories numerous times, but I still sat enthralled at his masterful delivery. And that is the second main insight I took away from Mike— part of the art of teaching relates to the craft of good *storytelling*.

Let me give you an example, one you are free to steal. In my own Intro to IR course, I have a section on the evolution of the international state system. For the lecture notes of one class, all I have written is "World War One was caused by love" and then some dates and facts that I can never entirely remember. I then begin the class by asking a student how World War I started. A sharp student will reference the assassination of Archduke Franz Ferdinand. If they are really good, they'll know that assassination happened in Sarajevo on 28 June 1914 (I had to go look that date up). But when I press them by asking what the Archduke was doing in Sarajevo and how his assassination led the Germans to invade France by way of

Belgium, they usually come up short. So with a grand theatrical flourish, I inform them that World War I was, in fact, caused by love. Which it was. For the next hour, I'll tell them about how Ferdinand was so in love with his wife Sophie that they constantly sought ways to travel outside of Vienna together, eventually leading them to Sarajevo. I will then tell the story of how this event led to the eventual outbreak of the war.

Yet, one thing I have learned is that good storytelling means never pointing out the lesson or moral of the story. A good story thrives on ambiguity. When telling the story above, I explicitly don't tell them what the story is about or what lessons they should be taking away. Afterward, I ask the students if I convinced them that World War I was caused by love. Inevitably one student will refer back to the love between Ferdinand and Sophie, which is the initial hook of the story. I'll respond by saying that that wasn't the love that I was talking about, shrug my shoulders, and dismiss class, hoping that they'll dig deeper into the story to think about what other forms of love contributed to such an epic tragedy. Because I had also talked about the ways in which the love of nationalism (the assassins), the love of rational planning (Schlieffin Plan), the love of masculinity and militarization, the love of racial supremacy, the love of secret diplomacy and alliances, the love for colonies and commerce, and the love for prestige and reputation, all factored into the outbreak of World War I.

Of course, sometimes I just want to tell the students what they *should* take away from the stories. When talking about recent US wars of aggression, I want them to all understand how misguided, counter-productive, and simply wrong these interventions have been. But I've realized that beating them over the head with the "moral of the story" is highly ineffective. Teaching, after all, is impossible. So I am constantly reminding myself to stick with the ambiguity, the contradictions, the complexities and messiness of the stories. But sometimes I give in to my proselytizing impulses. In my Intro to IR course, there is little ambiguity in my discussion about climate change and the epic environmental insecurity that we now find ourselves with. I find trying to give space to climate change naysayers is ethically impossible for me. Last year I go so emotional talking about the horrors that we are inflicting upon our world that I teared up. As I said to my students at the time, "If tears are not the proper response to this tragedy, then I don't know what the fuck is." Was I being overly proselytizing? Probably, but I'm OK with that because I was being ethically authentic, which is important for the encounter that Naeem speaks of.

HAVE A BIG AND VARIED TOOLBOX

Despite everything I just wrote, it is important to underscore the fact that lecturing is a really horrible pedagogical practice. Most of us all know this, but many of us still do it. I am still amazed that at academic conferences we give our presentations by sitting or standing in front of our audience and reading from our notes. We know this doesn't work on our students, so why are we doing it to our colleagues? I fear that many of us may, in fact, torture our students this way. I know I did for the first few years of teaching. Of course, the reality is that when you have a big class, you don't have much choice. For example, it would have been impossible to have small group discussions with those 200–300 students in Mike Corgan's Intro to IR course.

When I have big classes, I reluctantly rely on lecturing/storytelling more often than not. But for smaller courses, for the bulk of the classes I offer, lecturing is a horrible idea. But for the first few years of teaching, I treated my courses of 20–25 students the same as if they were filled with hundreds. Just me up there telling stories and occasionally asking questions. Fortunately, my partner Anna Creadick is a brilliant educator. She got a degree in Education, before going on to a PhD in American Studies. One thing I learned from her was to try doing something different every day you are teaching. If you lectured last time, then structure the next class around small group discussions. If you did that last time, then give them a role-playing exercise. Or give them questions from the reading and have them interview each other. Or use a "fishbowl" approach where you select a handful of students to sit in the middle of the class to have an intense conversation about the material before inviting the rest of the class to jump in. Or have the students debate a variety of positions you assign them as they walk into the classroom. Or cover the material by playing a game like Jeopardy or Family Feud. Or give them crayons and blank paper and have them draw "sovereignty" or some other abstract concept, then discuss why they drew what they did (this is actually one of my favorite exercises in my IR Theory class and it works exceptionally well for exploring how a concept like sovereignty is socially constructed).

The point is that it is important to *do something different every day*. If you did it last class, don't do it in the next one. This keeps the students engaged and interested, but it also keeps me engaged and on my toes. I fell into the trap of thinking that if something went well one time, I should repeat it often. But then it becomes routine and ineffective. "Oh great, we're playing Jeopardy *again*." I've found it important, especially in my smaller (less than 30 students) classes to have a diverse and varied toolbox to utilize. And don't worry about trying something that might result in extraordinary failure. I know that is easier to say from the far side of tenure, but I've learnt more from the failures than the successes. I've been in the middle of a role-playing exercise, realized it had completely come off the tracks, brought it to a premature conclusion, and then discussed with the students what went right, what went wrong, and why. I suspect students appreciate seeing the stumbles, in part because it makes professors more human and provides an awareness that they are part of an ongoing experiment/journey.

Of course, the path of least resistance is to simply identify the key concepts I want to discuss with the students and then go into the classroom and present them. It takes far more work trying to figure out new and interesting ways to present the material. And, yes, sometimes it feels gimmicky. And sometimes it is. If something feels too inauthentic, I won't do it again. Students are smart. They know when I am bullshitting and phoning it in, and will respond accordingly. If I want them at the top of their game, then I need to be as well. But if I'm being honest here, I've also gotten to the point in my career that I am really trying to keep myself interested and engaged in material that I have been presenting to 18–21 year-olds for almost three decades. I don't want to burn out. Part of that means actively upending things that have become too familiar and pushing myself out of my comfort zone.

You Gotta Justify Yourself

The best pedagogical experience I had was team teaching a course with Anna and our friend Nick Ruth, a studio artist. The course was a first-year seminar about developing a critical sense of place. Anna brought her commitment to doing something different every day. And Nick offered several pedagogical insights that have fundamentally changed the way I approach teaching and course design.

When we were putting the collective syllabus together, Nick would challenge every reading assignment I put forth. He would simply ask that I explain to him why any given reading was important for the students to invest their time and energy. And Nick was unrelenting. He would not accept answers such as "it's important" or "it's a classic." I would have to be able to articulate to him exactly what was important about that specific reading. If I couldn't come up with a convincing argument, then it wasn't assigned. Being a "classic" or "common" text wasn't enough. Nick insisted that we not assign any reading that was superfluous or that we could not articulate its value to ourselves and our students. Nick's position was driven by a desire for clarity on the part of the teacher and for the student. As he puts it, for the teacher, it's about knowing what the central insights of the material should be, and also about feeling confident about how the dots connect because you have curated the dots. It's for the student in the sense that you are promising not to ask them to spend time doing stuff that may not be useful and used and are, therefore, valuing their effort to actually do the things you ask them to do and showing them how it is useful. What resulted in that class was a reading list that was rather Spartan, but totally focused.

That was not the way I typically had done things. My syllabi tended to be reading-intensive, no matter what the course was. For my IR Theory course, I thought it important that students read all the "classics" as well as important contemporary contributions of significant debates. I had them reading Kenneth Waltz, Machiavelli, Alex Wendt, and scores of other "big" names. It was my view that they *had* to read these primary texts to understand what IR Theory was all about. It was almost a rite of passage. How could you take a course in IR Theory without reading them?

After teaching with Nick, I embraced his approach when assigning readings, asking myself to justify each and every reading I assigned. "Because I say so," wasn't an option. Nor was "because it is a classic." I could justify Machiavelli, but making my students read Waltz? No. That was more akin to a form of hazing. Same with Wendt and so many others. My reading list for all of my courses got pared down to the barest of essentials. Often I share my rationale with the students so they can understand why I am assigning particular readings, which also makes explicit the normative decisions at play within any course design. Did the students suddenly start doing all of the reading? Sadly no. But now I could clearly articulate exactly why I was assigning what I was. And having that clarity in my own mind gave the presentation of that material, and the entire course, a sharper focus. Interestingly in the IR Theory course, not only did the assigned reading shrink dramatically, but it also became less white and less male. So many of the dead (and undead) white dudes were included because I had some sense of obligation to include them as part of the Canon, despite my own feminist and postcolonial sensibilities. Waltz, Wendt, and Gramsci are all gone, but Fanon, Walter Rodney, Cynthia

Enloe, and Cynthia Weber are all present and accounted for. This kind of radical accounting of the assigned reading has had a major impact on how I design courses and has, undoubtedly, resulted in better courses.

The other thing that Nick did when we were collectively designing the course was to constantly ask how we were going to hold the students accountable for what we were asking of them. If we were assigning readings, how were we going to ensure that they had done it? If we wanted them to understand some concept, how were we going to assess if they actually did? What he was demanding of us was that we design mechanisms that held students accountable and ensured that they were comprehending what we were asking them to comprehend, but also that we should not create any assignment that did not explicitly do these things. There would be no "busy work." If we were asking the students to take a quiz, write a paper, complete some task, then we had to be absolutely clear to ourselves and to them why we were asking this of them. If we couldn't, then the assignment was cut. If we didn't have a mechanism for assessment, then we had to come up with one. This was an extension of valuing student effort, while also generating vehicles with which to assess whether or not the central ideas are being engaged and applied. The idea wasn't to limit what students can think about a given topic but to make sure that they deeply engage with the ways to think that are being presented.

This had the same impact as Nick's relentlessness on readings. On the one hand, in all my classes the assessment mechanisms became more numerous. But on the other hand, they became more focused and, to my mind, more interesting. For example, in my IR Theory course, I now assign multiple short papers. But they are explicitly geared toward having students apply concepts from the readings to current events. In my American Foreign Policy class, I want them to see how the specific policies that they are studying have real-life consequences in people's lives, so they now make short documentary films that require them to reflect on the readings and to interview members of the local community.

Both of Nick's interventions into my teaching really just revolve around *being more mindful and intentional* of everything I do within a course. I've come to realize how easy it is to lose perspective. At least it was for me. Over the years, I would add readings because I thought I should. I would assign research papers because that was what was expected. I would create busy work in order to make sure the students had something to do. It took a studio artist's intervention to make me a better social science professor.

I should also mention that whenever I would lead our collective class, Nick would stand in the back of the room and give me the finger. Or he'd walk into my section and knock my books onto the floor. Those were also great lessons in reminding myself not to take myself too seriously. That is an important lesson to keep in mind throughout your career.

Also, I think I probably started it.

AND THE MORAL OF THE STORY IS…

I still believe that teaching is impossible. But after almost three decades at a liberal arts institution I am trying to make what Naeem calls the "encounter with others" more productive for everyone involved, myself included. I am a different professor than the one who began a few days before 9/11, in large part because I became more self-reflexive about what I was doing in the classroom. That's because I made a lot of mistakes. And I continue to. But I've tried to find solutions by talking and paying attention to my friends and colleagues.

And if this essay has any type of takeaway (heaven forbid I tell you the moral of the story), it is this: if you want your students to learn, you need to be learning from others yourself. Talk to others about their teaching practices and philosophies. Not just your senior colleagues, but folks across all ranks, and, more importantly, from all disciplines and divisions. Go sit in your colleagues' classes and see what they are doing (and give them the finger from the back of the classroom). Ask your non-professor friends what inspired them in school, and what inspires them now. Always be looking for the kinds of innovations that will diversify and enrich your own craft.

CHAPTER 6

Teaching as Service: Losing and Finding My Identity in Global Classrooms

Jamie Frueh

Current institution: private liberal arts college
Typical classroom setting: interactive classes of 18–35 students
Typical pedagogical approach: collaborative learning, with lecture
Disciplinary identity: IR pedagogy, political identity

The first time I thought of myself as a teacher was, ironically, the most out of my depth I have ever felt. Three weeks after graduating from college, I left for an eighteen-month volunteer assignment teaching high school in the rural homelands of apartheid South Africa. I was there to serve humanity in some small way, so when the principal told me I would be teaching calculus and South African history, I said I would give it my best shot. Being about as far away from home as I could be and teaching subjects I only vaguely understood, I both lost and found an (incomplete, complex, and continuously emerging) identity as a teacher. It helped that my students (whose existence actually made me a teacher) were more interested in other, more politicized aspects of my identity, and that they were not conflicted in any way about either my teacherness or their studentness.

J. Frueh (✉)
Center for Engaged Learning, Bridgewater College, Bridgewater, VA, USA
e-mail: jfrueh@bridgewater.edu

J. Frueh (ed.), *Pedagogical Journeys through World Politics*,
Political Pedagogies, https://doi.org/10.1007/978-3-030-20305-4_6

I have always said that I learned a hundred times more from my experience than I taught, but now I can see how thinking of myself as serving my students created a particular identity as a teacher that continues to this day.

The engagement I experienced with my South African students sustained me through the doctoral program gauntlet and still echoes in the attitudes I bring to becoming a good teacher. For me, teaching is still about service, about empathizing with the individuals who come to class (more or less) ready to be engaged by the world, and about not just yielding, but actively challenging the authority that students have been trained to associate with those three little letters after my name. I think of teaching as serving not just my students and their futures, but the society (my society) and the world (my world) into which they will stride after graduation. With what I acknowledge is a huge dollop of hubris, I think that teaching can change the trajectory of the world. To be only slightly less trite about it, I think of what I do as giving emerging democratic citizens practice using the skills they need to call liberalism's bluff by actually remaking the world as individual and collective agents.

IMPUMELELO HIGH SCHOOL

I honestly did not know what I was doing, and yet I felt authorized and, in unguarded moments, a bit smug about doing it. I was a newly minted college graduate heading to an educational system where many high school teachers didn't have their own high school diplomas.[1] In the face of anti-apartheid student protests in the mid-1980s, my university had divested its endowment from corporations doing business in South Africa, but the university president wanted to do more. The result was a volunteer teaching program in the apartheid homelands, the 14% of South African territory where Blacks (about 83% of the population at the time) could own land. While the curriculum was the same "Bantu education" as in all Black schools, and all the (non-volunteer) teachers were paid by the government, Impumelelo High School was on the compound of a Catholic church and the facilities were paid for by funds from Europeans. I lived in the rectory

---

[1] One of the most pernicious institutions of apartheid, the structure of legalized racism that governed South Africa from the late 1940s until the mid-1990s, was the education system designed to stifle Black aspirations. The number of Black teacher training college graduates was kept well below what was needed.

with priests (a German and an Austrian) who spent their days ministering to dozens of widely dispersed congregations. The principal was a Black South African, as were the other teachers, and they answered to the KwaZulu Homeland Department of Education.[2] The school was surrounded by gorgeous hills and valleys, but little else besides a post office, café, and general store about a half mile away. It was a far cry from senior week.

I arrived with self-righteous indignation, a genuine desire to help, and a core commitment to service. I almost immediately got hit in the face by just how inadequate all that was. *Everyone* was genuinely appreciative that I was there (which I didn't feel I had a right to expect), and they were willing to let me pursue my quirky ways, such as refusing to use corporal punishment. But I was definitely lost. Mail took two weeks to get to the US and two weeks to get back. I had enough money for one international phone call a month, and that required the assistance of half a dozen operators. In ways big and small, it took intense energy to make sense of and adapt to my new environment, and countless times each day I felt I was failing.

But, I was there to serve South Africans by being a teacher. The principal assigned me a couple English classes along with South African history and calculus. I had just graduated from an IR school with a degree in International Relations, Organizations, and Law. The only South African history I knew was stuff I was sure wasn't in the government curriculum. My degree required economics but no math. Even my college English course was "Politics of the Novel." But I figured I must have learned all that grammar stuff at some point, I could read and explain what was in a history textbook, and I had taken calculus in high school, which was more than anyone else on the staff could say. Filtered through my service mentality, that seemed sufficient. At least it did during training, before real live students showed up expecting me to help them pass the year-end government examinations. What the hell was I playing at? More importantly, whose futures was I playing with?

I muddled through, but I sucked. I spent weeks teaching obscure English verb tenses because they were on the dusty government curriculum. I spent every night hunting justifications for apartheid in the ninth grade history book and wondering whether my students would fail their exams if I taught them otherwise. I relearned calculus the day before I

---

[2] Nominally each of the ten homelands had a degree of independence, but the bureaucracies existed mostly to create a class of Blacks beholden to the status quo, and their authority over policy was practically nonexistent.

walked in to teach it. But I put on my tie and stood in the front and hoped that the lessons would come out right. As a teacher, a font of knowledge and understanding, even wisdom, I sucked. I loved the students and they seemed at least to tolerate the hairy-legged *umlungu*. But I knew I was failing as a teacher.

What saved me, what taught me that I might one day become a good teacher, were the relationships with the students, not as abstract knowledge containers and future exam takers, but as people like me who had a hard time understanding things. Especially with calculus, I realized my greatest asset was that I understood how they might misunderstand, because I was, in real time, also in the process of figuring it out. It took a while, but it dawned on me that even in areas where there certainly were right answers—past present participles, the date of the battle of Isandlawana, the area under a parabola—it was OK to be a teacher and not know those answers. It was OK because we—teacher/students—could figure it out together. I started walking into calculus class saying things like "I couldn't figure this one out. Let's see if we can work it through together." I stopped obsessing about what I didn't know and started trying to teach *my* students—Bhekizitha, Musa, Precious, Lengiwe—how to learn stuff. I decided the skills that make a good teacher—figuring things out and explaining them to others—are processes that everyone should acquire, and that learning works better if we practice it together.

I also found that it is easier to build learning environments when I genuinely respect the others in the process, when I see them not as a backdrop for my soliloquies or an audience for my magic tricks (can I get a volunteer?), but as individuals with unique, creative minds. Because my students were boarders, and because there wasn't much else to do, and because I was genuinely there to encounter difference, I hung out with them after class. I asked them to teach me things—how to order a beer in Zulu, what a *tokoloshe* was, how to dance at a wedding. They taught me a joke about my whiteness that I still tell today.[3] I challenged the traditional teacher/student binary, along with a whole mess of the other categories of self/other that facilitated apartheid. They said (and

---

[3] The pattern of greeting in Zulu, like in English, involves an exchange of acknowledgements, (e.g. "*sawubona*") and inquiries after the other's wellbeing ("*unjani?*"). The routine is to respond, "I'm fine" ("*ngiya phila*"). Especially during apartheid when race was a marker of how one was doing in a deeper sense, in certain circumstances I'd answer instead with "*ngi mhlope*," which means, "I'm White."

it seemed to be the case that) they found my service useful. That service, along with all the privileges my other identities bestowed on me, earned me some credit I could play with. I was willing to take risks with my teacher identity in part because the job was so far outside my comfort zone, in part because of the power of my other identity labels (including a presumption of creative freedom), and in part because my first tentative, muddling steps in that direction seemed to work, both for me and for the students. The more I reflected and experimented, the more confident I became that I could make this kind of teaching work and that I enjoyed it.

AFTER IMPUMELELO

Teaching in South Africa convinced me that a career as a college professor would be fulfilling. I could bring my empathy and skills for understanding misunderstanding to American students who, I knew from experience, are rarely forced to genuinely wrestle with just how different the world can be. I could help others navigate and understand the challenges of otherness. And, as I mentioned, I could save the world. Along the way, I had tried retail and hospitality and realized that service industries are not really about service. They are about creating and catering to customer perceptions of value, and the compromises required were unsatisfying. So I enrolled in a doctoral program, knowing that my goal was a career in teaching. I enjoyed my research, and there are projects of which I'm quite proud. But since Impumelelo, I've been trying to be a teacher.

I could now indulge in a number of (what I think are occasionally entertaining) stories about how I made it through graduate school and landed a job at a liberal arts college, but the editor of this volume is a real stickler about word limits. Suffice it to say that my identity as a future teacher sustained me through some difficult personal challenges. It got me summer gigs running a volunteer teaching program in Jamaica, a State Department program for Greek- and Turkish-Cypriot university students, and another assisting high school students from Kenya. It earned me a teaching award and a temporary position at my doctoral institution teaching Cross-Cultural Communication. And after three years on the market, it landed me a job with a 4-1-3 teaching load at a wonderful regional liberal arts college where I have been ever since. It has also sustained me for two decades of disciplinary conferences where everyone else has written (and read) all the brilliant new books and spent their energy since the last conference creating and hashing through exciting new global political ideas. My identity as a teacher of IR has sustained me because it is a continuously creative project, because I believe that teachers can save the world, and because I am occasionally good at it.

But I certainly haven't always been good at it. Even after discovering a passion, a mission to serve, and an inflated sense of my role in the universe, I still regularly suck as a teacher. Continuously becoming a good teacher is hard work. By hard work I mean more than just dealing with embarrassing gaffes, misguided angry students, justifiably angry students, inabilities to communicate, failed classes/modules/semesters. I mean becoming a good teacher requires investing energy, not just in course content, but also in the process of creating good learning environments. The hard work involves exploring new teaching techniques in print, in workshops, and by visiting colleagues' classrooms. It involves asking students and colleagues to help identify learning impediments and create engaging ways to overcome them. Reflection, empathy, and creativity are work because they require time and energy. They can be *hard* work because they also involve admitting that my teaching needs help, which rubs against the predominant teacher persona. It helps to think of my investments as modeling a growth mindset and the attitude of "a lifelong learner." But the work of continuously becoming a good teacher is not a show for my students, colleagues, or review committees. It is an integral part of my identity.

I also believe that connecting my teaching practices to my ontological/epistemological commitments has helped. My identity as a teacher and my constructivism have grown up together, and they inform each other. As a constructivist, I believe that agents change social arrangements by acting in conjunction with other actors. Those social arrangements constrain and empower agents by attaching rules to actors through meaning-laden identity labels. Agents steer the trajectory of the social arrangements to the extent that their social power and rhetorical prowess convince other actors of descriptions, explanations, and imperatives. I don't believe in progress, but I like that I teach in a society that does, and I like that my students believe in progress, even if they don't know that they do.[4] The rhetoric of our Western liberal social arrangements emphasizes the power of the individual as an agent of change and argues that individuals should be rewarded or punished based on the social value of their creative acts. Even though

---

[4] By progress, I mean the inevitable improvement of societies through dialectic competition. I don't believe in a telos or that the circumstances of life necessarily improve over generations.

that rhetoric does a terrible job of describing the actual distribution of rewards and punishments, we do know some things about the kinds of acts that are supposed to make individuals successful. As a constructivist and a student of social change, I believe actors who understand existing patterns and who are adept at processes recognized as creative have a better chance of remaking the world and earning rewards. As a teacher of individuals in a liberal society, I have adopted as my overarching pedagogical goal educating individuals to be the best, most empowered liberal agents they can be. This goal, grounded in my ontological/epistemological commitments, organizes my pedagogical work and my teaching choices. As an administrator, it grounds the curricular and logistical work I do on behalf of my colleagues' teaching. My development as a teacher has consisted of hashing through the nuances of my commitments by testing them against my pedagogical failures and successes.

PROCESSES AND TECHNIQUES

The upshot is that I am committed to the empowerment of my students as agents, both as learners and as participants in liberal democratic/capitalist arrangements. I teach the limits of that agency and what it means to be critical and thoughtful participants in those arrangements. I teach how to delve beneath the veneer of simplicity upon which we all live most of our lives, and how to find, explore, and appreciate the complexity that undergirds late-modern life. In our society, I think an undergraduate education should be about seizing the agency inherent in these liberal processes. I have, however, decided to cede any authority I might have over what students should do with their agency. I often have strong opinions about what they should do, but I fear the implications for *their* agency if I insert my authority into our collective deliberations. My unwillingness to tell them what to think generates a good deal of confusion and ambiguity, conditions my students rarely associate with teaching, even if they do tend to associate them with the first stages of learning.

I teach liberal processes through global politics, a subject particularly well suited to teaching undergraduates about complexities. But I emphasize that complexity is a generic condition, and that a college education is (more or less) an opportunity to practice exploring all kinds of complexities. Late-modern societies (although, emphatically, not all individuals within those societies) are far enough removed from mere subsistence that individuals are able to specialize in particular complexities (such as teaching global politics). But individuals live richer lives if they are able to attend to a wide range of complexities and to continually find, explore, and appreciate new complexities. As my students are working through the complexities of global politics, they are practicing complexity exploration and I devote a lot of class time to teaching and celebrating those processes. After establishing the contingency ("squishiness") of global political knowledge, we investigate methods for sorting through competing knowledge claims. Individually and in groups, students practice evaluating knowledge claims concerning complex issues about which smart people disagree. They then try their hand at authoring their own knowledge claims and submit them for evaluation by the rest of us. Becoming proficient at these processes takes time and energy, and many students ultimately decide it isn't worth the investment. But even students who only take one IR course should learn to recognize global complexities and have a road map for how to interrogate them if they choose to do so in the future.

Most of my pedagogical work, therefore, involves exploring teaching techniques through which students learn the processes that make successful late-modern agents. Sometimes I have chosen to try teaching techniques because I thought they would help me accomplish my pedagogical goals. Sometimes I have tried teaching techniques because I found them intriguing and their success refined how I think about my pedagogical goals. Of course, I have tried techniques that didn't work for me, and their failures either helped me refine my teaching or they didn't. The techniques in my current repertoire remain because I think they contribute to an environment of respect for and engagement of Bridgewater College students. The approaches of collaborative learning are a good example.

I encountered the term collaborative learning in a pedagogy workshop run by a couple of colleagues who had attended a workshop on the topic. Collaborative learning is a set of techniques that reject the student as a passive receptacle of knowledge, judged on individual ability to master material. Instead, coursework is framed as a collective project, with students and professor working together to make sense of material. Student work is often completed in small groups, with incentives built on mutual interdependence rather than competition. "Base groups" of three or four students are established during the first week of class and persist through the semester. While some exercises use different groups—random or spatial groups, super-base groups, a single large group—the base group is the main locus of interdependence. For example, instead of individual essays on my midterm and final exams, my students take group oral exams in their base groups. I distribute nine essay-type questions a week before the exam so each group can work together to devise answers and prepare for their free-flowing 30-minute discussion that take place in my office. Every member of the group gets the same grade, based on the coherence and complexity of the conversation, the richness of references to course materials, and teamwork. Students do worry about grade interdependence, some groups work better than others, and these exams take longer than grading individual essays, but almost without exception students prefer group oral exams to individual written essays because the group preparations and negotiations expose them to deeper complexities and alternate perspectives that enhance their learning.

I use a number of similar group structures for interdependent collaboration—discussion leadership, paper presentations, exam question construction—and I have systems that usually, but not always, keep them functioning smoothly. With respect to discussions, for example, the first official act of a base group as a collective agent is to nominate rules to govern our class discussions. Over the course of the semester, base groups apply these rules in a dozen different discussion formats, and regularly evaluate the effectiveness of different systems of collaborative deliberation. "Public discourse" is not just a technique for delivering content. It is an explicit learning objective for the course, and base groups are an effective structure for practicing those processes. A quarter to a third of every class is devoted to learning practices that are not specific to global politics, such as group deliberation, critical thinking, analysis, written/oral communication, or how to author knowledge claims. Some grumble that my job as a teacher is to settle things for them, not to keep complicating things, and I have to keep reminding them that the high school model of education to which they are accustomed has not served them well. I assure them they will pick up knowledge about global politics, but that the point of the course is to use global political content to practice these processes. Several times a class, I draw their attention back to this meta-cognitive level and argue again that this system is better than a semester of me giving them "the answers."

While I invest a lot of time in these collaborative systems, I do not agree with some of my esteemed colleagues that lecturing is inherently ineffective or that teaching is impossible. I even use PowerPoint and some of my written exams require identification terms. The act of lecturing or showing outlines on a screen is not the problem; the problem is the attitudes that too often drive the choice of these tactics. Lecturing merely to convey knowledge reduces teaching to Freire's banking model of education or Ford's industrial/efficiency mode of workforce development, and it is alienating. But accompanied by both explicit instructions about how to use lecture material in service of ideas, and evidence of genuine respect for both students and the student/teacher relationship, lecturing (even with PowerPoints) can effectively model analysis and prepare students to participate in the deliberations that are the heart of my enterprise. While students must buy in to the learning project, teachers can teach students to learn. Through good teaching, students can experience (and become addicted to) the rush of sliding seemingly disparate pieces into place to create an idea, of owning that idea, and of explaining that idea to others (Grandma at the Thanksgiving dinner table, a roommate in a late-night conversation, me in a ten-page paper). I argue (at the beginning of my courses and regularly throughout) that a college course should be about playing with ideas in pursuit of arguments and explanations and decisions, the stuff of liberal agency. But playing deeply with global political ideas is best accomplished with some context and shared vocabulary. With many Bridgewater students, I find I can more efficiently get to perspective taking, public discourse, and the authoring of knowledge claims if I provide some of that context and vocabulary in a (short and deliberately planned) lecture. I think part of my job is to straddle the complexity divide and help translate, sometimes as an expert, but always as a listener who can empathize with how students might misunderstand (situations, theories, others' points of view). So I lecture in short bursts, interrupted by student writing, small-group discussions, student questions, film clips, and brainteasers. I use PowerPoint for visual learners, but distribute all the text on the slides at the beginning of class to make sure students focus on ideas instead of scribbling. There are many ways to be a good teacher. As long as I am thoughtful, true to my guiding principles/educational goals, honest with myself about the results, and flexible about fixing problems, I think I am a better teacher using a variety of techniques, including lecture.

ENGAGED LEARNING

The journey that began as I muddled my way through calculus with several dozen South African teenagers 30 years ago continues. Just a few weeks ago, I was again playing teacher in South Africa, this time with several dozen American students on a 15-day travel course. I'm on much firmer ground as a teacher now and the course is, some tell me, life changing. But even though this was the seventh time I've taught the course, I still experienced failures and missed opportunities. A few days ago, as is my practice at the end of every course, I wrote to my future self several pages of dense notes for the next time around. Along with proposed changes to timing and logistics, I wrote about still struggling to find the right balance between my role as an expert and my commitment to giving my fellow travelers space to figure South African normality out for themselves. At the heart of my pedagogical philosophy is a commitment to structuring environments in which students are responsible for their own learning. I do all the extra work to run a travel course because it epitomizes why I teach global politics—to help students learn how to find, explore. and appreciate difference. I know they will get so much more out of their experiences if they discover South Africa for themselves, but I have to balance that against my responsibility for their safety and the limited time they have in the country.

So in the notes to my future self, I wrestled with being too ready to show off my expertise. On the one hand, it took me years of study to feel like I understand a few of the nuances of South African society, and, in most cases, I understand them BECAUSE someone with more expertise answered my questions. AND answering earnest questions with hard-earned knowledge is exactly what teachers are supposed to do. AND explaining things is much more efficient, especially if these students will never return to South Africa. BUT I am suspicious of the impulse. I am a little too proud of what I think I've got figured out, and answering their questions makes me feel not just smart, but wise. The efficiency/philosophical tensions are evident in a range of explanations I could provide— how to use a foreign ATM, why even the poorest dwellings are surrounded by fences and walls, whether people are genuinely being nice to us. But in all my courses, I struggle with this tension between a responsibility to give *my* answers and a responsibility to empower agents to find *their own* answers. Where is the line? Who is responsible for student learning and what are the implications of that responsibility? I have my own tentative answers, but these are questions on which all teachers should gnaw, with other teachers if possible.

Having taken on some administrative duties, part of my job now is to facilitate those kinds of conversations between my colleagues. While I still teach (it is important for me to say that), the current stage of my journey is as director of Bridgewater's Center for Engaged Learning, an administrative position that oversees the college's interdisciplinary academic programs (general education, the honors program, study abroad, the first-year seminar, the senior portfolio, the career center), and four endowed institutes. I spend most of my days solving logistical problems on behalf of my colleagues, our curricula, and of course our students. One of my jobs is to explain the concept of engaged learning at open houses, orientations, alumni and donor events, and at lots of meetings. This suits me; my interpretation of engaged learning embodies the mission I have been working to flesh out since Impumelelo. Engagement is a feeling of flow, a rush, a sense of focused presence in the moment, a willful investment of energy and concentration in the challenge at hand, not because it needs to be done, or is supposed to be done, or because it will make the doer a better person in ten years. Engagement is embracing a challenge for the joy of it. My job is to make sure our programs help students find the engagement in their college education, to get addicted to the joy of playing with ideas. You, dear reader, know that intellectual challenges concerning global politics can be engaging. For a whole host of reasons, however, you should assume that the vast majority of the students in any undergraduate class have yet to be convinced of this. I don't know how to teach curiosity or joy, but I can explain the project of education as a search for engagement. I can model the joy, and I can build exercises, classes, courses, and curriculums that make engagement more likely. And on top of making college more fun and lives more fulfilling, engaged learning also makes liberal agency more likely. Helping people find the engagement in their learning engages me, and I feel lucky to have a career built around it.

CHAPTER 7

Confessions of a Teaching Malcontent: Learning to Like What You Do

Jennifer Sterling-Folker

Current Institution: large state research I university
Typical classroom setting: large lecture, graduate seminar
Pedagogical approach: lecture, Socratic, active learning
Disciplinary identity: International Relations theory, research methods

It's hard to write a pedagogy statement when you've never taught a class, harder still if you were never trained to be teacher. Combine that with a general lack of desire to even be a teacher and one's first pedagogy statement for the job application or tenure file is a bit nightmarish. Pedagogy? What the heck, I thought, was that? And why did one have to write about it? Wasn't teaching at the college level about standing at a lectern and pontificating about facts and ideas? Certainly it had seemed that way in my own college and graduate school experiences so why did those activities necessitate a statement involving a personal "philosophy" of some sort?

Unlike many people in the profession, teaching was never a "calling" for me and it certainly didn't come naturally. Frankly, I didn't much like the idea of dealing with other people's children, many of whom seemed to

J. Sterling-Folker (✉)
University of Connecticut, Storrs, CT, USA
e-mail: jennifer.sterling-folker@uconn.edu

J. Frueh (ed.), *Pedagogical Journeys through World Politics*,
Political Pedagogies, https://doi.org/10.1007/978-3-030-20305-4_7

actively resist the idea of learning anything. It was a bit of a shock, then, when the summer before my tenure-track began the department administrator asked, "What do you want to teach this coming year?" Teach? They expected me to teach?

My naivety is amusing now but at the time I was in a real panic. I had been lucky enough to land the "big one"—a tenure-track at a university that aspired to Research I (R1) status in New England, where I had grown up, still had family and had wanted to work. I only had to teach two classes a semester and spend the rest of my time writing and publishing for tenure. Easy-breezy, right?

Of course what they didn't tell me was that my class sizes would be twice the size of my husband's, who taught four courses each semester at a local teaching college capped at 20 students a piece. My "Introduction to International Relations" lecture course, on the other hand, had 250+ students in it, and that was complemented with a second course of 40+ students. Now it was my turn to stand at the lectern and pontificate about facts and ideas. For someone who didn't intend to be a teacher, and who doesn't like public speaking in general, stepping up to that lectern to find so many eyes staring at me was a weekly exercise in managing stage fright. I was so stressed by the experience that first year that a kindly colleague noticed my distress and bought me a book on stress management techniques. Yet no amount of visualization, deep breathing, massage or regular exercise alleviated the physical and mental anxiety I felt every time I was at the lectern.

The central problem, I felt at the time, was that I didn't feel I had any mastery over the facts and ideas of my chosen field of study, and nothing about my Ph.D. training had prepared me to teach IR to others. I had been fortunate enough to attend an excellent graduate program, albeit one that didn't have the standard teaching or research assistantship arrangements in exchange for tuition and scholarship funding. There were no program expectations that Ph.D. candidates gain experience teaching at the college level before graduating with the degree.

In addition, my ambitions in attending graduate school lay in the policy and practice realm. In my 1978 high school graduation yearbook, my stated ambition had been to be the first female Secretary of State, a fairly radical notion at the time given how men thoroughly dominated the foreign policy establishment. In college, I briefly considered taking the State Department entrance exam until one of my American Politics professors pointed out the glass ceiling for civil servants. The real policy-making action was with the political appointees at the top of the bureaucratic food chain. Professors were often pulled from academia for advising stints in the White House, the National Security Council and so on depending on their political affiliations. It seemed the Ph.D. and a university position could be the stepping stone for foreign policy-making at the very highest echelons, and I was ambitious enough at the time to imagine enjoying that.

Of course my imagination was fueled more by Hollywood movies than the realities of foreign policy-making, and I would have been very ill-suited for such a position, but the point is I saw the Ph.D. as a stepping stone to policy practice, not teaching. Thus, I imagined that I would be a "sometimes" professor, cloistered in a brick and ivy-covered office surrounded by musty, well-worn books while sycophantic students and reporters made pilgrimages to my office to hear my policy-making experiences and wisdom. At other times, I would be in Washington or some distant international capital talking with my policy-making counterpart about heady affairs of state, much as I had imagined Henry Kissinger, Zbigniew Brzezinski, or Anthony Lake had done.

Now, however, as I embarked on an actual tenure-track position in 1994, reality set in. My new employers didn't care that I imagined being a policy-maker of the highest repute someday. They wanted to know what I could teach in two months and, oh by the way, what was I going to publish in the next year in order to keep my tenure-track position? UConn's tenure expectations were comparable to other R1s but the process of meeting them seemed unnecessarily grueling. Prior to tenure, one's university contract was renewed annually. This necessitated the submission of a hefty report every September that documented all tenure-worthy accomplishments one had undertaken the prior year. This was followed by an annual, nerve-wracking promotion committee meeting to clarify what scholarship you were working on next. The possibility of being fired midstream was real, as I discovered in my third week on the job when the contracts of two tenure-track professors were not renewed for lack of sufficient progress toward tenure standards.

In such an environment, the promise of memoirs by a renowned but future policy-maker obviously weren't going to cut it. Nor were my new employers interested in policy-related publishing. I'd actually have to publish for other academics. And because I was used to thinking about big ideas, I gravitated toward a subject like International Relations (IR) Theory which can make for dense, unengaging material in a large lecture course. These difficulties were compounded by the masculinized expectations of the student body—international relations was a field for men, not some 33-year-old female assistant professor fresh out of graduate school who had no experience teaching.

Although this last statement was not entirely true. I *did* have some teaching experience prior to attending graduate school. I was a substitute teacher at a private high school in Massachusetts for three years. Eventually, they asked me to teach an American Politics course to sophomores, and I developed a research methods course for graduating seniors. Thus, when I applied to graduate school, my application was replete with the evidence of teaching promise—copies of my syllabi, exams and classroom exercises. After receiving my doctorate, I adjuncted at three different universities and spent a year as a Visiting Assistant Professor at Wheaton College where I taught courses as varied as Japanese politics, Introduction to Data Methods and Analysis, and US Foreign Policy.

But my prior experiences in the classroom had not been particularly positive. The middle school classes I regularly subbed had delighted in playing catch with their shoes whenever my back was turned to the board. Being no authoritarian myself, I struggled to command the kind of respect and appropriate classroom behaviors that, much to my shame, only seemed to occur when the principal appeared suddenly at my classroom doorway and a shuddered hush fell across the room. The high school classes I subbed and taught had a different problem—boredom. Rather than throwing shoes for entertainment, many of the upper class men had mastered the art of sullen rebuke and resignation (along with much note passing). Learning how to find information in the pre-digital age or in what ways the US Constitution still sets the stage for daily American political life seemed exciting to me but not to them. Despite the variety of teaching exercises and "fun" activities I experimented with to promote engagement, the vast majority remained disinterested.

My experience at the college level was only slightly better. Yes, the students were even politer now and certainly there were gems among the crowd who genuinely wanted to learn about the subject. But when pressed the vast majority admitted it was the need for required graduation credits, not the subject matter, which had led them to my courses. And I found my authority in the classroom frequently challenged by some of the young men, who liked to pontificate during class discussions as a demonstration of their knowledge, seemed to delight in asking questions to which I clearly didn't know the answers, and often quite directly challenged my knowledge of the subject matter. "There is no evidence of a causal relationship between the Great Depression and Hitler's rise to power," one young man asserted vehemently during a pause in one of my lectures. Huh?

Worse yet were the number of young men who tried to cheat during exams and whom, despite my quiet and discreet efforts to save them embarrassment, would instead create a loud scene in the middle of an exam disrupting everyone's concentration. On more than one occasion a male student would insist loudly and forcefully that, despite my actually holding his cheat sheet in my hand, he hadn't cheated at all. Young men were also more likely to cause a scene when I handed back graded assignments, sometimes yelling out at me angrily or storming out of the class room.

Those teaching experiences had reinforced my worst ideas and fears about teaching. It seemed to me that within the classroom, students as a collective tended to be an unruly mob of anti-intellectuals who were more interested in socializing with one another than listening to me. They could even be dangerous if confronted with their own mistakes and inappropriate behaviors. I was pretty skeptical of this entire "teaching" enterprise and the need to articulate "my" conceptions of learning as a result.

That said, my early teaching was not all bad, in fact, by the admittedly low comparative standards provided in University-wide student teaching evaluations (SETs), I was considered a good teacher. It helped that initially I tended to be enthusiastic at the lectern. My voice brimmed with excitement as I described arcane historical events that shaped our world. I was constantly scribbling on the white board and it was a running joke that I had to frequently stop the lecture to decipher my handwriting for note-takers. If nothing else, the students were initially entertained by my boundless energy and zeal.

It also helped that I liked students as individuals and enjoyed learning about their unique personalities and interests. I became particularly adept at cultivating advising relationships with the more interested and eager among my undergraduates. And in smaller classes, I often used class time for one-on-one appointments so I could get to know each student individually. Friendliness, I discovered, could take one pretty far in academia, particularly if you are a woman and even if you aren't a particularly effective teacher.

And as with any new faculty member, I quickly learned techniques from more seasoned colleagues on handling college classroom disruptions. Make the students sit every other seat to prevent exam cheating. Insist students wait at least a day before asking about a recent grade to prevent raw emotions from producing tears or anger. Ask for at least one male graduate assistant whose presence seemed to calm some of the young male student's worst tendencies. Of course these are just classroom management techniques. They helped but they weren't about pedagogy or how to teach well. And, in any case, I was at an R1 institution, which emphasized research over teaching and service. Publicly, we were all encouraged to be good teachers, but behind closed doors we were reminded that the real focus had to be our research. The SETs just had to be good enough and, as one senior colleague advised me, "You can worry about learning to be a good teacher after tenure."

Unfortunately by the time I got tenure, I had come to loathe the entire process of teaching. Despite having taught IR for several years by then, I still felt like I had no real mastery of my subject matter and lived in constant fear that the more astute undergraduates would intuit this. To avoid this possibility, I regularly worked late into the night composing notes on the next day's topic. I also set aside time prior to each class session to review and memorize notes, dates and events, as if I were preparing for a stage performance. After class I assessed my performance according to whether I thought I had effectively held the audience's attention. If I felt the performance had failed, I redoubled my preparation efforts.

This worked for a time and got me through tenure, but it was stressful, exhausting and unrewarding. For one thing, the nature of the subject matter was always changing, thus requiring constant preparation, and for another, there was so darn much of it! How could one hope to master and then teach a subject as enormous, elusive and ever-changing as IR? And my brain was such that I couldn't easily recall basic facts or retain them from one semester to the next, thus necessitating constant preparation and rehearsal for my classroom performances. I preferred the open-ended, leisurely pace of a Socratic graduate seminar in which we discussed ideas without coming to any particular conclusions. For undergraduates, on the other hand, wasn't the point that there were facts and ideas they needed to know? Wasn't I supposed to be the authority on the subject matter in the room? Wasn't it my responsibility to know the answers and provide those to the students? And how could I ask them to recall course material on exams if I couldn't recall it easily myself?

Over time, I fell into a lot of bad teaching habits that were ultimately self-defeating. The teaching experimentation I had engaged with as an assistant professor, including role-playing exercises, small-group activities and the like ceased altogether. I began to stress rote memorization over critical analysis because it was easier to grade and subject to fewer grade challenges. I rarely encouraged class discussions, preferring straight lectures that I alone could control. I avoided eye contact with the students as a way to discourage questions lest my classroom authority and subject matter knowledge be tested. I couldn't bear to look at my teaching evaluations since just one negative comment could send me into a crying fit of humiliation and despair. I resented the students' lack of appreciation for all my hard work in preparing my performances on their behalf. I came to dread the start of each new semester.

In fact, I grew to hate teaching as I had come to understand it and stated those feelings openly to family and friends. I looked for ways out of the undergraduate classroom, taking on more graduate courses, serving in administrative positions and taking on journal editorships since these latter roles provided undergraduate course releases. They also allowed me to work on what I considered to be the "real" substance of my profession.

Looking back, I now understand that I was suffering at the time from a bad case of Imposter Phenomenon (IP). IP involves "intense, secret feelings of fraudulence" and leads its sufferers to believe they do not "have what it takes to complete important work and are in constant fear of failure" (Sanford et al. 2015: 31). IP sufferers among higher education faculty are often young women who tend to "believe themselves to be less competent and intelligent than others perceive them to be" and can suffer from anxiety and depression due to "the constant pressure of living up to the successful image that the impostor has crafted" (Studdard 2002: 30). In other words, the IP sufferer lives in constant "fear that others will discover that they are living a lie" and "often pressures herself to maintain the appearance of success, but is constantly anxious that her incompetence will be discovered" (Studdard 2002: 29–30). Sound familiar?

My lack of self-confidence in my own expertise combined with my preconceived but erroneous notions of what it meant to be a professor produced a vicious psychological and behavioral IP cycle. I thought being a professor meant it was my responsibility to know everything, but that placed the "burden" of learning on me rather than the students. I thought if they weren't "fooled" then my professorial performance had failed, yet over time this effort led me to fear and resent the undergraduates as a classroom collective. I had, in effect, made the students judge and jury for my own professional expertise and abilities in the classroom. No wonder I was so miserable teaching.

A turning point in my attitude came in 2009, almost 14 years after I had begun teaching at UConn. I would hardly be in any position now to offer you any teaching advice if I hadn't experienced an epiphany of sorts regarding my own self-defeating teaching attitudes and behaviors. Unfortunately, I can offer no replicable magic elixir for achieving personal insight. My own came during a long-term illness and, as a result, a particularly exhausting semester. I was approached by a student after the final exam who wanted to tell me, kindly I might add, that he had been excited to take my course but it had not met his expectations and he was disappointed. I suspect the illness made me less defensive and more receptive than usual because I didn't internalize the criticism. Instead, I engaged in a 30-minute conversation with him about what teaching styles he had experienced and preferred. In other words, for the first time in my career, I actually listened to what an enthusiastic student wanted me to do as his *teacher* rather than what I thought I was supposed to do as a *professor*.

Our conversation led me to really engage for the first time with the question of why I did not like teaching. I had always blamed my dislike on the expectations of the students, their potential challenges to my authority, and the need for constant preparation. Yet here was a student who was asking me to teach him in an entirely different way. So what was I doing wrong? It was my therapist who pointed out the obvious when I recounted the story to her later. "No one ever taught you how to teach and it's stressful to publicly engage in an activity for which you have no preparation." Why hadn't I ever thought of it like that before?

Obviously the process of obtaining a Ph.D. does not involve teaching pedagogy per see, it's about the mastery of one's subject area. I had conflated that mastery with good teaching but the fact was, I didn't have a clue what went into being a good teacher. I had just been copying what I'd seen my own professors do and trying to live up to an idealized professorial vision in my own head. And so for the first time in my professional career, I was receptive to the idea that if I was going to become a better teacher, I needed to get some training.

That, in fact, is my first piece of advice. Learn how to be a teacher, which is a separate activity from mastering the subject matter you teach. Take advantage of teaching training that might be available at your institution, read books on the subject, watch teaching tip videos online and continue to get training even after you feel comfortable in your own teaching skin. You are never too old to learn new techniques and ideas for working with your students and providing fresh instructional experiences. Had I undertaken training earlier, I might have recognized that I was approaching the job in an unhealthy manner and saved myself a great deal of grief.

One of the central insights I gained from my teaching training is my second piece of advice. Teach the student, not the subject matter. This is a common saying among K-12 teachers, often to underscore the need to cater to individual student learning styles. That seems unrealistic in large lecture courses but also counter-intuitive at the college level—isn't the point of a Ph.D. to focus on *the* subject matter? Alternatively, I understand the phrase to mean two things as it relates to my university teaching.

First, consider what people need in order to learn in general. There are a whole host of things that get in the way of student learning that have nothing to do with the teacher. These can include learning disabilities, varying attention spans, diversity in learning styles and preferences, and financial, personal, and/or family problems. These are the kinds of issues that people who are trained as K-12 teachers learn about when earning their degrees. But as a Ph.D. with absolutely no teaching training, it had never occurred to me that a student who was failing might have an undiagnosed learning disability. Nor did I realize that the class fidgeting 20 minutes into my lectures was the result of normal human attention spans, not my own lecture performance. And it was a complete revelation to learn that students were often afraid of professors, of performing poorly in our classes, and of not living up to their own expectations or those of their parents and friends. I thought I was the only one with classroom jitters!

The techniques I had been utilizing up to this point were all about classroom management and control, not student learning per see. Meanwhile there were a wide variety of techniques for addressing these kinds of learning issues, even in large lecture classes. Stopping the lecture every 15 minutes and having students confer with their neighbors on lecture notes for several minutes allowed for attention spans to reset. Providing content variations and choices for required exercises, homework and even absences accommodated different learning styles. Flipping the classroom (a common technique in the sciences) so the lecture is online and class time is reserved for small-group activities allowed for more engaged, active learning. Encouraging a student with suspected learning disabilities to come to office hours to discuss exam and assignment preparation afforded the opportunity to point them in the direction of appropriate university services.

The second way in which I understand the phrase—teach the student, not the subject—is to avoid passing personal judgment on individual students. Of course as teachers we are expected to grade student performances and fairly apply instructional criteria. What I am referring to instead is the all-too-human tendency to pass judgment on the personal abilities and character of specific students. Much of this judgmentalism seems to arise from an idealized vision each professor develops of what a "good" student is supposed to be. Students who are perfectly willing and able to learn are often labeled as bad students not based on any objective assessment, but on a professor's personal ideas and preferences regarding what a student is supposed to be and do.

I myself engaged in a form of judgmentalism when I assumed that my authority was constantly suspect and subject to challenge, particularly by young men. Of course it was not all my fragile ego and imagination. Numerous studies have documented how female professors experience greater challenges to their authority than their male counterparts (Dion 2008; Kardia and Wright 2004; Rudman and Kilianski 2000; Rudman and Glick 2001; Scola and Lupo 2010). These studies also indicate that there are clear gender biases at work in higher education—male professors are expected to be assertive and agentic, female professors are expected to be kind and nurturing. Women who buck these gendered expectations risk lower teaching evaluation scores, which can endanger their future advancement in the discipline (Baldwin and Blattner 2003; Martin 2016; Tindall and Waters 2017).

But because I was so terrified of being discovered as an imposter, I tended to prejudge *every* student question and comment as a potential challenge to my authority. Thus the type of undergraduate student I preferred, often rewarded, and thought of as a "good student" were the quiet ones, whether male or female, who never rocked the boat, only answered or asked easy questions and remained solicitous and polite. Because I had made teaching about me, not the student, I couldn't see that most students weren't actually challenging me.

And really, was it such a bad thing if a student did challenge my authority? Wasn't the point of being an educator to help the student learn, not protect one's own fragile ego? So what if I didn't know the capital of Kenya or the relative Gross Domestic Product of Mexico off the top of my head. Those were just facts and easy to look up on the internet. They hardly constituted a more sophisticated, critical understanding of what made the world tick, which was something I could actually offer the students. And if some student didn't want to learn from me because they held implicit gender biases or other erroneous ideas about how professors were supposed to behave, ultimately that was their loss, not mine.

My more relaxed attitude was helped by the fact that I was now a full professor and finally felt like an expert, not an imposter. I was also a lot older so I tended to fit naturally into the "nurturing mother" profile that many students seem to implicitly prefer for their female professors. The challenges and angry behaviors of young male students from my early teaching days gave way naturally, it seemed, to greater deference. And I had a teenager of my own at home now whose own education made me more aware of differences in learning styles and the frustrations good students often felt when encountering a teacher who prejudged their learning abilities and potential.

These aspects combined with my teaching training helped me realize that I had never given any real thought to what students needed prior to the subject matter itself. The bottom line, it now seems to me, is the need to respect each student as individuals with their own unique personalities, experiences, strengths and weaknesses. That doesn't mean designing individual lesson plans for each student or applying different grading standards. Nor does it mean giving into gendered biases and expectations. It means thinking carefully about and trying consciously to overcome our own preconceived notions of a one-size-fits-all "good" student so that we can more effectively teach, and appreciate, a wider variety of students.

This leads me to my third and final piece of advice. Empower students to take responsibility for their own educational successes and failures; don't do the work for them, but do so in a way that works for you personally. This sounds so obvious, but through the haze of my own tangled ego and fears, I did not understand earlier that I was doing all the learning for them, blaming them for my exhausting preparation work, and then feeling demoralized when they didn't enjoy my lectures, performed poorly on exams or challenged a paper or exam grade. In other words, I made the process about me and internalized all their behaviors as my responsibility, not theirs. In so doing, I was largely depriving students of responsibility for their own learning, their own behaviors and their own egos.

Yet how you empower students depends a lot on your own personal preferences, weaknesses and strengths. If there is no one-size-fits-all good student, then that is certainly also true of good teachers. For too many years I carried an image in my head of professors as subject authorities and classroom authoritarians whose presence automatically commanded respect in the classroom. In trying to live up to that image, a construct of my own gendered biases about authority in the classroom (Rudman and Kilianski 2000), I made myself and many of my students miserable. Now I understand that it's OK to let your own strengths and weaknesses shape your pedagogical aspirations and practice. For me that has meant I don't have to be an authoritarian or a know-it-all in order to generate respect and enthusiasm among my students.

Again it was training that exposed me to this simple truth. One of the speakers at a large lecture training session was a UConn Business Professor who regularly taught accounting to more than 500 students. As he recounted the different techniques he utilized to keep control of and engage such a large class I was struck by how differently he approached these tasks than I had. At the start of each class session he asked students to ponder a meditation or self-help quote such as "If you want to conquer the anxiety of life, live in the moment, live in the breath" (Amit Ray), or "Minds are like flowers, they only open when the time is right" (Stephen Richards). Did students like that? Yes, because it helped ground their thoughts and reduced their nervousness about the impending class session. In fact, they often emailed him with quotes for the start of class. His request for the students to put away their cell phones wasn't a stern command. Instead, he explained they had so little time together each week that he wanted them to focus on his lecture, not their cell phones, so they could succeed in his class. Did the students turn off their phones? Without hesitation. And each semester he barely slept the night before his first class due to nervous excitement about getting back into the classroom with the students. It had never occurred to me that nervousness could be recast as excitement (rather than as an indication of something to avoid).

Listening to him, I realized this professor behaved less like my imagined professor and more like a minister tending the intellectual and emotional needs of his flock. No wonder he was one of the most effective and well-liked teachers on campus. He couched his expectations for relatively rigorous work and respectful behaviors in terms of caring about their success. If he could teach with his own style, demeanor and frame of mind, why couldn't I?

And so I began the transition from subject authority figure to subject facilitator and mentor with the goal of assisting students on their own educational journeys. The focus of my teaching now is to provide the tools and experiences to help students succeed in achieving their *own* goals and dreams, not mine. I now feel confident that I have important professional knowledge, experiences and analytical skills to share with students. And I want to share this knowledge not because information is an end in itself, but because it can facilitate the student's own intellectual and professional journey.

This means the students are free to decide whether learning these skills is right for them. There is no longer any judgment on my part, either of myself or of them regarding their choices and decisions. Their education is their responsibility, my role is to serve as their guide as *they* explore and try to understand the subject matter. I facilitate this learning process by listening more carefully to what students hope to achieve (both in the classroom and after graduation), being clear with regards to my learning goals for them in light of their dreams, adopting a flexible attitude toward class activities and appropriate assignments, and respecting them individually for their unique talents and interests.

Does this transformation in my teaching style make me a great teacher now? No, but I am better, I now enjoy teaching more, and my students have a better learning experience as a result. Because I adjusted my own expectations of what makes for good teaching, my relationship with the undergraduates has changed in significant, positive and more self-affirming ways. In other words, even if you don't think of yourself as a natural born teacher, it is possible to learn how to do it better and to like what you do.

References

Baldwin, Tamara, and Nancy Blattner. 2003. Guarding against Potential Bias in Student Evaluations: What every Faculty Member Needs to Know. *College Teaching* 51 (1): 27–32. https://doi.org/10.1080/87567550309596407.

Dion, Michelle. 2008. All-Knowing or all-Nurturing? Student Expectations, Gender Roles, and Practical Suggestions for Women in the Classroom*. *PS: Political Science & Politics* 41 (04): 853–856. https://doi.org/10.1017/S1049096508081110.

Kardia, Diana B., and Mary C. Wright. 2004. *Instructor Identity: The Impact of Gender and Race on Faculty Experiences with Teaching*. University of Michigan's Center for Research on Learning and Teaching, 19: 1–8.

Martin, Lisa L. 2016. Gender, Teaching Evaluations, and Professional Success in Political Science. *PS: Political Science & Politics* 49 (02): 313–319. https://doi.org/10.1017/S1049096516000275.

Rudman, Laurie A., and Peter Glick. 2001. Prescriptive Gender Stereotypes and Backlash toward Agentic Women. *Journal of Social Issues* 57 (4): 743–762. https://doi.org/10.1111/0022-4537.00239.

Rudman, Laurie A., and Stephen E. Kilianski. 2000. Implicit and Explicit Attitudes toward Female Authority. *Personality and Social Psychology Bulletin* 26 (11): 1315–1328. https://doi.org/10.1177/0146167200263001.

Sanford, Amy Aldridge, Elaina M. Ross, Shawna J. Blake, and Renée L. Cambiano. 2015. Finding Courage and Confirmation: Resisting Impostor Feelings through Relationships with Mentors, Romantic Partners, and Other Women in Leadership. *Advancing Women in Leadership* 35: 31–41. 2015.

Scola, Becki, and Lindsey Lupo. 2010. *This Lecture Might be Messy: The Role of Gender in Academic Life*. Presented at the 2010 APSA Teaching and Learning Conference, February 5–7, Philadelphia.

Studdard, Scarlette Spears. 2002. Adult Women Students in the Academy: Impostors or Members? *The Journal of Continuing Higher Education* 50 (3): 24–37. https://doi.org/10.1080/07377366.2002.10401202.

Tindall, Natalie T.J., and Richard D. Waters. 2017. Does Gender and Professional Experience Influence Students' Perceptions of Professors? *Journalism & Mass Communication Educator* 72 (1): 52–67. https://doi.org/10.1177/107769 5815613932.

Teaching in Capitalist Ruins

David L. Blaney

Current institution: private liberal arts college
Typical classroom setting: small classes, never larger than 20 students
Typical pedagogical approach: reading, writing, discussion
Disciplinary identity: international relations and political theory

When I arrived at Macalester College in 1994, I found I was a good teacher. This wasn't a complete surprise, but it was far from a forgone conclusion. My experiences at another liberal arts college (not named; hereafter LAC) seemed to foretell a different conclusion. My first year at LAC (the 1989–90 AY) was very nearly a total disaster. There is a temptation to tell a story of learning that connects the two data points, but the story may be more about place and time.

Warning signs were evident during my interview at LAC. Faculty I met seemed scarred by their isolation from the rest of the world and within the college. The older Indian couple that picked me up at the airport was strangely hesitant, even passive, as if there selves had been worn away by

Thanks to Naeem Inayatullah, Jamie Frueh, and Lisa Mueller for insightful and occasionally painful comments on earlier drafts of this essay.

D. L. Blaney (✉)
Macalester College, St Paul, MN, USA
e-mail: blaney@macalester.edu

© The Author(s) 2020
J. Frueh (ed.), *Pedagogical Journeys through World Politics*,
Political Pedagogies, https://doi.org/10.1007/978-3-030-20305-4_8

91

years of small affronts and lack of recognition. The other two, and much younger, faculty of color, neither of whom would be at LAC the next year, complained that the faculty took on the provinciality of the small town no matter where they came from. During my interview, the President asked if I could communicate with conservatives and suggested I read Russell Kirk. I learned later that he was recruited via the Boards' connections to the Hudson Institute and that he had been the equivalent of VP for Academic Affairs at Hillsdale College when it fell afoul of the American Association of University Professors (AAUP) for violations of academic freedom. All kind of startling, but what in retrospect astonishes me is that the President himself was involved in interviewing candidates. LAC was small, the political science department even smaller. I didn't understand what that would mean, though later I found myself reading articles about the intellectual isolation you can feel in small colleges. But the department was not uninviting (one of its members perhaps the best colleague I have had) and there were other interesting faculty (the guy in history who worked on the I-Ching and the radical sociologist, though both, like me, moved on or were moved on). I felt crushed by the heavy teaching load (3-1-3 or 3-4), magnified by the fact that I was still revising my dissertation during that first year and trying desperately to write myself out of the job I had just accepted.

I took the job, for the usual reasons. I was not having great success on the job market. This was only my second interview after nearly two years of applications. My options seemed limited and those limits felt structural, the character of the discipline and my own choices seemed to foreclose the possibility of a successful career. I did work as a political and social theorist, but came from a graduate program in International Studies that, by definition, did not produce political and social theorists. That's not to mention that I wasn't properly credentialed as a political scientist. Not helpful either was writing a dissertation on Marx, as a non-Marxist and at a moment when Marx was being declared irrelevant and others theorists were becoming all the fashion. My graduate advisers either were in a different field (e.g. an economist) whose letters could carry little weight or they were negligent. I felt on my own, and with little hope. I felt the same discouragement and desperation that I seemed to see in the eyes of many of my grad student colleagues when we crossed paths at the cubbyholes assigned to us for the American Political Science Association job fair (no cell phones or email then). Spending another year on the market would have meant more debt and I felt lucky to have an offer at all; taking this job seemed the price of working in the field. I now doubt my judgment; I was panicking, but that's not the teaching story.

Everything seemed wrong that first year. Many new preps, maybe five, and I was teaching in areas well beyond (and some that remain beyond) my competency. These courses were assigned to me and I made things worse by accepting the pedagogical goal of cultivating student mastery in these subjects—from World Politics, International Law, International Organization, and Global Political Economy (more down my alley) to that bane of the discipline, Introduction to Political Science, which unexpectedly turned into my favorite course. I also should add that I had very little actual graduate school training in IR. I shied away from those courses in grad school. (This seems a pertinent fact, since I have made my career in and around IR and that my task here is to tell a story that assists those beginning careers as teachers of IR.) My lack of mastery in these courses showed, particularly the first time through; I worked to evade teaching some, like International Law, a second time.

I also failed to connect with the students. It is tempting to say that I shot over their heads, which falls too easily into lamenting their academic preparation and intellectual curiosity. But I clearly failed to meet them where they were. And, more importantly, I completely failed to identify what kinds of topics and texts I was good at teaching. Nor had I settled into a pedagogical style that suited me. These might be common early career problems, though maybe less so with the somewhat greater emphasis on pedagogical training and self-consciousness in graduate programs, but still problems I might grow out of. My teaching evaluations were far from stellar, though I thought they showed I was not beyond redemption. In this case, my failings were potentially more devastating since LAC did reviews every two years: my first review occurred just after this less than amazing first year, and before a committee that was unimpressed by the fact that I presented two conference papers that year, suspecting rightly that I was not their kind. I escaped the ignominy of nonrenewal, but only because my department went to bat for me.

Eventually I left on my own: I quit, *before* I had found the job at Macalester, something I now find difficult to imagine—an act of faith or maybe desperation. I took a year to write. Naeem and I were back to collaborating by this time and Nick Onuf agreed to read my work and, then, to write a letter of recommendation for me, a debt I will never be able to repay. And I went back on the job market, but now with a much stronger file. Maybe not about teaching, but you can practice the vocation of teaching only when you have a job teaching.[1]

I might now say that I found my vocation as a teacher in the Introduction to Political Science course at LAC; and this a result of (1) throwing up my hands in despair of trying to make sense of what this course would usefully cover; and (2) consulting with one of my dissertation committee members, who shared his syllabus, which served as partial inspiration for my own. I began to make the course about reading, thinking, and writing, instead of being about political science; whatever that might be, I was pretty sure I was against teaching it. (Again, pertinent facts: I was a political science major as an undergrad and I didn't like Introduction to Political Science the first time. And, as above, I didn't get a PhD in political science, a fact that doesn't amuse my colleagues at Macalester, when I remind them. The uncomfortable truth is that, now, they would not hire someone with my profile. A strong department, unlike the one into which I was hired, wouldn't take such a risk.)

I realize that I have told this story wrong. I just found the syllabus, recovered from a file folder left over from my interview at Macalester. By the winter term of 1993, the course was called "Politics of the Modern Age" and it was a reworking and renaming of the course by the two of us responsible for teaching it. In my section, we read Locke and some Smith and Marx and some Milton Friedman; we read many excerpts from political and social theorists in Nancy Love's excellent collection; and we read novels: Dickens, *Hard Times*, Sinclair Lewis, *Babbit*, and, more immediately relevant in the Reagan-Bush I era, McInerny's *Bright Lights, Big City*. I had forgotten until I just looked at the syllabus that this course was largely my little introduction to political economy, finally allowing me to teach what is closest to my heart and my expertise. And just when I became motivated by what I was teaching and how I was teaching, so did the students. (Naeem helped articulate the principles: if the space is dead for the teacher, it cannot but be dead for the student; if it is alive for the teacher, it doesn't matter what s/he teaches or how. And: content does not matter, always.) In any case, I connected; I started to develop a loyal, though still somewhat small, following. But that small following altered how I was seen and how I felt about myself as a teacher.

To discover that you are a good teacher, after some years of doubt, is a joyful experience. And maybe I did know what I was doing by 1994, when

---

[1] An insight Naeem insisted on here.

I stated at Macalester, but I must distribute credit and acknowledge the weight of time and place. In a recent article on pedagogy,[2] I wrote about my Macalester students as "very strong, relatively well prepared and generally willing to take on whatever I throw at them. They are concerned about their career prospects, but also with trying to figure out who they are and who they want to become." Students like that compensate for many faults. It is not that Macalester students teach themselves, but that my job is easier in some key respects. I often serve as a facilitator and sometimes my job is to point at some target and then get out of their way, until they ask for help. Because they take their education seriously, they are also demanding of me—particularly of my time and energy, which I have given mostly willingly for 25 academic years. And I remain grateful for the opportunity that Macalester afforded me.

As an aside, toting up the demands of the job at Macalester would involve counting the tutorials conducted, the Honors projects supervised, the hours in consultation with students about research projects for courses, not to mention the "career/survival in an inhospitable world" advising time. I was shocked when I heard an enumeration of my numbers by the Macalester College President in 2011, on the occasion of giving me the college's teaching award, only roughly a year after I had experienced a serious psycho-bio-social crisis, a feeling of collapse, a disorganization of my brain chemistry to the point that I found it challenging to do the job that I once thought I had mastered. I soldiered on. The students never knew and I shared with only select colleagues, just in case they would have to step in. Here, some of the joy ended. "Adjustment disorder," a counselor called it (it had to be called something for insurance purposes), which I took to mean a failure of my body any longer to cope with the expectations placed upon it, particularly those I placed on myself. Every year, I faithfully teach (and reread carefully) Kathi Weeks' brilliant chapter on the work ethic in her *The Problem of Work* (Durham: Duke University, 2011) as a reminder of what I should learn about my self-imposed workload, but never do. My wife can't even be reminded of this teaching award without becoming furious—again. From a seat in the audience, she reacted with fury when the award was given, but she was the only one who really knew what my work had done to me. The recognition/insult/comedy continued as I was awarded a named chair the following year, only to be given

---

[2] David L. Blaney, "International Politics: as it is, as it might be," *Critical Studies on Security* 1:3 (2013), 275–6.

another, more prestigious one, just a few years ago. It took nearly four years to feel anything like normal (a normal which was the problem), but I have never quite regained the confidence that came with promotion and the publication of my second book. I recognize that this "adjustment" is not an aside to my career, but an integral feature of it, though I originally hid it away as a footnote. Readers forced it into the text.

Looking back to those early years at Macalester, I doubt I was conscious that my pedagogy revolved principally around "reading, thinking, and writing" or my energy and enthusiasm about the material, somewhat indifferent to the ostensive topic of the course. I may be reading that back into a moment, when it would make sense that I was aware of what I was doing. I have no evidence: Nothing on my current computer dates before 2003. And rummaging through my current department's file cabinets, somewhat illicitly, revealed only my LAC syllabi, from my original application, but no teaching statement. Did I even include one? Was there an equivalent in the cover letter? I have no idea. And Macalester College seems to have nothing readily available from the file I submitted for tenure review in 1996. The disks on which earlier stuff might be found appear to have been discarded, along with paper copies. But then, I found my disks. And credit must again be distributed: my wife found them and I suspect she, having the soul of an archivist, saved them, when I tried to throw them away. And the relevant ones were right in plain sight. But the evidential difficulties remain. I can't read them, despite having an external disk drive and an old PC that should read them.

The most recent teaching statement I can access was prepared for promotion review at Macalester College (dated December 2005), perhaps explaining why I find it so banal and largely unworthy of repeating, except with serious commentary that makes me seem less foolish. Among other things, I claim a commitment to:

1. Providing "intellectual challenge," meaning something like assigning amongst the "best works" written on a topic, an indication that I am a person of the book (that is, of books) and not inclined to multi-media engagement, however much I am told about current student learning styles. And that I am a hard grader, with an average GPA far below the college's average, though I have been "softening" in recent years.

2. "Teaching within a curriculum," meaning roughly, my current self would say, that I recognize that I coordinate with others—that I am

not a lone wolf, or, better, that I know that wolves like me run in packs. We call them departments—maybe disciplines. (I do like the wolf image, which is a translation I just made, but I would revise this statement more fundamentally now. Recently, I have come to think of myself as teaching in a community of teachers more broadly. I feel more confident about what I do as a teacher because others do differently, because their strengths reach beyond my limits, that they serve students whom I fail. I don't have to be everything to every student, a form of hubris that befalls those of us who aspire to the dangerous task of teaching.)[3]

3. "Sequencing skills" across my courses, which I guess mean something like emphasizing "reading, thinking, and writing." But, in my mind, I now associate talk of "skills" with preparing students to perform a research project at a high level in their senior year. This focus on senior research feeds, rather unfortunately, into scaffolding and assessment, and ignores the multi-genre world of writing that students are entering (a discovery that I seem to have made only very recently myself. And

4. Engage "real questions," which I describe "as preparing students to engage the unanswered intellectual questions of the ages and our time." Though I now have less confidence that I can identify such questions. I do remain certain that these intellectual questions "are always also ethical and practical questions" and that "because at least some of these questions engage and puzzle me too," I can "not only pretend that the classroom is a site of real intellectual engagement," but we actually can be "engaged in a real conversation about open questions."

I do find in this statement an idea that I have written about and continue to ponder. At this point, I called it "humility," an odd label given the earlier claims I made, exposing a "performative contradiction" perhaps endemic to the teaching philosophy genre itself. I write:

My attempt is to "model" in the classroom a process of reflection on intellectual and ethical matters that is careful and circumspect—alert to the

---

[3] Something like this revision came out when I was asked to say a few words on the occasion of receiving that teaching award in 2011, the occasion of the enumeration of my self-exploitation described above.

complexities of issue and problems and resistant to facile gestures.[4] At one level this means disempowering students to an extent,[5] robbing them of certainties, easy answers, secular tenets of faith. It means dislodging knowledge as much as adding to it.... [T]his may also create a certain kind of empowerment – more quiet, more patient and plodding, more humble in its goals and perhaps more effective in producing outcomes. At least that is my faith.

This idea of disempowerment I still take seriously, though I am grow increasingly concerned about my students' growing and simultaneous empowerment/disempowerment.

I developed my defense of disempowerment in a 2002 article, responding to claims about the empowering character of global education. I argued for a strategy that worked to disempower students focused on their relation to the rest of the world, especially those with the desire to help. In a footnote, I qualified this somewhat, situating my argument in relation to my placement at a highly selective liberal arts college, with a tradition of commitment to internationalism and civic engagement.[6]

I put some of what was in this statement better and in a more politically pointed[7] fashion some years later, in a forum Jamie organized and edited.[8] In response to the question, "Is it part of a professor's academic responsibility to teach students right from wrong on some political issues?," I wrote:

> My classes ... end with anti-climax. There is no revelation on the last day—only the warning that, if I have done my job well, I have left them with more questions than answers (and hopefully with enhanced skills for tackling the serious problem of how one is to live in this world in relation with others). Hopefully, these are the kinds of questions that last a lifetime, that inhabit our very souls, that haunt every decision we make, and that, importantly,

---

[4] I should have referenced Foucault here, in light of the growing role of footnoting in teaching statements.

[5] I am quoting myself: David L Blaney, "Global Education, Disempowerment, and Curricula for a World Politics," *Journal of Studies in International Education* 6:3 (Fall 2002), 268–82. I think Himadeep Muppidi suggested this language to me.

[6] Blaney, "Global Education," 278.

[7] I may not have been willing to put it quite this way in materials to be read by a promotion committee.

[8] Jamie Frueh, David Blaney, Kevin Dunn, Patricia Goff, Erik K. Leonard, and Simona Sharoni, "Political Beliefs and the Academic Responsibilities of Undergraduate Teaching," *Journal of Political Science Education* 4:4 (2008), 447–62.

lead us to do less damage in the world. ... Some have appropriately called this a rather dismal political project, but it is not simply defeatist. Arguably, the desire to do good informs much that is destructive in today's world, or at least the capacity to delude oneself and others as to the goodness of one's motives and actions underlies much of what appears to me as evil in the world.[9]

No political detachment here and not so much humility either. I would still defend these positions, but with less enthusiasm and weighted with more doubts.

I have more doubts because my students don't seem as hyper-empowered any more. The demands on them seem to have escalated beyond reason and into paradox. Getting an entry-level job now requires three to five years' experience. Getting into a college that will make you competitive for jobs requires a resume beyond what in the past one could hope to have on finishing college. The pressure put on today's college students to publish may now be spreading to high school students. Fueled by these fears, most messages students receive seem to undercut the vocation of the liberal arts itself, even those sent by liberal arts college presidents. This is not to mention that the state of the world itself seems to call for unsustainable demands for doing good just when it seems so much harder to get a job doing good, or even to know how to do good. Now properly chastened by contemporary sensitivities to difference, including through my own teaching and writing, they are less confident about their ability to navigate in a world of difference. And the idea of doing good is freighted with concerns about their own survival in an era of shrinking opportunities and the sense of a future foreclosed by an impending multi-faceted ruination. And the prevalence of mental health issues on campus makes disempowerment seem a cruel pedagogy. I feel like I am teaching in a new place and time—in capitalist ruins, to borrow from Anna Tsing.[10]

I walk lines and strike balances a bit differently now. I am more circumspect in using grades as a way of pushing students. My average GPA, faithfully reported to me by our institutional research department, has crept closer to college averages the last few years, though my reputation remains.

---

[9] See Naeem Inayatullah on the problem with helping: "Why do some people think they know what is good for others?" in Jenny Edkins and Maja Zehfuss (eds) *Global Politics: A New Introduction* (Routledge, 2008), pp. 344–69.

[10] Anna Lowenhaupt Tsing, *The Mushroom at the End of the World: On the Possibility of Life in Capitalist Ruins* (Princeton and Oxford: Princeton University, 2015).

Recently, I find myself policing more and more how students engage texts, encouraging more generosity to the author and a gentler mode of critique that leaves something intact at the end, so that the texts we read are not left in ruins along with our own spirits by a misguided commitment to ruthless criticism. (Naeem and I have defended this generosity of reading as crucial to our scholarly orientation,[11] though we haven't always lived up to the precept.) I find myself insisting on this more forcefully, more cognizant of the fragility of my own books and my own body. And perhaps sharing my students' feelings of fragility and anxiety, though I will see much less of the future than they, I find an uncomfortable breaking down of a divide—a distancing—that I have maintained between myself and students that seemed necessary to my performances in the classroom. I find myself sharing a bit more of my own experiences as a student/teacher/scholar, including my own thinking on issues, though rarely my own writing, which would reduce the distance further. Much of this sharing comes laden with irony and humor, perhaps to sustain some distance and some equanimity in the face of a darkening shadow of the future.

This darkening shadow also seems, like Anna Tsing's Matsutake mushroom, thriving in patches in damaged forests, to bring forth the best I have seen in students. Planning a life in capitalist ruins can foster genuine wisdom and I have drawn on this recently as I plot a line of flight from my current job. I am unlikely to be (fully) employed by Macalester beyond the 2020–21 academic year. I can make this move at age 63 because of Macalester's generous phased-retirement plan—a basic income when full-time work loses its appeal. I imagine a future where I shift from 30 years as a teacher-scholar at liberal arts colleges to a scholar-teacher, who can now return to plans for perhaps two books (or more, when I allow my fancy full flight), a return to ambitions that were swamped by my own frailties and demands connected to finding myself a senior scholar, like writing chapters for edited books. I hope also to take better care of myself. I have begun to share my plans, first with those in the field I trust the most, and now more broadly. I hear myself describe my vision and I test the reactions in the eyes of my interlocutors. I have turned recently to a few of my students, sharing my thinking about my own past and future as a teacher and scholar, in conversations ostensibly about advising, but in

---

[11] See "Tea and Text: Cultivated Intuition as Methodological Process," for Johnna Montgomerie, major author and editor, *Critical Methods in Political and Cultural Economy* (London: Routledge, 2017).

which I also search their reactions for guidance. A few members of my department have reacted with incredulity, but most of my peers respond with greater understanding. My students react with the least surprise: they no longer expect any job to last that long and they seem the most attuned to how the demands on all of us accumulate in our bodies. Where vocational paths have been disrupted or appear unbearable wisdom might be found and shared.

REFERENCES

Blaney, David L. 2002. Global Education, Disempowerment, and Curricula for a World Politics. *Journal of Studies in International Education* 6 (3): 268–282. https://doi.org/10.1177/102831530263007.

———. 2013. International Politics: As it Is, as it Might be. *Critical Studies on Security* 1 (3): 358–360. https://doi.org/10.1080/21624887.2013.850227.

Frueh, Jamie, David L. Blaney, Kevin Dunn, Patricia Goff, Eric K. Leonard, and Simona Sharoni. 2008. Political Beliefs and the Academic Responsibilities of Undergraduate Teaching. *Journal of Political Science Education* 4 (4): 447–462. https://doi.org/10.1080/15512160802413725.

Inayatullah, Naeem. 2008. Why Do some People Think they Know What Is Good for Others? In *Global Politics: A New Introduction*, ed. Jenny Edkins and Maja Zehfuss, 344–369. London: Routledge.

Inayatullah, Naeem, and David Blaney. 2017. Tea and Text: Cultivated Intuition as Methodological Process. In *Critical Methods in Political and Cultural Economy*, ed. Johnna Montgomerie, 23–27. London: Routledge.

Tsing, Anna Lowenhaupt. 2015. *The Mushroom at the End of the World: On the Possibility of Life in Capitalist Ruins*. Princeton: Princeton University Press.

Pedagogies of Discomfort: Teaching International Relations as *Humanitas* in Times of Brexit

Felix Rösch

Current institution: large public university
Typical classroom setting: seminars
Typical pedagogical approach: community of learners
Disciplinary identity: International Relations Theory, History of International Relations

INTRODUCTION

At the beginning of October 2012, I lectured for the first time to a group of undergraduate students. Considering my anxiety prior to and during the lecture, I do not think that my performance was particularly noteworthy, but the room I was teaching in bears significance for what I hope to achieve in my teaching. The lecture hall is situated on the fourth floor of a building, offering a beautiful vista over Coventry Cathedral. Today, the old cathedral only exists in ruins after Coventry was bombed by the

F. Rösch (✉)
Coventry University, Coventry, UK
e-mail: ab3522@coventry.ac.uk

© The Author(s) 2020
J. Frueh (ed.), *Pedagogical Journeys through World Politics*,
Political Pedagogies, https://doi.org/10.1007/978-3-030-20305-4_9

German Air Force in November 1940, and a new brutalist one, designed by Basil Spence, was erected next to it during the late 1950s. In the aftermath of World War II, Coventry Cathedral quickly came to be recognized as an international symbol for reconciliation, epitomized in the *Cross of Nails* and Josefina de Vasconcellos' sculpture *Reconciliation*, copies of which are to be found, for example, in the Chapel of Reconciliation in Berlin and the Hiroshima Peace Memorial Park.

Passing in between the two cathedrals on my way to work, these striking sacral buildings remind me that teaching International Relations (IR) is not only about communicating to our students the ins and outs of the discipline, but also about encouraging what Karl Jaspers (1959: 53) believed to be a "spontaneous by-product" of higher education: *humanitas*. For Hannah Arendt (1958), this concept stands for the active and collaborative engagement in the public sphere. Public engagement is a venture (*Wagnis*) (Arendt 1958: 2) because, although people may not be fully aware of all the resulting potential discomforts, they know that being in the public sphere puts them in a vulnerable position. *Humanitas*, therefore, crystallizes in agonistic, yet responsible dealings with the other (Arendt 1958: 3). In the case of Coventry, *humanitas* meant collectively rebuilding the city after World War II. Instead of taking revenge, Coventry has built bridges to former enemies like Dresden for a peaceful cohabitation. This "by-product" is of particular importance for our discipline because, after all, we teach the horrors that international politics can entail. In my classes, I ask students to think and talk about war, genocide, terrorism, slavery, and colonialism in order to help them imagine life-worlds differently. By identifying what unites people, rather than what differentiates them, differences (Inayatullah and Blaney 2004) can be experienced as creative sources for an agonistic, but more peaceful world.

While agreeing with Jaspers that *humanitas* cannot be the main purpose of studying any social science, aiming to induce spaces that facilitate it is indispensable at times. Particularly in the Anglophone world, the commodification of life no longer stops short of universities and we experience a degradation of degrees that Jaspers (1959: 123) was already concerned about more than half a century ago. As a consequence of this educational crisis, people often lack the criticality that *humanitas* sustains and that allows them to oppose the "populist obstruction of reality" (Behr 2017: 73), such as the decision of the United Kingdom to leave the European Union (Brexit). For such dehumanizing tendencies (Rösch 2015), IR teaching has to provide a counterbalance.

To highlight the importance of this by-product for IR teaching and show how I am to achieve such a counterbalance with my students, this chapter proceeds in two steps. First, Jaspers' *Idea of the University* (1958) and its connection to *humanitas* is further expounded. The aim of this section is to demonstrate that, despite recent concern (Schick 2016: 28) about the prospects of a Socratic education, as brought forward by many early twentieth century German intellectuals like Jaspers, this kind of pedagogy allows for a criticality that challenges dehumanizing "dominant cultural values of self-sufficiency, self-achievement and mastery" (Schick 2016: 26). Second, echoing Brent Steele (2017: 211), it is demonstrated through the discussion of modern dance that particularly the aesthetic turn can be a "productive and transformative" implementation of Socratic education, as it "exposes instructors and students to a vulnerability" in collectivity that can instill *humanitas.*

HUMANITAS AND THE IDEA OF THE UNIVERSITY

During the Weimar Republic, higher education was fiercely debated, as many intellectuals thought is epitomized a much larger cultural crisis. Jaspers' frequent pre-war interventions demonstrate that he was no stranger to this concern. Having been banned from academic work during the Nazi period because his wife was Jewish (Östling 2011: 115), he returned to questions of tertiary education in Germany (Habermas 1987: 3), as evidenced in his extensive involvement in the reestablishment of Heidelberg University in 1945. During the early days of the Federal Republic of Germany, Jaspers reintensified his public engagement, promoting universities as key sites to democratize Germany. *Humanitas* was central for his ambitions.

At the heart of *humanitas* stood for Jaspers (1959: 23) a commitment to honesty, knowing that "science unmasks illusions with which I would like to make life more bearable." Rather, "science disperses half-truths which serve to hide realities I am unable to face." As such, *humanitas* requires reflexivity and (self)criticality because only then, science "will truly humanize" (Jaspers 1959: 32). Stressing the flexibility of reason highlights that *humanitas* for Jaspers does not prioritize assumptions of rationality based on the mere accumulation of knowledge in which the other is being objectified by the self, as Kate Schick (2016: 30) is concerned about with respect to contemporary cosmopolitan education. This is because *humanitas* does not happen in solitude, but evolves in a very specific spatio-temporal condition. The space "in which our thought is at home," as Arendt (1958: 4) beautifully put it in her laudation for Jaspers on the occasion of his receiving of the Peace Prize of the German Book Trade in 1958, is "never unpopulated," but consists of a "community of thinking" (Jaspers 1959: 62; similar Rösch and Watanabe 2017).[1] Hence, central for *humanitas* is unrestricted relationality, meaning that these communities are not conditioned through their intellectual or ethnic background. Rather, they are conditioned through very hard work in the sense of intellectual modesty that encountering the other requires in order to avoid essentializations. This facilitates the acceptance of the other in her/his subjectivity by learning to understand other perspectives in their relational contextuality. However, it also means to make oneself aware of the potential vulnerability this stepping into the public entails. In what Fred Dallmayr (1993: 512) identifies as an "agonistic dialogue," people get a grasp of reality that, while being perspectivist, bears validity for their specific spatio-temporal context. In achieving this perspectivist objectivity, they are forced to investigate, expose, and renegotiate their identity foundations in collectivity. In this process, what the self considers to be her/his subjectivity—hence, what the self believes is objectively tangible—is challenged (Arendt 1958: 3) because the other perceives the self in a way that has not been disclosed to the self before. As Schick (2016: 31) maintains, this can also imply having to acknowledge an involvement of the self in "violent structures and norms" that one would have rather not concealed to oneself. This can be a deeply unsettling experience.

To alleviate this unsettledness, Jaspers (1959: 52) proposed a Socratic education to organize these dialogues. While this form of education cannot establish equality between scholars and students, as some form of hierarchy will persist between them, it still can inscribe "respect" (Jaspers 1959: 51) for each other by taking seriously all contributions to the community of thinking as valid attempts to further truth, helping to avoid making the teacher the narcissist "primary object of concern" (Schick 2016: 30). Jaspers (1959: 45) suggested that through asking questions, students can be accompanied in learning about themselves, others, and their life-worlds. Stimulating this (self)reflexive process is not intended to arrive at convictions of ultimate truth, but the realization that one's identity and life-world are in constant flux. The other is then no longer experienced as a threat to oneself, but as someone whose different outlook on life can provide the stimulus to imagine different, potentially more peaceful life-worlds that one is currently living in.

---

[1] All translations are by the author.

THINKING IN MOVEMENT: PEDAGOGICAL PROSPECTS OF AESTHETICS

To further *humanitas* in my teaching, I have found the aesthetic turn in IR to be promising. The use of movies, comics, paintings, literature, and even music is now standard in many classrooms (Weber 2001; Hawn 2013; Lobasz and Valeriano 2015), but the pedagogic prospects of the aesthetic turn are yet to be explored in more detail, as recent scholarship maintains (Grayson et al. 2009: 159–160; Steele 2017: 212). The purpose of this section is to demonstrate how the aesthetics of modern dance helped open up thinking space in a concerted effort with my students to sensibilize them for the prospects of vulnerability and ambiguity, helping to sustain the public sphere.

More than 15 years ago, Roland Bleiker (2009: 33, 87) popularized the aesthetic turn with the aim of transcending "the narrow realities" of "high politics." It was meant to challenge the often Western-centric view of international politics as the dealings between two or more nation-states, disregarding other actors in the international realm. Bleiker (2009: 2) argues in this respect that aesthetics "is about the ability to step back, reflect, and see political conflict and dilemmas in new ways." In doing so, we gain "a different dimension to our understanding of the political... since art is not the language of the habitual, since it searches for the new, the different, the neglected." Art encourages people "to reflect upon and rethink what has been taken for granted, to move beyond dogma and promote debate about issues that would have otherwise remain silenced or marginalized" (Bleiker 2009: 11). More recently, he was even more poignant, stressing that "aesthetics offers us possibilities to re-think, re-view, re-hear, and re-feel the political world we live in" (Bleiker 2017: 260).

As Aida Hozić (2017: 201) rightfully stresses, key to the aesthetic turn is the understanding that politics is to be found in the gap between representation and represented. Following Oliver Marchart (2004: 102), this gap exists due to the "original lack" of democratic societies. People will always be represented by a smaller group who cannot transmit the will of the people in total. This lack constitutes the space where politics—embodied by different actors—is being staged (Marchart 2004: 101), making it ephemeral and contingent, as politics is subject to contestation. Politics, therefore, "becomes a transient affair" (Marchart 2004: 107), exposing people to ambiguity and heightening their vulnerability. This is because on the political stage also power is being performed. Demagogues play with people's "deeply rooted desire for security and invulnerability" (Schick 2016: 26) by distracting them from the unsettledness that "no unequivocal take on the real" (Bleiker 2009: 9) can be offered. My students and I experienced this first-hand in the run-up to what ultimately led to Brexit, the UK government's decision to trigger Article 51 and leave the European Union. Since then, many British newspapers as well as politicians and public figures actively misled the public about the EU and stirred anti-European sentiments to influence the advisory referendum and later to conceal their promulgation of what in today's parlance would be called "alternative facts." One example is the claim on the now infamous red buses that the £ 350 million the UK spent each week on the EU could fund the National Health Service instead. It was retracted the day after the referendum.

With aesthetics, I try to sensibilize my students for the gap between representation and represented, stressing ambiguity and the vulnerability of life, but I also want to provide hope. The Japanese-American conductor Kent Nagano recently confirmed in an interview (Komma-Pöllath 2013) that "hope manifests itself in art; it becomes visible and concrete, because it touches our innermost feelings." This hope is not to be understood in a naïve way, but as a "critical hope" (Schick 2016: 41) in the sense that realizing this transience of politics can produce more just societies. Only when people start acting together, the public emerges in which people have the possibility to find compromises that allow them to canalize their antagonisms productively. Exposing oneself to vulnerability in collectivity helps them to accept the ambiguity of life and, by negotiating the fluidity of their own identities, putting power back into the collective action of people, away from the reification of demagogues. Simply put, we may consider ourselves British, support Arsenal, Aston Villa, or Liverpool, and be engaged in many more groups or causes that make us as a person, but these belongings are constantly evolving and so are our identities. We might be British, but still appreciate the peace that the EU has brought to a conflict-ridden continent or feel appalled about the UK government's treatment of the "Windrush" generation. We might support Arsenal, Aston Villa, or Liverpool, but this support can decrease or increase over time, triggered by successes, defeats, memories, or catastrophes as the 1989 Hillsborough disaster in the case of Liverpool.

To accompany my students in realizing this fluidity and engage with it positively as part of our *humanitas*, I incorporate, among other tactics, contact improvisation into my courses. This modern communal dance, that evolved at institutes of higher education in the United States in the early 1970s when a group of students under the supervision of professional dancer Steve Paxton started to question traditional forms of dance and their enshrined gender and power hierarchies (Cooper Albright 2013: 212–17), is notoriously difficult to define, as it is an evolutionary dance that resists more conclusive definitions. Still, Daniel Lepkoff (2008: 285) provides a useful approximation by suggesting the need to conceive contact improvisation as a "duet dance form that creates a frame for observing the functioning of the body's reflexes and our innate abilities to respond to the unusual physical circumstances of the touch of a partner and the floor on any surface of the body." In performing contact improvisation, my students can experience, with the support of Coventry University's Centre for Dance Research, the gap between representation and represented, learn to negotiate their ambiguity, and embrace critical hope by taking ownership of their relations and the space they perform them (Rösch 2018). Students put themselves in vulnerable positions, as they have to deal with their emotions in public and to potentially face critique from their peers (Marchart 2014: 44). By performing dance movements together, students learn to understand the other while at the same time become willing to (re)negotiate their own positions in order to successfully perform these moves.

In the following, I give a short overview of movements typically conducted during the workshop (adapted from Rösch 2018: 76–7). First, students can familiarize themselves with the dance studio and their peers within it. Exercises include sensing the space of the studio while walking through it with closed eyes. For most of the workshop, however, students do exercises in duets with changing partners, such as *escort down*. This move helps students manage the force of their own weight in relation to the weight of their peers. *Escort down* asks them to stand back to back to each other with the intention to move their bodies simultaneously down to the floor and back up again. It helps build trust among students, and they gain a first indication of alternative modes of power, as *escort down* can only be conducted successfully if both partners develop a sense of their own weight and that of others. At the end of the workshop, students engage in a collective exercise in order to further stimulate their questioning of common conceptualizations of power and to incite their imagination to consider different realities through alternative forms of power. Such movements include, for example, a variation of the *round robin* exercise, in which students form a circle, looking at each other's backs. They then put their arms on the shoulder of the person in front of them, while having their eyes closed. This is followed by simultaneously going down to their knees and sitting on the lap of the person behind them, with the aim of standing up again. Only when students sense the intention to move of the persons in front and behind them, while having an awareness of the distance to these other two students, and having the trust that the person behind them will support them in sitting on his/her lap, can this movement be completed successfully.

Certainly, modern dancing may be unsettling at first. It is not what you would normally expect from an IR course. Moving away from the security that a static understanding of the self and the other seemingly provides, they have to accept the imaginativeness of ambiguity. However, to alleviate concerns, I introduce my students to the intended learning outcome prior to the workshop and my dance colleagues explain contact improvisation further, focusing on its specific movements and the wider socio-political and historical context. Following the workshop, a feedback session takes place during which students can share their experiences. I learned from these feedback sessions that it helps that "acting is fun," as Arendt contended (Marchart 2014: 43) because it takes away some fears and helps my students to act together, eventually finding compromises and give them the power to create. It is in this way that "thinking in movement" (Sheets-Johnstone 2017: 1) takes place.

Conclusion

Trying to teach IR aesthetically to foster *humanitas* is not without its risks, as Steele (2017: 213) highlights, and I certainly encountered some of them ever since I entered this lecture hall on the fourth floor in October 2012.

By dancing with my students, I try to make international politics not only visually and affectively experienceable, but also tangible for students. I do this, knowing that some students find it too estranged from what they perceive to be the very heart of the discipline: nation-states, diplomacy, and foreign policy. The Westphalian system of nation-states is still a commonly accepted reality (Carvalho et al. 2011) and international politics is presented as a realm of anarchy in which nation-states as black boxes prevail, making some students struggle with alternative narratives in which they are supposed to engage with their own emotions and those of others. For this reason, I have decided against incorporating the dance workshop within the first year. Some might find opening up to oneself and others problematic, as vulnerability is not perceived as something positive. It certainly helps that dancing is fun and that it is part of most if not all cultures regardless of religious or socio-political constellations, but one cannot rule out the possibility and has to consider ways to avoid students feeling emotionally or intellectually overwhelmed (Holland 2014: 269). Finally, we also have more and more students affected by the neoliberal colonization of higher education (Steele 2017: 213) in which grades and degree classification matter, but they matter less if students have been educated to foster the critical hope of *humanitas*. However, if all that matters are grades, there can be resistance in engaging with an exercise that deliberately challenges students emotionally and intellectually.

Still, IR scholarship should not shy away from getting engaged with the "humanistic endeavor" (Hajo Holborn) in its teaching—and doing it aesthetically is just one way. After all, it is ever more needed in a world in which the neoliberalization of private and public life is only accumulating and fanaticism is making a return to world politics, as evidenced in Brexit.

References

Arendt, Hannah. 1958. Laudatio. Humanitas. In *Friedenspreis des Deutschen Buchhandels. 1958 Karl Jaspers*, ed. Börsenverein des Deutschen Buchhandels, 2–6. http://ow.ly/t0MB30duJ8Q. Accessed 10 July, 2017.

Behr, Hartmut. 2017. The Populist Obstruction of Reality: Analysis and Response. *Global Affairs* 3 (1): 73–80. https://doi.org/10.1080/23340460.2017.1302309.

Bleiker, Roland. 2009. *Aesthetics and World Politics*, Rethinking Peace and Conflict Studies. Houndmills/New York: Palgrave Macmillan.

———. 2017. In Search of Thinking Space: Reflections on the Aesthetic Turn in International Political Theory. *Millennium: Journal of International Studies* 45 (2): 258–264. https://doi.org/10.1177/0305829816684262.

Cooper Albright, Ann. 2013. *Engaging Bodies. The Politics and Poetics of Corporeality*. Middletown: Wesleyan University Press.

Dallmayr, Fred. 1993. Self and Other: Gadamer and the Hermeneutics of Difference. *Yale Journal of Law & the Humanities* 5 (2): 507–529.

de Carvalho, Benjamin, Halvard Leira, and John M. Hobson. 2011. The Big Bangs of IR: The Myths That Your Teachers Still Tell You about 1648 and 1919. *Millennium: Journal of International Studies* 39 (3): 735–758.

Grayson, Kyle, Matt Davies, and Simon Philpott. 2009. Pop Goes IR? Researching the Popular Culture—World Politics Continuum. *Politics* 29 (3): 155–163. https://doi.org/10.1111/j.1467-9256.2009.01351.x.

Habermas, Jürgen. 1987. The Idea of the University – Learning Processes. *New German Critique* 41: 3–22.

Hawn, Heather L. 2013. Utilising Popular Music to Teach Introductory and General Education Political Science Classes. *European Political Science* 12 (4): 522–534. https://doi.org/10.1057/eps.2013.37.

Holland, Jack. 2014. Video Use and the Student Learning Experience in Politics and International Relations. *Politics* 34 (3): 263–274. https://doi.org/10.1111/1467-9256.12022.

Hozić, Aida A. 2017. Introduction: The Aesthetic Turn at 15 (Legacies, Limits and Prospects). *Millennium: Journal of International Studies* 45 (2): 201–205. https://doi.org/10.1177/0305829816684253.

Inayatullah, Naeem, and David L. Blaney. 2004. *International Relations and the Problem of Difference*. New York: Routledge.

Jaspers, Karl. 1959. *The Idea of the University*. Boston: Beacon Press.

Komma-Pöllath, Thilo. 2013. Abschied vom Sehnsuchtsort. *Frankfurter Allgemeine Zeitung* (August 5). http://ow.ly/sTWX30dDSQB. Accessed 14 July 2017.

Lepkoff, Daniel. 2008. Thoughts on Contact Improvisation: An Issue of Definition. In *Contact Improvisation Sourcebook II: Collected Writings and Graphics from Contact Quarterly Dance Journal 1993–2007*, ed. Contact Quarterly, 284–285. Northampton: Contact Editions.

Lobasz, Jennifer K., and Brandon Valeriano. 2015. Teaching International Relations with Film and Literature: Using Non-Traditional Texts in the Classroom. In *Handbook on Teaching and Learning in Political Science and International Relations*, ed. John Ishiyama, William J. Miller, and Eszter Simon, 399–409. Cheltenham: Edward Elgar.

Marchart, Oliver. 2004. Representing Power. Public Space, the Artist, and the Body of the Leader. *Österreichische Zeitschrift für Geschichtswissenschaften* 15 (3): 95–110.

———. 2014. Dancing Politics. Political Reflections on Choreography, Dance and Protest. In *Dance, Politics and Co-Immunity. Thinking Resistances*, ed. Gerald Siegmund and Stefan Hölscher, 39–57. Zurich: Diaphanes.

Östling, Johan. 2011. The Regeneration of the University. Karl Jaspers and the Humboldtian Tradition in the Wake of the Second World War. In *The Humboldtian Tradition Origins and Legacies*, ed. Peter Josephson, Thomas Karlsohn, and Johan Östling, 111–126. Leiden: Brill.

Rösch, Felix. 2015. *Power, Knowledge, and Dissent in Morgenthau's Worldview*, The Palgrave Macmillan History of International Thought. 1st ed. New York: Palgrave Macmillan.

———. 2018. The Power of Dance: Teaching International Relations Through Contact Improvisation. *International Studies Perspectives* 19 (1): 67–82. https://doi.org/10.1093/isp/ekx002.

Rösch, Felix, and Atsuko Watanabe. September 2017. Approaching the Unsynthesizable in International Politics: Giving Substance to Security Discourses Through *Basso Ostinato? European Journal of International Relations* 23 (3): 609–629. https://doi.org/10.1177/1354066116656764.

Schick, Kate. 2016. Unsettling Pedagogy. Recognition, Vulnerability, and the International. In *Recognition and Global Politics. Critical Encounters Between State and World*, ed. Patrick Hayden and Kate Schick, 25–44. Manchester: Manchester University Press.

Sheets-Johnstone, Maxine. 2017. Moving in Concert. *Choros International Dance Journal* 6: 1–19.

Steele, Brent J. 2017. Recognising, and Realising, the Promise of The Aesthetic Turn. *Millennium: Journal of International Studies* 45 (2): 206–213. https://doi.org/10.1177/0305829816684254.

Weber, Cynthia. 2001. The Highs and Lows of Teaching IR Theory: Using Popular Films for Theoretical Critique. *International Studies Perspectives* 2 (3): 281–287. https://doi.org/10.1111/1528-3577.00058.

I Love Teaching: It Is Fun!

Rosemary E. Shinko

Current institution: mid-sized private research II university
Typical classroom setting: seminars (<19), survey courses (<25)
Typical pedagogical approach: mini framing or summary lectures (no
  PowerPoints, no more than 10–15 minutes), discussion around textual
  (in the broadest sense) analysis, small group-based activities
Disciplinary identity: political theory, IR theory, theoretical approaches
  to peace and identity

I have read many sanctimonious commentaries on teaching and at some
point not too far into the book or article, I give up in frustration and drop
it onto a pile of what I thought were promising reads. Teaching is really
challenging and even when you think it went really well, it might not have
according to your evaluations. And that is when I admonish myself, "You
know what, this isn't about me, but about the students and how they
understand what just happened over the course of the semester."
Sometimes I will leave class thinking about how powerful or significant
the themes and ideas were that I presented and at some point during my
self-congratulations, I stop and ask myself how much of the discussion was
taken up by me. Did my power and position as the professor suck up all of

R. E. Shinko (✉)
American University, Washington, DC, USA
e-mail: shinko@american.edu

© The Author(s) 2020
J. Frueh (ed.), *Pedagogical Journeys through World Politics*,
Political Pedagogies, https://doi.org/10.1007/978-3-030-20305-4_10

the oxygen in the room? How much space was opened for student reflections and responses? In those moments of critical self-reflection, I realize how I am evaluating class on the basis of my performance and how I feel and not, more importantly how my students may have experienced it. This is my internal check to keep reorienting my teaching back to my students. Yes, I am passionate and vested, but the key is to help them identify their own passions and enable them to become vested in the class.

MY SOCRATIC COMPLEX

When I first started teaching, I thought all I had to say was "I use the Socratic Method," which in retrospect is amusing on so many levels. Where to start on that one? Well there is the fact that Socrates only had male students of means who could afford to sit around locked in endless debate, that rationality had a particular cultural and gendered cast to it, and that topics for debate were tethered to a circumscribed range of public/political issues that ignored the larger swath of so-called private concerns. Which makes one wary about the whole intellectual context within which one adopts role models and their pedagogical remit. But seriously, I initially thought teaching really just revolved around me learning how to ask questions and to keep the whole thing going with me firmly conducting the orchestra of responses. The key here was that all of the responses came back to me. Yes, my students generally found it more interesting than a lecture, but oftentimes more confusing because it did not have the logical order of a lecture. Eventually I got better at conducting, but that ended up with me being even more firmly embedded at the center of my student's learning experience as the discusser-in-chief. Here's the thing, I was really good at this, I enjoyed it and took a lot of satisfaction in really developing this approach, and I did this for years.

I prided myself on how adept and nimble I had become in the classroom and how I could so dexterously respond to even the most bizarre responses from students, which in retrospect feels a lot like giving everyone a trophy regardless of their response. I suspected that this approach was not the end-all-be-all of good teaching, but kept it up because it had become so easy and comfortable for me to do. Students were confirming my own hesitations in their course evaluations. While, overall, my evaluations were positive, there were indications that I really needed to reconsider and re-craft what I was doing and how.

Sometimes students felt as if my questions were merely asking them to fill in the blanks and that I had a clear expectation of the desired response. Class became more of a game of charades. I was soliciting answers I wanted them to give to questions I posed rather than letting them engage with the materials. I was narrowing the range of responses to conform to the conclusions I expected them to draw. This is not only limiting and problematic, but also ultimately driven by the professor's own ideological or intellectual commitments. In those instances, I realized I was not creating an intellectual space of competing ideas but carefully scripting and imposing my version of the correct interpretation on my students. At other times, I erred on the opposite end of the spectrum by allowing the discussion to range too far afield and we all lost sight of what the heck we were supposed to be discussing. This is all compounded by the fact that I really hate pausing to write on the board because it disrupts the flow of ideas. I managed to fix that by asking my teaching assistant to serve as the scribe and keep track of the key themes and ideas on the board. I also tried to solve the problems by beginning each class with a statement of the class theme and points to be covered for the day that I wrote on the board before class began. But these were basically minor tweaks to an overall approach that really required a serious reevaluation and overhaul.

A Disaster in the Making

Perhaps the real moment of clarity occurred after I taught a large 500-student class. The course was "Western Political Thought" and it was my first and last foray into the large lecture hall format. Since I was so wedded to the Socratic method, I could not envision any other approach to teaching. Furthermore, if I am brutally honest, I did not want to change my style as it had become central to my own sense of identity as a professor. I enjoy hearing what students think and how their responses prompt my own and challenge me by raising different insights. This is what makes the class a shared journey that has a direction but enables us to explore paths I might have overlooked or not considered taking at all. It is the shared aspects of the Socratic dialogue that I find most rewarding and fulfilling. But I plunged ahead and adapted my discussion format to the large lecture hall. It actually wasn't the disaster it could have been and surprisingly my evaluations were not far off from where they had been, right in the middle of the range. That being said, some of the criticisms were stinging as I clearly ran afoul of what students expected by enrolling in this type of class. There were students who found the reliance on a more dialogic style engaging, but as you can imagine, the problems I previously mentioned were merely magnified. These included a clear lack of direction, a sense that at times I was merely asking students to fill in the blanks and confusion on the part of students who did not know what to make of disparate strands of comments from so many different students. I could have just stayed the course and doubled down on my approach, but I had learned some important things about myself and what I love about teaching. I really dislike preparing and delivering lectures, I balk at having to rely on PowerPoint and I genuinely believe teaching is a conversation. Lecturing feels like talking to myself or treating students like a captive audience hopefully wowed by my carefully scripted presentation. I admire my colleagues, who are really good at effective and engaging lecturing, but I am not, nor do I care to become so. This is the one aspect I have retained from my Socratic complex that I refuse to jettison. The other important lesson I learned was that substituting variations on the theme of Q & A was just as deadening, from the opposite side of the spectrum. The large lecture format drove this point home because I did not have the time to follow students down their own conceptual pathways, nor could I keep everyone else on point while one student rambled on. I wasn't really engaging them at all, save for those few who could hear their own voice offering up answers to my very circumscribed questions.

Change Can Be Daunting

So what to do? And how to catch the baby as one throws out the bath water? This is the scary part because this has huge implications in terms of one's own advancement and reputation and there is always the fear that change may not be productive, progressive or effective. While I am basically a risk adverse person in terms of actions, that is not the case in terms of ideas. When I returned to graduate study later in my career to work on a Ph.D., my first class was with a postmodern political theorist. I felt as if I had been living in a cave and all of the referent points by which I had navigated IR theory had radically shifted. I was more than a little confused and wary, but the more I gave myself the space to get over my attachment and supposed comfort in the way things had been when I exited the field, I discovered that I did have a greater capacity to take intellectual risks than I had given myself credit for. So I had to turn off one side of my brain to encourage the other that finds "out-there ideas" so inviting and compelling.

I realized that these two moments in time were similar and that the same leap into postmodern/post-structural IR as a conceptual frame of reference could be brought to bear on my teaching. So what would it look like if I upended my circumscribed reliance on the "Socratic Method" for something more akin to my own intellectual discovery of postmodernism, in other words, a pedagogical approach that more accurately reflected and took inspiration from my own intellectual journey? And how to do this without thinking of or recreating my students as mini me's? Their journey is not mine, but my journey can hopefully inspire them to take risks and to embrace the scary yet productive aspects of change. I am constantly wary of placing myself at the center of their intellectual journeys. I strive to be an interlocutor and more of a guide than one who would dictate the terms of their journey, limit what they encounter along the way, or constrain their ability to create their own pathways. Now if you think the rest of this article is going to demonstrate how I have figured all of this out, you probably should stop reading now and consign me to your own dustbin of disappointing reads.

I will, however, share with you how I arrived at what I think is a more nuanced and holistic view of teaching, but with the caveat that it never fully settles into a place of comfort or self-assurance. Each semester is a new opportunity to "get it right" but also a risk that things may go awry. They usually do go awry at some point or another and the key is to figure out how to positively respond and recover.

Reorienting My Teaching

My journey to where I am today is really reflective of a series of leaps, trial and error, and a willingness to experiment. How could my teaching capture the fact that I really love being with students, admire their youth, energy, humor and potential, and draw on that as a way to inform my pedagogy? I tried to analyze what I really found compelling in teaching and to identify what deep strands of self-satisfaction and self-worth it fulfilled. This is true not only for me but for my students as well. How could I structure my courses to acknowledge and develop these facets of learning?

The first thing I did was to question why I approached my syllabus as one piece of whole cloth of linear learning punctuated by assignments, exams and essays. The radical shift I made was to begin thinking of each class as its own discreet learning experience. It wasn't that I was fracturing the overarching structure of the course, but I tried thinking about how to construct an interrelated series of activities and assignments that provided unique opportunities for learning that were intellectually linked across the semester. This change in perspective was coupled with an honest acknowledgment that just because I say something in class or it is covered in the readings does not mean that students understand it, learn it and can apply it. Thinking about how I learned and improved as a teacher, I realized it was by iterative practice and repetition across the semesters and years. Now admittedly, we don't have years with our students, we have a semester or two. But how can I replicate this in an accessible way in only a semester? And how to accomplish this in a way that does not merely become repetitive or formulaic?

Postmodern theory really pushed hard against my entire sense of linearity and it occurred to me that learning is far from linear. I began to conceptualize education as a series of ever widening and deepening circles unfolding across the semester. I saw teaching and learning as simultaneously a movement backward to capture and incorporate what has been previously learned and a movement forward in order to apply and do something with the information learned. There was a moment when it quite literally dawned on me that I needed to structure my classes so that learning and doing were entwined and practiced across the semester.

I did not achieve this overnight nor have I fully realized or perfected this. But each semester and for years now, I have kept at it and continue creating a repertoire of materials, strategies and plans that I can draw upon and swap in and out of various classes.

LEARNING AND TEACHING: BRINGING NEW APPROACHES TO YOUR CLASSES

My first foray into this new approach was captured in my teaching article *Thinking, Doing and Writing IR Theory* (Shinko 2006). Writing this article really was a foundational moment that set me on a new course in my own approach to teaching and learning. It enabled me to explain to others and myself not only how I taught but also why I thought this strategy of blending thinking, writing and doing was so important. By writing the article, I acknowledged that these three components were seminal to my own development as a professor. In this respect, the article was my own thinking, doing and writing moment that I could share with my students and colleagues.

The basic structure of my new approach to teaching emerged out of my experimentation with different assignments, writing projects and discussion formats in my IR theory courses. Once I settled on this tripartite framework, I intentionally organized every subsequent IR theory course as a set of overlapping circles with essays, midterms and finals cumulatively designed for application and synthesis. Each segment of my class was built around a key theoretical lens, spanning realism to postmodernism that afforded students multiple opportunities to read, discuss and engage various facets of this theoretical approach in a variety of ways. The basic design of each subsection of my class remained relatively constant across the semester enabling students to have some stability via the organizational framework while introducing new sets of readings and conceptual frameworks. The topics and themes shifted but the engagement strategies, the doing and the requirements for their analysis essays, the writing, remained constant.

Each section of the course was built around key theoretical readings and application exercises in class so students could try out the theoretical lens, grapple with and think about the ideas and concepts, draw the materials together and select their own current event, and write their own analysis essay. The midterm provided the students with an opportunity to apply the lenses they had learned by that point in the semester and to write an analysis essay on a topic I selected and draw upon each of the lenses in turn. The writing assignments were intentionally designed to give them an opportunity to synthesize their observations, critiques and insights across all of the various readings discussions and class activities. The essays enabled them to practice the work of a theorist/analyst and to set them up for a final project or exam where they could demonstrate the various critical thinking and writing competencies they had developed and refined over the course of the semester.

The final project consisted of an IR Theory Conference where students worked in small teams representing each theoretical perspective in order to analyze a common topic that was student-selected. The analysis unfolded in class verbally as students represented, defended and challenged the various approaches highlighting their strengths, weaknesses and conceptual limitations and blind spots. The final exam closed the circle by offering the students one more opportunity to practice synthesis and analysis across all of the theoretical lenses in a comprehensive application essay on a topic I selected. My pedagogical objective is to enable my students to think, write and do. I create a learning environment where they can practice, practice, practice, make mistakes and learn from them, but most importantly succeed.

I currently teach a class on Identity, Race, Gender and Culture and I have adapted my basic framework to this class in a slightly modified format. The class is organized around the three basic themes of the subaltern, discourse and visuality. The essay prompts for each section are given to students at the outset so they can begin to organize their thoughts and become conscious about how their own ideas develop and change over the course of our readings and discussions of that theme. Students write three essays, which cover each theme and that enable them to practice analysis and synthesis.

After we have covered all three themes, they write a reflection essay that asks them to discuss their own personal intellectual engagement with our three themes, to identify the key insights they have discovered and some of the critiques or challenges they would like to raise about the various conceptual frameworks we studied. This lays the groundwork for our final two class activities. We read aloud the play *Disgraced* and then they write their final essay. The final essay asks them to analyze the play through each of our three themes. They are expected to be able to draw upon seminal authors, concepts and ideas using the play as the basis for their application. It is this final exercise that brings the course full circle and by design, they have been practicing these intellectual competencies and critical thinking and writing skills across the semester. The final essay then offers them an opportunity to bring all of their learning together and to demonstrate how they can apply their knowledge in this new context. In short my approach is based upon thinking, doing and writing, whether I am teaching a first year seminar or a senior capstone.

This basic framework has worked well for my students and for me because we both can directly observe their progress over the course of the semester. When I compare their initial essays with their final exam, the qualitative and substantive evidence is undeniable. To prepare for the final exam and summary class discussion, students go back and reread their previous essays as a way to prepare and identify what they may need to review, but most importantly to enable them to reflect on their own intellectual growth and development. This framework continues to shape how I approach teaching and learning. I organize each class by asking two basic questions: what should they understand today and how can they apply or use it in a context that is new or different. Student learning occurs when they have opportunities to play with the ideas in class, to struggle and write about them in their own essays and then to be able to bring them all together in summative projects or writing assignments.

CHALLENGES AND DRAWBACKS TO THIS STYLE OF TEACHING

So perhaps this all sounds foolproof, but I would not be honest if I did not share with you my own struggles with teaching in this way and the demands and challenges it presents for my students. This type of teaching demands an intensity of focus and preparation from both the student and the professor. I fully acknowledge that some students will calibrate their level of preparation for class and come to rely on others to help shape the information for them. I have no real way of knowing the actual degree of preparation of my students, but can get a sense of this through their reactions and responses to various discussion prompts and their degree of participation in small group assignments. I walk around during the small group work and take note of the materials students are using and if they are referring to reading notes or marginal comments on the articles and, of course, if they even have the assigned materials in front of them. I should add that I continuously share critical reading strategies with them, calibrated to match the types of materials they are asked to engage with, and share a section or two of my own marked up copy of the day's assigned materials. And I acknowledge those students who have notes and annotated assignments in front of them and provide positive feedback on their preparation for class. I provide students with data that backs up the reasons for this type of actual physical interaction with the assigned materials. And I constantly reiterate how these are transferable skills across a lifetime of career paths. I have also designed the essays in such a way that this type of engaged interaction with the assigned materials is essential to the analysis and synthesis required in the essay. After the first essay assignment, we discuss the challenges they faced in writing their essays, how their reading strategies can either hinder or support their writing, and how their preparation for class and quality of participation in the discussion also help to establish a context that helps them organize and structure their writing.

One strategy that seems to encourage and support this type of intense and engaged focus is the fact that I post the essay assignments along with the introduction and assignments to each thematic section of the course. This helps frame their preparation for class and reinforce why I require that they learn how to synthesize all of the assigned materials into their essay. They know the essay questions up front and that they are going to have to figure out how to draw the materials together in order to craft their essays. Students have indicated in my teaching reviews that they really appreciate this type of structure, but that the real challenge for them

124 R. E. SHINKO

is, of course, related to the skills of synthesis and analysis. I do get push-back about my requirement that they incorporate all of the material into their essays and I acknowledge that this is challenging. My goal is to encourage deep learning, the kind that sticks with you because you are encountering it over and over again but in different contexts and ways. This requirement is designed to draw them back into the texts and to think about what emerges when they look for strands that overlap and ideas that butt up against one another. I believe that deep learning occurs in these interstices of working through a variety of materials, written, visual and auditory, but perhaps most significantly, they are the conductors who draw all of the threads together in a way that makes sense to them and that enables them to puzzle out and develop what they think and why.

The biggest drawback for me is the time I spend grading these essays and the level of detailed commentary I provide. I will say that most of my students appreciate the commentary, but a few of them feel overwhelmed by it. I try to temper the amount of my comments so I am not jumping on every word and sentence and I give them room to develop and try out their ideas and arguments. I am conscientious of pointing out what they are doing well and where their arguments and supporting proof are effective and well crafted. I genuinely appreciate the fact that the majority of my students are working very hard but also acknowledge the relativity of that personal determination and its variance across my students. Students will always try to calibrate how much effort they need to put into the assignments, so I am very conscientious about ways in which I can encourage them to be fully present and prepared for class.

There is no magic formula for this, but I am convinced that it is related to the relationships I create between us in the classroom, the ways in which I acknowledge their efforts and take seriously their ideas. I am not afraid to share with them my own passions regarding the subject matter and my own struggles and questions that I too grapple with. But the real key is my focus on them, their learning, their passions, their interests and commitments. They understand that I care and I want them to flourish and succeed and that is why most of them will get fully vested in this semester long journey. They appreciate the fact that I constantly remind them that we are making this up together, we are creating our class and the experiences we have together each and every day. I fully acknowledge the various degrees of preparation and effort that different types of assignments require and I am transparent about this. I also acknowledge the degree of effort this type of class structure requires, so I am very conscious of breaking things up to include some assignments that lighten things up.

A course can't be all broccoli! I strategically vary the types of materials so there is an ebb and flow so that there isn't one academic article after another with no room to breathe. I know which theoretical/academic materials are the most challenging and so I design more student-engaged ways of working through it. And when I do get the sense I have pushed them too hard, I insert some type of a break, which could involve me selecting the various aspects they could focus on or asking them to choose the one they most want to explore. The class time is used to help them practice the art of synthesis by working through how to draw threads together. Or I can organize class around some pop culture item that provides an effective focal point for class discussion and this also helps demonstrate how relevant the class materials are to these broader trends and aspects of our lives. I try to make class fun and I have found that they really enjoy learning how to identify the weak spots in the arguments and how deconstruction can be effectively used to expose bias or unacknowledged assumptions. I do let my passion for postmodern critique guide my style, but I am also conscious that I have to temper the bleakness and sense of futility that type of critique can engender. I blend the critical with the encouraging and try to maintain a balance between what is wrong and what might be moving in a more positive direction.

It's All About Practice

It is very easy to become discouraged and focus on what your students can't do or what they are failing to do, but I keep two important things in mind: learning is an uneven process that unfolds over time and all of the things we are asking them to do require practice, application and opportunities for reiteration. I think we tend to forget how long we have studied, how much effort we continue to expend in order to do so, and that they are not us. That being said, learning is a practice and we need to craft our courses in ways that enables them and us to practice, make mistakes and improve. We need to teach them how to read critically, how to think critically and how to engage critically through writing. This requires iterative course design, iterative assignments, iterative class applications and discussions that help them constantly practice and improve. The key here for me is to scaffold this across the semester, thinking intentionally about where students are at the beginning of the semester and how I can help develop their competencies and intellectual capacities in a stepped fashion that keeps challenging them and progressively drawing them forward.

A final note of caution, just as our students are not us, you are not me and my approach might not suit you. Teaching and learning is a process of trial and error and you should seriously think about how your own teaching could be scaffolded by building throughout the semester various creative approaches that are clearly linked to your learning objectives and outcomes. Think about the class as a journey and what you are looking forward to, what might be the difficult or challenging parts of the journey, where you might get lost, but most importantly where and in what condition you hope to arrive at the conclusion of this semester's intellectual trip. We all know the positive energy we have at the beginning of the semester and the trick is to think about how to nurture that enthusiasm, recognizing that it will wax and wane. The main goal, however, is to create a shared intellectual journey consisting of memorable moments of shared challenges, hard work, enjoyment, fun and accomplishment.

REFERENCE

Shinko, Rosemary E. 2006. Thinking, Doing and Writing International Relations Theory. *International Studies Perspectives* 7: 43–50.

CHAPTER 11

"Come on Down!" Pedagogical Approaches from *The Price Is Right*

Jeremy Youde

Current institution: large public research university
Typical classroom setting: seminar discussions, lecture (30–75 students)
Pedagogical approach: collaborative/interactive
Disciplinary identity: IR/comparative, sub-Saharan Africa, global health, international organization/global governance, international development

True story: I'd never stepped foot in an Intro to IR classroom until the fall of 2010.

By that time, I'd earned the bachelor's, master's, and doctoral degrees in political science—the last of which specifically focused on international relations. I had held faculty positions at three different institutions. I had published two books and a dozen peer-reviewed articles, including one on pedagogy in international relations.

And yet…that core foundational course remained elusive. Through the combined quirks of timing, study abroad, and curricular reform, I never took Intro to IR as an undergrad. During my years as a teaching assistant (TA) during graduate school, I somehow never got assigned to Intro to

J. Youde (✉)
University of Minnesota Duluth, Duluth, MN, USA
e-mail: jyoude@d.umn.edu

© The Author(s) 2020
J. Frueh (ed.), *Pedagogical Journeys through World Politics*,
Political Pedagogies, https://doi.org/10.1007/978-3-030-20305-4_11

IR. At my first two faculty jobs, the departments already had people teaching Intro to IR. It wasn't until my third year at the University of Minnesota Duluth (UMD) that I finally got my chance.

This is not to say that I was removed from international relations as a teacher. I had been teaching upper level IR-related courses in departments of political science or as parts of various interdisciplinary programs—but I hadn't taught (or even been a part of) that core foundational course. That may have contributed to some of my initial negative attitudes toward IR. When I entered grad school, I had no intention to study IR because, as far as my 20-something-year-old brain had convinced itself, IR was merely about counting guns and bombs. I overcame that attitude in grad school when my IR seminar professor provided me with a constructivist epiphany, which has since led me to the fame and glory I now possess. (*Ed. Note: I don't possess fame and glory.*)

So here's my problem: I'm teaching a brand new course for the first time in my life. I'm teaching a course that any yahoo with a degree in international relations should be able to teach in her or his sleep. I'm teaching a course in a subject area that, when I was these students' ages, I considered boring and "beneath me." (*Ed. Note: I wasn't always insufferable as an undergrad, but I definitely had my moments.*)

That's when it hit me: this is my *The Price Is Right* moment. I'm being called to come on down to Contestants' Row to see if I can make it on stage (or even to the Showcase Showdown). In fact, the more I reflected on it, I came to realize that my teaching philosophy is basically modelled on *The Price Is Right*.

JOHNNY, WHO'S OUR NEXT CONTESTANT?

My love of game shows runs deep. When I was six and my parents asked me what I wanted to be when I grew up, I told them that I wanted to be a game show host. (*Ed. Note: I also wanted to be a farmer and a McDonald's franchisee...so I naturally went into academia.*) As a kid, there were few things I loved more than watching shows like *Sale of the Century*, *The Joker's Wild*, *Family Feud*, *Press Your Luck*, and *Card Sharks*. *The Price Is Right* was a favorite during summers or when I was home sick. The excitement of guessing prices at an age when I barely understood the concept of money! The novelty t-shirts the contestants wore! The idea of spinning the wheel! The elusive thrill of the rare Double Showdown winner! As an awkward and shy kid (who has grown into an awkward and shy adult), I marveled at Bob Barker's ease in interacting with everyone. As I got older,

I gravitated more toward *Jeopardy*, but my residual affection for *The Price Is Right* remained. When I started working at Duluth, I reconnected with *The Price Is Right* because it would be on at the gym when I went to run on the treadmill. Trying to guess the price of a can of tuna packed in oil is a great way to take your mind off the absurdity of running on a treadmill.

It was at this same time that I was grappling with how to put together an Intro to IR course and make it work for me. I felt like I was flailing around without any grounding. This led to trying a few different initial strategies that seemed like good ideas at the time. My first false step was to do something that a lot of us do: ask my really smart friends for copies of their Intro to IR syllabi in the hopes that I could simply copy what they had done. In my fantasy, one of my friends had already crafted such a jaw-droppingly amazing syllabus that I could walk into the classroom, deliver the course and inspire young minds so intensely that, at the end of the semester, they would cheer and carry me out of the classroom on their shoulders. I was looking for the Intro to IR equivalent of *Rudy*.

Surprisingly enough, this did not happen.

This isn't because I don't have smart friends who have incredibly well-developed courses. Rather, it's because these smart friends are not me. What works for them does not necessarily work for me—simply because we are different people with different interests and teaching styles. Furthermore, context matters. A course that worked well at my friend's large R1 flagship institution wouldn't necessarily work at my tuition-dependent regional comprehensive university on the shores of Lake Superior. For example, one of my friends frequently used in-class quizzes with clickers as a way to check in with students during his lecture. I could do that! Except clickers were not used at my school, so I'd have to ask students to shell out an extra $70–100 for a device that would only be used in one class. And I was dealing with a class of 50–80 as opposed to more than 300. And my classes did not have separate lectures and discussion sections. If my friend had tried to use his syllabus with my students in my department, it would not have flown. Now imagine if someone else (also known as me) tried to deliver his syllabus in my department. Right. You see where the problems emerge.

My second false step was a function of my pack-rat tendencies. Going through my files, I found a copy of the application that I had sent to the good folks at UMD—the application materials that got me the job (or at least got me the interview that led me to get the job). Included in that was my teaching philosophy statement. "Surely," I thought, "this will unlock the secrets and allow me to reconnect with my true thoughts and feelings about teaching."

It did not.

There's a difference between *having* a teaching philosophy and *writing* a statement of teaching philosophy. When I went back to read mine, it gave me nothing practical. It did not unlock any secrets. It did not tell me anything I didn't already know about what I do in the classroom.

What Do You Bid?

It was at this point that I realized that I was going about this in the wrong way. Intro to IR wasn't that radically different from courses I had already taught. I had developed a persona in the classroom. I knew the rhythms of my classes—both in terms of what I tended to do in each individual class and in terms of how students navigated the semester. I knew what sort of experience I wanted my students to have and the tools that I could use to try and achieve that.

In other words, what I learned in my despair about trying to create this course that should have already been in my wheelhouse was that I already had the building blocks. I realized that the specific bits of information that I wanted students to learn about classical realism or the end of the Cold War mattered less than the experiential element of my teaching. Rather than planning everything that I wanted students to learn and then trying to shoehorn that into a framework, I reversed that option. I know how I want to teach, and I know various techniques that I've used successfully. I want students to have a good experience that will allow them to learn. If I start with that, I can figure out the specifics that make sense in that context.

I can make most subject matters fit within the framework of how I teach. What I can't do is present different versions of myself to different classes. For me, this was a key moment in my own pedagogical development. If I'm going to be effective in the classroom and achieve as many of the learning outcomes that I have as possible, then I need to be comfortable in my own skin. When that happens, students can sense it—and they can be comfortable in their own skins. When that happens, it's far more likely that they will engage, develop their critical thinking skills, and foster a respectful environment than if I try to be incredibly overt about this.

At this point, I decided to take a step back and think about what I really value in the classroom environment. What is it that I try to do, even if I haven't previously articulated it? I came up with a list of five values and expectations:

- I want to employ a broad repertoire of engagement strategies.
- I want to build and facilitate interpersonal relationships, getting to know and value my students as people and not just nameless bodies.
- I want to embrace the diversity of my students and make sure they know that they are respected.
- I want to continually experiment and try new things in my classes, even if my efforts occasionally fail.
- I want to be enthusiastic about my teaching, and I want that enthusiasm to be contagious.

Where had I seen these behaviors modelled? Why, when I watched Drew Carey asking contestants to guess the price of a pair of skis or explaining the rules of Flip Flop. I doubt that the show's producers sit around their studio at CBS Television City thinking about the pedagogical elements of one of America's longest-running game shows, but their approach to their show helped me to think about how to structure Intro to IR—and my teaching philosophy more broadly.

Spin the Wheel!

I promise: analogizing my teaching philosophy to a daytime game show was not an example of me trying to be cheeky or dismissive. Let me flesh out how these ideas about how I want the classroom experience to go mirror my boyhood dream.

First, it is important to **develop a broad repertoire of engagement strategies**. On *The Price Is Right*, everyone knows the basic outline of the show, but there is a wide variety of different games used to get the contestants and audience members involved. It would be boring if every contestant played Plinko. It's the same when I teach. At the beginning of each class, I explain what I want to accomplish during that period. How we get there, though, will vary. I will use different strategies to reach out to and engage my students because each student has a different learning style. Furthermore, it bores students to just sit there and listen to me drone on and on every class period. In my Introduction to Comparative Politics course, for example, I will occasionally lecture with PowerPoint slides, but I'll also use visual aids (particularly a giant dinosaur and a Scooby Doo-shaped Chia Pet) to illustrate theories about the origin of the state. Other days, we'll watch clips from *Monty Python and the Holy Grail* or *The Simpsons*, and then break into small groups to discuss the political issues raised. By mixing things up, I try to adjust my teaching strategies to reach as many students as possible and to keep everyone interested and engaged.

Beyond visual representations, I try to incorporate very tangible experiences into as many of my classes as I can. Most commonly, these take the form of simulations. In an Intro to IR course, for example, I might develop a simulation where students work in groups to represent the members of the United Nations Security Council to consider how to address North Korea's nuclear program. The specifics of the topic and how the simulation will work vary each semester, but I use the exercise to make students embody a particular worldview and advocate for it publicly (even though it may not accord with their own beliefs). I also want students to understand two seemingly contradictory ideas—that achieving agreement on big issues in international relations is a lot more difficult than it may seem at first glance, and that there are more opportunities for agreement and cooperation than commonly assumed. In essence, the simulation is an effort to crush some measure of both students' idealism and cynicism.

Using simulations has also brought home for me the difference between focusing on learning specific facts over the course of the semester and focusing on the experience. Simulations generally take about a week of class time for the simulation itself and the debriefing afterward. They generally take place toward the end of the semester, too. In the span of a normal semester, taking an entire week out for a single activity involves trade-offs, especially in an introductory course where you want to make sure that the students get enough information so that they can take upper-division IR courses. It means that I can't fit as many issues into the course as I may like, and I may not be able to use all of the readings that I would like. Those are both definite costs, but there are so many benefits that the simulation provides for me. It gives the students a direct experience that they may not get in their other courses. My friends in the natural sciences often tell me that students don't really understand chemistry or physics until they get in the lab and can see it in action. I want students in the social sciences to have those same sorts of hands-on experiences—even if it means that I have to sacrifice subject matter breadth. I want students to walk away from my classes with that experience, even if they never take another international relations or political science again in their lives.

Second, you have to **build interpersonal relationships**. Whenever Bob or Drew brings a contestant on stage, he asks that person a little about him or herself—where home is, what brought them to the show, and what they were hoping to win. Building a rapport makes people feel comfortable and more able to engage in the matter at hand. The same principles work in my classroom. Even in larger classes, I pledge to at least know each student's name and a little something about them—their hometown or their major or an activity with which they are involved. Doing this demonstrates to my students that I'm interested in them as people, not just faceless masses. It makes it easier for students to approach me with questions about the class material and speak up in class. It also lets students know that people in the college care about their whole being. I've had students come out to me, approach me about personal problems, and open up about difficulties they have faced making the transition from high school to college. Showing that I care makes them feel comfortable so that they can succeed—both in my class and as adults.

Third, you can't succeed unless you **embrace diversity**. Bob Barker never knew who was going to end up on Contestants' Row next, and he could not predict which contestant would make it on stage with him. That didn't matter. Everyone who might play the game had something they could contribute. In my classes, I get a wide range of students, and I do everything in my power to make sure that everyone feels comfortable, respected, and able to contribute. I don't hand-select my students, so I am always anxious each semester to see what sort of diversity we'll have. I want students to draw on their lived experiences to interpret and process the material we are discussing. I also want to eliminate any barriers that may prevent students from fully engaging with the material. I've been fortunate to receive recognition for my efforts on this front, such as being awarded a Certificate of Appreciation from UMD's Office of Disability Resources in 2011 for accommodating a variety of student needs.

Fourth, **don't be afraid to try new things—even if you fail occasionally**. *The Price Is Right* doesn't rest on its laurels. It introduces new games. It retires old ones. It changes the format occasionally. It keeps up with the times while still remaining firmly grounded in its underlying ideals. I do the same in my classroom. I introduce different techniques to make material resonate with students— and sometimes those attempts do not work. One time, in Theories of Comparative Politics, I tried to create a *Family Feud*-style game to generate some discussion of a chapter. It did not go over well: I didn't explain the rules well, students were confused, and the subject matter did not lend itself well to questions with a "right" answer. Instead of throwing up our hands in collective despair, though, we shifted class on the fly and talked about the material and why the game didn't really work with a chapter on Max Weber. Trying something new and failing led to an even better classroom discussion, and it gave students a sense of ownership in the class. Later that semester, students suggested other activities that we could use to discuss our material.

Finally, **let your enthusiasm be contagious**. Bob Barker loved hosting *The Price Is Right*, and it was clear to everyone that watched the show. Drew Carey evinces the same joy on the show today. He smiles. He laughs. He has fun. He shows contestants that they can understand the game and play it successfully, and the contestants respond with their own enthusiasm. It isn't much different when I step into the classroom. I love political science, and I want to share that love with my students. I know that not all of them will love it with the same fervor that I do, but I want them to see that the material can be fun. It's not just about having fun for fun's sake, though; when I'm enthusiastic about the material, it helps put students at ease that they, too, can have fun with it. On an essay exam in Introduction to International Relations once, I asked students to use three theories of international relations to suggest how the international community would respond to a zombie outbreak. When students saw the question, I heard laughs and saw smiles. I saw stress melting away. Nearly two years later, I still have students ask me about that essay prompt. It was indeed fun. Far more importantly, though, scores for that essay were far higher than those from traditional essay questions. The enthusiasm and fun aspect of the question let students relax, engage with the question, and demonstrate that they really knew this material. At the end of a semester, I want a student to walk out of my classroom feeling like they had an enjoyable time and that they learned something. I want them to tell their friends that they need not be scared of political science. I want them to see that college isn't just about getting a degree, but about having enriching experiences and opening up to new ideas in new ways.

CONCLUSION, OR BE SURE TO SPAY OR NEUTER YOUR PETS

A few years ago, I had to write a statement of my teaching philosophy as part of my application to become a Senior Fellow in the Higher Education Academy (UK). This was a challenge for two reasons. First, I hadn't written a proper teaching philosophy in years. Even though I had taken the time to figure out my teaching philosophy, I hadn't actually committed it to paper. Second, and perhaps more importantly, I was writing for a UK-based accreditation body while based in Australia. *The Price Is Right* is not a staple of Australian television like it is in the US. It hasn't been on air in Australia since 2012, it has its own combination of games, and the logo is not the same. Would the references make sense? Would it be serious enough?

After taking the appropriate amount of time to panic, I realized that the core of my teaching philosophy—those five bullet points from above—remained regardless. *The Price Is Right* is a hook for understanding my approach, but the real substance is in the experiences that I want my students to have. I can explain those by taking specific examples from my experiences teaching Intro to IR and other courses—even without discussing the finer points of *Range Game* or *Safe Crackers*. That strategy worked, and I received Senior Fellowship designation in early 2017.

Saying that my teaching style replicates one of America's longest-running game shows is not the sort of thing that is likely to appear in a university guidebook, and it's not something that I would tell students over the course of the semester, but it's an effective way for me to conceptualize what I am trying to do. It helps me to tackle new challenges like teaching new courses in the midst of all sorts of other competing pressures. The only thing missing is a giant wheel to spin.

From Two-Time College Dropout to Full Professor: The Non-traditional Route to Teacher and Mentor

Eric K. Leonard

Current institution: small private liberal education university
Typical classroom setting: seminar discussion
Typical pedagogical approach: collaborative learning with some Socratic method
Disciplinary identity: International Politics, Foreign Policy, Political Philosophy

PERSONAL BACKGROUND

To say that I was not the best of students in high school and my early college years is an understatement. I had no interest in academia, reading, critical thinking, writing or any of the attributes that make for a solid Ph.D. prospect. Instead, I was more concerned with learning to surf, playing soccer and enjoying my college years. After dropping out of college twice and failing to find any profession of interest to me, I found my way

E. K. Leonard (✉)
Shenandoah University, Winchester, VA, USA
e-mail: eleonard@su.edu

© The Author(s) 2020
J. Frueh (ed.), *Pedagogical Journeys through World Politics*,
Political Pedagogies, https://doi.org/10.1007/978-3-030-20305-4_12

back to a small state school near my home at the age of 23. It was at this institution that I discovered my love for political science, but more importantly, realized the impact a college professor could make on a student's life. In this chapter, I lay out my non-traditional path to the academy and the effect it has had on my career decisions. Teaching was why I came to academia, but the path to becoming a successful teacher is difficult. In fact, honing your pedagogical craft and becoming successful in the classroom is one of the tougher things academics can accomplish. Throughout my career, I have clung to the fact that the quest for good pedagogy is often fraught with failure, but also rewarded with a positive impact on students that is hard to quantify.

My journey to academia began when I was 23 years old, working for my friend's landscaping company and failing to see where I was going or even where I had been in life. To that point, I was a mediocre student who upon completing high school got into some excellent universities because I played soccer, not because of my SAT scores. I played soccer, surfed and occasionally attended class for two and half years at a Division I school before tearing my ACL and leaving university for home. Another short stint at a local college failed to inspire an academic spark, more as a result of my personal situation than the college itself. At 23 years old I decided, with some prodding from my father, that it was time to try college one more time. You know what they say, the third time is the charm; and in fact, it was. At the same local college I had attended a few years earlier, I stumbled into a set of political science classes that energized and excited me. I fell in love with the discipline, with the process of learning and with the thought of affecting others the way the faculty at William Paterson College had impacted me. Why do I start with this personal story? Because it is essential to understanding how I teach my courses and what I hope to achieve in the classroom.

What Do You Want from This Profession?

In considering graduate school, it is imperative that you have some sense of your postgraduate goals. When I realized my desire to pursue a Ph.D., I knew that the primary purpose for that pursuit was to teach. I enjoyed the research and writing aspect of the discipline, but my passion was teaching. In particular, teaching at the undergraduate level at an institution similar to my alma mater. Thus, when looking at graduate schools, I wanted an institution that would help me achieve that goal. I did apply to some Ivy League and Big Ten institutions, but in the end, the University of Delaware provided me with everything that I was looking for, even though it did not have the "big name" standing of other political science programs.

Primarily, Delaware provided me the opportunity to hone my teaching skills. This process began with my time as a teaching assistant and evolved into my own classes. My biggest piece of advice for graduate students that wish to succeed in the classroom is that you need to get into the classroom. All the pedagogical reading and training cannot prepare you for what it is like to be in front of a class. When teaching your own class, so many things go wrong, so many issues arise and so many failures emerge. But despite the pain, and sometimes embarrassment, of those lessons, I would not trade them for anything because it was through those moments that I became a better teacher. If Delaware had not provided me those opportunities, I would not have been as marketable to the types of schools where I was seeking employment, and I would have been inexperienced if offered a job at a teaching-oriented school. The problem with the latter scenario is that I would have been making those pedagogical mistakes while my tenure clock was ticking; resulting in a weak promotion portfolio in the exact area where it needed to be strongest.

I also realized that my pedagogical goals were in teaching students who had an academic background similar to my own. I never intended on pursuing an academic career at an R1 institution. My desire was to teach, and to teach students who were also seeking their academic potential. In order to fulfill that desire, I applied for jobs at two types of institutions: mid-level state schools that required a 4/4 or 4/3 teaching load, and smaller private universities with low teacher to student ratio. But it is important to note that the latter category did not include the elite liberal arts institutions. At the smaller private universities the teaching load is high, and the amount of double preps is low. A typical teaching load at these smaller private schools is seven different preps per academic year. For scholars focused primarily on their research, this may sound like a nightmare scenario. For me, this was the dream.

Learn and Evolve

One of the most important things to remember about becoming a good teacher is that you never stop learning—it truly is a process of "becoming." It is crucial that professors, who spend a lifetime constantly studying all of the nuanced changes in their area of research, also study the continuous dialogue on pedagogical method. It is safe to say that where your pedagogical method starts when teaching your first class is not where it will end.

My first class was a winter session Introduction to American Government class. It was a general education class taught over 5 weeks, 2.5 hours per day, 4 days per week to approximately 50 students. I was still a graduate student and had never prepped my own course. In preparing the syllabus, I completely focused on content and all of the facts that the students needed to learn. Although this was an American Government course, I know that if this were an Introduction to International Politics course I would have taken the same approach. The course began and for my very first course, it did not go completely off the rails (and to some degree that is the low bar you should have for your first class).

However, as the course proceeded, I realized that what the course was providing students was an excellent opportunity to win at a Trivial Pursuit game or some other multiple-choice style assessment on American government. I was simply spewing facts at them, writing lists on the board, asking them to engage in an almost purely rote-learning exercise. If I were to place my assessment of the class into the vocabulary of my current philosophy of teaching, students were not learning, they were memorizing. One week of a professor spouting off facts and figures about American Government, followed by a multiple-choice exam with some short answer questions, to only continue the same process the following week. If I were a student in that class, I would have been thoroughly bored and uninterested. Luckily, these students were kinder to me than I was on myself, and the teaching evaluations did not reflect how poorly I taught the class. However, I would hypothesize that those evaluations had more to do with a comparative analysis of how other professors taught their classes, rather than the pedagogical proficiency of the class relative to a higher standard. In many ways, the personal recognition of how much better the course could be, coupled with the positive student evaluations told me that expectations were far too low among today's college students. It appeared as if the typical lecture style format paired with a regurgitation style assessment was satisfactory as long as the instructor was not fumbling over their words and was fairly well organized. However, I felt that students deserved more and this poorly executed course began my quest for an improved pedagogical method. It also initiated my journey into a study of what constitutes learning and the broader question of what exactly am I hoping to accomplish in my classes.

THE MESSY SEARCH FOR METHODS AND OBJECTIVES

It was at this point that I began to codify what I wanted to achieve in the classroom in the form of a teaching statement. What I now find interesting is that the general premise of that initial philosophy has not changed, but the means and primary objective of it has. As a result of my first foray into teaching, I knew that learning was not the same as memorization and regurgitation of facts. For me, rote learning was insufficient because it did not produce an understanding of the material, just a factual knowledge of it. I was searching for a way to get my students to understand the material in way that they could make it their own.

It was at this point that I was fortunate enough to serve as a teaching assistant for Bob Denemark in his Introduction to International Relations class. In this class of almost 100 students, Dr. Denemark introduced me to an active learning exercise that transformed not only my teaching but also my approach to pedagogy—case studies. I watched Dr. Denemark direct the first case study of the semester and instantly realized that he had reached these students in a way that most traditional methods could not. The case study method necessitates student interaction with the material, both in terms of understanding the content of the case; but more importantly, in the analysis of the case and its relationship to the broader course material.[1] From my perspective, it was the point in which learning occurred.[2]

This method became the backbone of my pedagogy for years. I used it in the majority of my classes and even published my own case study on the International Criminal Court.[3] However, I soon realized that the pedagogical method was not the important aspect of the course, but what I was seeking was the outcome of that method. In other words, I began to

---

[1] GUISD case study material accessed at Georgetown University Institute for the Study of Diplomacy. "Case Studies." https://isd-georgetown-university.myshopify.com/

[2] Vicki L. Golich, Mark Boyer, Patrice Franko and Steve Lamy, "The ABCs of Case Teaching," http://researchswinger.org/others/case-method-teaching.pdf is an outstanding resource for those wishing to understand how to employ the case study method. This was originally found on the GUISD site, but is now accessible at the link provided. Vicki L. Golich, "The ABCs of Case Teaching," *International Studies Perspective*, 1, no. 1 (2000): 11–29, also provides an excellent resource.

[3] Eric K. Leonard, "Establishing an International Criminal Court: A New Global Authority?", Institute for the Study of Diplomacy, (2000), https://isd-georgetown-university.myshopify.com/products/establishing-an-international-criminal-court-the-emergence-of-a-new-global-authority

understand that the method was not the important part of my pedagogy. I always advise my peers to avoid employing a new method just because it seems novel or engaging. I realized that the method was only as good as the outcome it provided and that outcome, in terms of student understanding and behavior toward the course material, was what I wanted to achieve. And as I embraced this quest for positive outcomes, I recognized that active learning, in whatever form I could provide it, would produce the desired outcome of understanding the course material, rather than just memorization.[4] Active learning promotes a classroom environment in which students are engaged participants in the learning process, not simply vessels that the instructor is filling up with knowledge. This environment promotes self-learning, collaboration and engagement with the material in order to understand the material instead of just memorizing it.

Thus began my messy journey to achieving the outcome of student understanding. If one wants to become a good teacher, it is important that you are willing to take pedagogical risks. This is often difficult, especially early in your academic career. For anyone in academia, the primary professional goal is tenure. Before achieving this goal, the notion of taking risks in the classroom is nerve-wracking. You are constantly thinking, if the pedagogical method does not work, what will that do to my student evaluations? Or how will my colleagues perceive me? Or what impact will this have on my future class enrollment? (The last of these is a very real danger when teaching at a small, private institution.) I was fortunate to have the support of my institution in trying new pedagogical methods, but the prospect of poor student evaluations still loomed large. Despite this danger, it is important that new professors play with different active learning methods to discover what works best in their classroom and with particular classes. Personally, I have used in-class simulations, online simulations, games, policy papers and whatever else I thought might assist my students in understanding the material.[5] In the end, I found that different methods worked well in different classes, but I eventually found my way back to a reliance on case studies. What is important to understand about this process is that it is a personal one. Do not allow someone else's success to

---

[4] Jeffrey S. Lantis, Lynn M. Kuzma and John Boehrer (ed). *The New International Studies Classroom: Active Teaching, Active Learning.* (Boulder, CO: Lynne Rienner Publishers, Inc., 2000), provides a look at multiple means of active learning.

[5] A large number of the methods I employed came from my time attending professional conferences and workshops. The APSA Teaching and Learning conference was extremely helpful, as were the career workshops held at the annual ISA conference.

dictate your methods. A colleague may use a particular method in her/his classroom with tremendous success, but that does not necessarily translate to your classroom context, the type of students in your institution, your teaching style, etc. Because there are so many variables in achieving classroom success, it is important that instructors find their own path and their own method in assisting students to understand the course material.

What I Learned from AAC&U

Just as my methods evolved and became more inclusive, my outcomes also began to shift. Part of this evolution is the result of my interaction with AAC&U and their Liberal Education and America's Promise (LEAP) initiative.[6] Approximately 12 years ago, I attended a one-day conference at Washington & Lee University on the LEAP initiative. At the time, I was the Director of General Education at Shenandoah University and was attending the conference in this capacity. However, I realized that the LEAP initiative extends far beyond a student's initial foray into college through the general education curriculum. In fact, for LEAP to truly achieve its goals, the initiative must proceed from general education to major curriculum as a means of providing students with the skills necessary to succeed in their post-college life.

The LEAP initiative focuses on a set of essential learning outcomes. These outcomes include: knowledge of human cultures and the physical and natural world, intellectual and practical skills, personal and social responsibility, and integrative and applied learning.[7] In essence, the purpose of these outcomes is to meet "the demands for more college-educated workers and more engaged and informed citizens." As further explained on the LEAP website, "Today, and in years to come, college graduates need higher levels of learning and knowledge as well as strong intellectual and practical skills to navigate this more demanding environment successfully and responsibly."[8] This is an attempt to invigorate higher education with a liberal education model that "helps students develop a sense of

---

[6] American Association of Colleges and Universities (AACU). "About Leap," https://www.aacu.org/leap

[7] https://www.aacu.org/leap/essential-learning-outcomes provides an overview of these outcomes, along with the skills that each outcome contains.

[8] AAC&U, "About LEAP," https://www.aacu.org/leap

social responsibility, as well as strong and transferable intellectual and practical skills such as communication, analytical and problem-solving skills and a demonstrated ability to apply knowledge and skills in real-world settings."[9]

How does this affect my own pedagogical approach? My acceptance of the LEAP initiative as part of my own classroom means an embrace of the skills that undergird that program. These include oral and written communication skills, critical and creative thinking, information literacy, quantitative literacy, ethical reasoning, teamwork and problem solving, civic knowledge and engagement, and intercultural knowledge and competence. What I have learned through my 20 years in the classroom is that these skills are what I value and what the research tells us employers' value as well.[10] As a result, the impact I could make in the classroom began to shift from a content-driven perspective, to a skills-based one.

It is important to understand that this shift in emphasis does not mean that my pedagogical method does not value the content that our students achieve in a political science program. It remains vital to our students education that they understand the main theories of International Relations, how foreign policy power is distributed between the branches of government, what the difference is between a first past the post and proportional representation election, how the United Nations Security Council works, among so many other things. However, this shift does mean that I value the skills they ascertain in achieving this content knowledge as much as the content itself. The reasons being that these skills are transferable to a variety of employment opportunities and to the attributes needed by the citizenry of a flourishing democracy. This pursuit of democratically articulate students is sometimes overlooked in our profession. We get so wrapped up in preparing them for a job that we forget that we are also preparing them to be knowledgeable participants in society. I like to emphasize, both to my fellow faculty and my students, that my role in the classroom extends beyond just assisting students in their ability to land a job. My role is to also provide a learning environment that promotes the attributes of a good citizen; and by engaging them in a culture of critical reading, critical

---

[9] AAC&U, "What is a Liberal Education?" https://www.aacu.org/leap/what-is-a-liberal-education

[10] AAC&U, "Falling Short? College Learning and Career Success," https://www.aacu.org/leap/public-opinion-research/2015-survey-results

thinking and objective analysis, I feel that students can achieve this vitally important role.

If one reflects on the students in their survey level courses, it seems reasonable that many of the students are not political science majors, have a limited interest in studying the political system, and are fulfilling a general education requirement by attending the course. Even at a smaller private institution like Shenandoah University, this is often the case. This often makes the task of "selling" the class to these students a difficult one. I do believe it is important to sell the importance of the class to students, because if your goal is an interactive learning environment, there must be student buy-in. The typical way one achieves this buy-in is a discussion of the course content and the need to understand this stuff because it will affect their lives in a globalized world. However, a supplemental way to sell the course is to discuss the way in which the course and its pedagogical method will prepare them for future employment, regardless of their major. The reality is that we work in an environment that is becoming more geared toward work-related skills and knowledge. Parents and kids want to know how a particular class will help them get a job.[11] An acceptance of the liberal education model in your pedagogical method provides an answer to this question, without sacrificing the content of the program goals.

ADOPTING A NEW METHOD

One way I have embraced this initiative in my classroom is by moving toward a set of assessment methods that provide students with the ability to practice the skills listed above. This provides a conscious move away from multiple-choice exams and toward a constant process of writing and a greater emphasis on individual and applied learning. In my survey level classes, I achieved this goal via the final point of evolution in my pedagogical method, the implementation of a hybrid-style delivery model.

In all of my 100/200 classes, and the occasional 300 level course, I employ a delivery method in which I meet with students in a traditional brick and mortar style classroom on Monday and Wednesday, and then in

---

[11] Pew Research Center, "Is College Worth It?" http://www.pewsocialtrends. org/2011/05/15/is-college-worth-it/, although a bit outdated, this survey provides insight about what the American public sees as the purpose of college, with 47% saying that "the main purpose of college is to teach work related skills and knowledge."

a virtual world on Friday. The benefit of this method is the constant inter-action that students must have with the classroom material. Although this constant interaction is possible in a variety of methods, I have found that this way works best for my students because they feel as if they are getting something out of the method (Fridays online) that offsets the level of work they must complete to succeed in this course.

So, what do Fridays look like? In order to meet the contact hours for this class time, students will engage in some exercise related to the current course content. This may take the form of an online lecture with a short assignment to show their understanding of the material, an applied assign-ment that asks them to engage a topic discussed during the classes on Monday and Wednesday, a discussion board or a variety of other assess-ment methods. One example is a recent assignment in my Introduction to Global Studies class in which we were studying nation-state identity and the fragmentation of these political entities because of secessionist move-ments. I asked students to provide some basic definitions of the concepts we discussed in class and then find a secessionist movement and answer the following questions:

1. What is the name of the nested polity or separatist movement?
2. Where is the movement located? What state?
3. Why do they desire political independence? What makes their iden-tity different from that of the state? Explain this in detail.
4. Do you think the movement will be successful? Why or why not?
5. Why would the state want to retain this group if they do not wish to remain part of the state?

Upon returning to class on Monday, we engaged in discussion of these political entities and the students' answers to the prompt. This method provides me with the fulfillment of many of my pedagogical goals—critical reading, critical and creative thinking, written communication, informa-tion literacy and oral communication. It also forces students to actively engage the course content in a way that differs from the traditional 50-minute classroom method. However, before initiating the hybrid method in their course, the one thing that professors should recognize is the fact that this method takes a lot more effort and time than the tradi-tional pedagogical method. I am grading student assignments on a weekly basis, working on new means of assessment and constantly honing creative methods of engaging students in the course material. However, if one's primary objective is to increase student learning and not just memorization, this may be a pedagogical tool worth exploring.[12]

ALWAYS LEARNING

After 20 years of teaching, if I could impart one piece of pedagogical wisdom to young academics it would be to never stop learning. The process of becoming a good teacher is one that never ends and as a result, your engagement of new and different pedagogical methods should never end. There is a plethora of resources for academics to engage in their attempt to improve their teaching. There are blogs on teaching,[13] workshops at professional conferences,[14] individual conferences on pedagogy,[15] most universities have a center for teaching and learning, along with more literature on pedagogical method than ever before. If you hope to become an excellent teacher then you must approach that job as you do your research. Our graduate programs constantly remind us to stay current on the literature in our area of study, read often and continue to write and publish. Your approach to teaching should be the same—stay current on the methods of teaching, read often and widely, experiment in the classroom and yes, publish! It is important that we continue to cultivate a community of professors that value teaching. As stated at the outset of this paper, the reason for pursuing my Ph.D. was not research or publications, but teaching those that looked like me when I was an undergrad; and the only way to do that well is to continue my education on pedagogy.

---

[12] Jay Caufield. *How to Design and Teach a Hybrid Course: Achieving Student-Centered Learning Through Blended Classroom, Online, and Experiential Activities.* (Sterling, VA: Stylus Publishing, 2011); Francine S. Glazer (ed.). *Blended Learning: Across the Disciplines, Across the Academy.* (Sterling, VA: Stylus Publishing, 2012) are two excellent introductory resources to this method.

[13] "Active Learning in Political Science" http://activelearningps.com/

[14] There are several at the current ISA conference (2018). I will be attending one entitled, Teaching the Intro Course.

[15] The APSA Teaching and Learning conference has been the biggest pedagogical conference in our discipline for years, but starting in fall 2018, ISA will be holding its own pedagogical conference. International Studies Association, "Innovative Pedagogy Conference," https://www.isanet.org/News/ID/5580/Innovative-Pedagogy-Conference-2018

REFERENCES

Active Learning in Political Science. Blog. http://activelearningps.com/

American Association of Colleges and Universities (AAC&U). About LEAP. https://www.aacu.org/leap

AAC&U. What is a Liberal Education? https://www.aacu.org/leap/what-is-a-liberal-education

AAC&U. Falling Short? College Learning and Career Success.

Caulfield, Jay. 2011. *How to Design and Teach a Hybrid Course: Achieving Student-Centered Learning through Blended Classroom, Online, and Experiential Activities.* 1st ed. Sterling: Stylus Pub.

Georgetown University Institute for the Study of Diplomacy. Case Studies. https://isd-georgetown-university.myshopify.com/

Glazer, Francine S., ed. 2012. *Blended Learning: Across the Disciplines, across the Academy.* Sterling: Stylus Pub.

Golich, Vicki L. 2000. The ABCs of Case Teaching. *International Studies Perspectives* 1 (1): 11–29. https://doi.org/10.1111/1528-3577.00002.

Golich, Vicki L., Mark Boyer, Patrice Franko, and Steve Lamy. 2000. *"The ABCs of Case Teaching," Pew Case Studies in International Affairs.* Washington, DC: Institute for the Study of Diplomacy. http://researchswinger.org/others/case-method-teaching.pdf

International Studies Association (ISA). Innovative Pedagogy Conference. https://www.isanet.org/News/ID/5580/Innovative-Pedagogy-Conference-2018

Lantis, Jeffrey S., Lynn M. Kuzma, and John Boehrer, eds. 2000. *The New International Studies Classroom: Active Teaching, Active Learning.* Boulder: Lynne Rienner Publishers, Inc.

Leonard, Eric K. 2003. *Case 314 – Establishing an International Criminal Court: A New Global Authority?* Washington, DC: Institute for the Study of Diplomacy. https://isd-georgetown-university.myshopify.com/products/establishing-an-international-criminal-court-the-emergence-of-a-new-global-authority

Pew Research Center. Is College Worth It? http://www.pewsocialtrends.org/2011/05/15/is-college-worth-it/

CHAPTER 13

Teaching Writing as Social Justice

Amy Skonieczny

Current institution: large public comprehensive university
Typical classroom setting: seminar discussions, >35 students, writing and research courses, senior thesis/capstone
Typical pedagogical approach: active learning, group collaboration, mini-lectures with discussion
Disciplinary identity: US Foreign Policy

MY BEGINNING

During my Ph.D. program at the University of Minnesota, I spent far more time thinking about International Relations Theory than teaching. When I did think of teaching, I imagined myself opening young minds and inspiring students to question conventions and stereotypes—to rethink American power in global terms and to spark curiosity about things they had never thought about before. I imagined inspiring change like my former professors did for me. I thought I would teach about justice, and invert hierarchies. I never once thought I would need to teach how to write a paragraph or why re-reading your own writing is a necessary and critical step in a research paper.

A. Skonieczny (✉)
San Francisco State University, San Francisco, CA, USA
e-mail: askonie@sfsu.edu

© The Author(s) 2020
J. Frueh (ed.), *Pedagogical Journeys through World Politics*,
Political Pedagogies, https://doi.org/10.1007/978-3-030-20305-4_13

My first year as a full-time visiting faculty member at Macalester College while finishing my dissertation was nothing like I imagined. Yes, I did have far more opportunities to inspire amazing, talented, private school students who were thirsty for understanding and hungry for justice in the world, but I rarely delivered. Instead, I badly 'prepped' five new courses and taught every day Monday through Friday in a harried, in-over-my-head collision with very prepared undergraduates who were used to top-notch experienced, seasoned professors. I was eaten alive. I would spend hours preparing for my US Foreign Policy class and successfully fill 50 minutes on Monday only to have absolutely nothing for Wednesday or Friday. Not to mention the two classes I had never taught before that were on Tuesday and Thursday. I showed random movies that I'd never seen too many times to count and either ended 20 minutes early because I was out of material or spent nearly the whole class period on the first three of 20 slides. I was stressed, incoherent and felt like a complete failure.

Yet, what at the time felt like failing was also learning. I learned that over-preparing did not always mean success and that I could sometimes successfully think on my feet—yes it stemmed from desperation but it sometimes worked. One of the best days I had in that same US Foreign Policy class was a day I had no material and no time to prepare. Fifteen minutes before class started, I was in my office panicking and considering cancelling class when I decided to throw together a mock UN simulation that was very bare bones but required that the students work in groups and negotiate with one another. It loosely related to the day's topic of climate change and was without much structure or background information. It worked! The students were on fire—crafting plans, huddling in groups, shuttling notes back and forth. At one point, nearly all of the 25 students were crammed into a small corner of the room adding comments to a joint statement they had written. I stood back in awe—once I was 'out the way', they directed their own learning. They were engaged, inspired, collaborative and worked together. And, it had taken less than 15 minutes for me to plan and prepare for that day. From then on, I spent more time thinking about student-directed learning than 'preparing to teach' and found I had more time and greater success. But this was just year one. And this was at Macalester College, a top-ranked private liberal arts school with fewer than 2500 students.

Shortly after fall semester started at Macalester, so did the job market. I applied to my 'dream job' at San Francisco State University (SFSU) back in my home state of California and was extremely lucky to get an interview.

It was 2006, when you could still apply for a tenure-track job while All But Dissertation (ABD). I was deep into my dissertation at that point and Minnesota had prepared me well for my job talk but it was my sink or swim stint at Macalester that got me the job.

By the time I came in for the interview, I had just wrapped up what I felt like was a dismal first semester of full-time teaching. But then came the interview. So many questions about teaching! I confidently answered questions about assignments and exams, and gave specific examples of failures and successes. I handed out five syllabi for the five different classes I prepped for my year teaching at Macalester that were not just mock-ups. I relayed real experiences and discussed what I planned to do in the upcoming semester to improve. I easily prepared a 45-minute teaching demo on the flight to California, which felt like nothing compared to winging it five days a week in three different classes. Despite my own feelings of failure, I was able to connect with the search committee about real students, in real class settings and real struggles to teach a wide variety of classes with little or no time for preparation. I could tell from the faces of the committee as they nodded, smiled and even chuckled at my stories about my first experiences teaching that while my idealism had clashed with the realities of teaching, it had prepared me well for the teaching-intensive environment of a non-R1 public institution. I would be battle-tested by the first day and they were confident I could survive the 3-3 teaching load. I was offered the job. By the next year, I felt excited, more prepared and ready to channel what I had learned into my new institution. This would be the year I would actually deliver on what appeared in my teaching philosophy. I would prepare more active learning assignments, deliver on a student-led pedagogy, inspire change and open minds about the world.

THE NEW WORLD OF THE LARGE PUBLIC INSTITUTION

One of the biggest adjustments in moving from a small, private liberal arts college to a huge, public institution was the wide-range of diversity in the classroom—diverse in ethnicity, education, age, preparation, language and country of origin. I had students who struggled with English and had only just arrived in the country and students who went to top high schools and could academically compete with any college student in the country. I had to learn to adjust my teaching to a multi-level approach to reach the student who was just hoping to pass and the one planning on applying to graduate school at Berkeley. Teaching became more challenging but also more stimulating than I imagined. I had to think through what was most important about each block in the syllabus and contemplate how to engage everyone in the classroom at the same time.

But by far the most frustrating aspect of teaching in this environment was the often very low level of student writing. This aspect caught me off-guard and I felt resentful, often angry and vastly unprepared to teach writing. In those early moments, I never imagined that this would become some of the most important work I do in the classroom.

Like many professors of Political Science, I had always been a good writer. It came easily to me and I didn't spend much time thinking about organization or structure. In fact, as an undergraduate, I wrote nearly all of my papers the night before they were due. I never once had a class that required multiple drafts and didn't use outlining. I was a procrastinator and wrote mostly without notes. I skated through undergraduate writing assignments with only complements and hardly ever received suggestions or advice on how to improve my writing. I acted as an impromptu editor for my friends and after I graduated from college, one of my jobs was proofreading faculty grade reports at UC Santa Cruz. I considered myself an expert at identifying poor writing but quickly found this didn't translate into teaching students how to be better writers.

My first year at San Francisco State, my assignments were freshly tested at Macalester College and in every class I taught, I had some sort of writing assignment—a country case study in US Foreign Policy, a policy report in International Political Economy, an essay in IR Theory. At SFSU, I was also assigned to teach the undergraduate 'writing across the discipline' course and a Senior Thesis course. The International Relations department I had joined required ALL majors to write a 45–60 page Senior Thesis as a core requirement, regardless of ability, GPA or desire. At Macalester, I found most of the papers I had assigned to be pretty good. I never considered assigning a draft or even having a detailed explanation of the assignment beyond basic information such as choose a country and write a 5–7 page paper on bilateral relations between it and the United States. Pretty straightforward, right?

I quickly learned that at SFSU, my assignments did not garner the results I expected. It would take me days to grade instead of hours because I would range from so despondent I contemplated a new career to enraged at what I interpreted to be lack of attention or care on the part of the student to basic spelling, grammar or just plain comprehension. I once called a student into my office and made her re-read one of her particularly poorly written paragraphs out loud—it didn't make any sense at all, it was not even readable, how could she turn something like this in as part of a college assignment? She cried. I felt bad, but also a little justified—like 'you *should* cry' and 'I practically cried when I read it too'. I would post snippets of atrocious writing to Facebook just to get some sympathy—and I always received an outpouring of comments and commiseration from my graduate school friends. What had we gotten ourselves into? We endured our Ph.D. program for this??!!??

For my first few years I kept going but got more and more cranky. I assigned writing, dreaded reading it, blasted it in comments on the paper, and on social media, and blamed students. I would meet up with colleagues, and we would complain about how bad the student writing was and some shared with me that they had simply given up. Tests only, no papers. I almost dropped my policy report assignment from my IPE course—the other sections only had a midterm and final. Why was I killing myself by assigning a paper too? In a low moment, I realized that something had to change. I decided that if I was going to assign writing, I needed to teach exactly how I wanted it done. At first this felt beneath me somehow—like now I would have to teach how to write a paragraph or spell out exactly how long an introduction should be? I wasn't trained to teach writing nor did I really think we *should* be teaching writing. Wasn't someone else supposed to do this?

When I lamented my realization to one of my colleagues, she seemed surprised that I was even thinking of incorporating more writing instruction in my courses. She seemed adamant that that was not our job. I knew where she was coming from, but from my conversations with my students, I also knew that most of the ones who struggled the most with writing simply could not hear or see their own mistakes. They did not know how to read their own work or structure a paper. Sure, they'd taken the required English 214, but nonetheless here they were in my class, unable to write coherently, and in the last semester before they graduated and were released into the world—didn't I need to try harder to teach them more about writing so that they'd be prepared to enter the workforce? How would their voices be heard if they couldn't communicate? They had important takes on international relations but all I could see was their poor writing. Wouldn't others feel the same way?

This led to a radical rethinking of my responsibility in the classroom and an important break-through in my pedagogy. Rather than complaining, mocking or berating students about their writing, *I* was the one that needed to rethink my teaching. I needed to reframe my own thinking about 'teaching writing' not as something 'less than' teaching Political Science but as critical social justice work that allowed more voices to be heard in the field of IR. I needed to think of teaching writing as *the* most important skill they would learn in college. Most of my students would go on to all different kinds of careers in a wide variety of fields—but all of them would have to write in at least in some capacity. I came to think of teaching writing as teaching a life-long skill that would transform students' abilities to effectively communicate with others, whether it be in a research paper, a cover letter or an email. I needed to see effective writing as a way to make a difference in students' lives—I came to embrace this part of my teaching rather than fight against it.

Changing Perspectives: Writing as an Opportunity

The next year, I restructured my class assignments, made space in the syllabus for working on writing, and made writing an important part of the class content rather than something taken for granted that somehow just happened as students learned about international issues. I reflected on my own experiences with writing and acknowledged my own fears, weaknesses and difficulties with writing, particularly in writing bigger projects and assignments. I opened up to my students and mostly, I listened to them talk about writing. What fears did they have when writing? How did they overcome procrastination especially when sitting down to write? What past experiences with writing impacted them? What worked in learning to write more effectively? What were they willing to risk to try something new?

I thought more carefully through my own struggles with writing my dissertation and developed the strategies I eventually used to complete it into parts of assignments, tasks and goals for my undergraduate thesis students. I challenged them to break with convention and try a new strategy for one week and share what happened in online posts and in class. I took time with them to talk about busy schedules, finding time to write daily and to shift from 'all-nighters' to short 30-minutes writing stints on a regular basis. I held writing challenges where for a week at a time we all logged our writing time and daily word counts. I revealed my own personal struggles with negative self-talk and even loathing when writing didn't go well or when I never even opened the document on my self-proclaimed writing day. I noticed that students nodded and could relate to what I was saying—especially the women in the room. I had students thank me afterward for sharing my personal stories and tell me that they thought they were the only ones who felt this way about writing. Many students tried something new and began to see writing as a learnable skill rather than a natural talent that either you had or you didn't. This opened the door for them to 'see' themselves as writers and to keep going even on the tough days when nothing seemed to happen.

I also broke down writing assignments into much smaller pieces where I could give more detailed feedback early on. Instead of whole papers or even partial drafts, I shifted to online forum posts where I would ask students to post 2–3 paragraphs of writing and I could then give more detailed feedback and comments on editing before they went on to write more. I would ask students to rewrite and repost on the same thread so that they could immediately revise and begin to see the improvement. Moreover, the writing was posted to the class so that everyone could begin to see others' writing and also my comments and feedback and start to notice patterns and common mistakes, but also smooth, more polished writing. I would then pull the posts up during class and discuss ones that reflected common issues or point out particularly strong revisions. I also talked through the emotions of writing and revising and coached students toward common goals rather than seeing rewriting as failure. I pushed students to see rewriting as an essential part of the writing process—early writing failures are part of the process and feedback on weak spots is not personal but a path toward improvement.

I gave out detailed hand-outs with very directed instructions such as 'the research question must go in the 2nd or 3rd paragraph of the introduction' and provided an outline of the precise six paragraphs that should make up the introduction to a thesis. I had students bring printed pieces of their drafts and use different color pens to underline things like 'a claim' and 'corresponding evidence' or circle citations (Should there be a citation? Why isn't there a citation? When was the last citation?) or write in the margins of each paragraph what the one main point of the paragraph was (or should be). I used these in-class exercises to discuss reorganization of main ideas and how revision improves readability and flow. I had them bring in the draft on a due date only to work immediately in groups on peer review of each other's work and then allow them to take the drafts home, rewrite them and turn them in for a grade two days later. I called these drafts 'zero drafts', and said I wouldn't see them but I was sure glad that they'd happened.

A Change in Teaching Changed Me

My changes in attitude and approach to writing in the classroom worked. Instead of feeling overwhelmed by student writing, I became energized by it. I felt that sharing my own personal stories touched students in a way that my old teaching style never did. I could easily grade 2–3 paragraphs of writing and even provide extensive comments if necessary and still finish grading in a reasonable amount of time. Once I had worked on a few of these short assignments early on in the semester, I often didn't need to assign short pieces of writing again. The later drafts I received were considerably improved and most of the early mistakes weren't repeated. I would get nearly instant gratification as students reposted much more polished and readable work. By the time the 'final' papers came in, I had read nearly all of the writing and could grade much more quickly. Plus, the papers were so much better—grading an excellent paper takes far less time than grading one that is terrible. I rarely felt hopeless while grading, and instead felt extremely proud of what my students accomplished.

I also could not believe the overall difference in student writing. In fact, since 2010, when I began to institute writing as a critical part of my classes, I have sponsored ten undergraduates to present at the ISA-West conference in Pasadena. In 2015, one of my undergraduates won the undergraduate paper award at ISA-West competing against USC, Stanford and other prestigious universities. This particular student was not a typically 'outstanding student'. In fact, she came to her last semester Senior Thesis course with a 2.5 overall GPA. Through careful development of her thesis idea and step-by-step writing work, her thesis went from preliminary to award-winning in one semester. While I certainly cannot take credit for her outstanding final paper, I know that my former approach to the class would not have allowed her to flourish and to develop as such an outstanding writer and contributor to the discipline.

Many of my students have used portions of their papers for scholarships, graduate school applications and even to gain internships. Last year, SFSU started an undergraduate research showcase where students present their work for the SFSU community and two of my undergraduates presented during the inaugural year. My Dean was so impressed with their presentations, he asked me to join the committee and help grow the showcase for next year. In 2013, a student who also was not a particularly strong writer initially, and had a GPA slightly below 3.0, came up with a thesis idea that matched my research interests at the time and through his hard work and dramatic writing improvement over the course of the semester, we went on to co-author a revision of his thesis into a book chapter. In part due to this publication, he went on to receive a prestigious full-scholarship at Johns Hopkins for his MA degree. The impact of teaching writing went far beyond the realm of the particular course and I could see that my teaching could have real, long-lasting impacts on students' lives.

The student results speak for themselves but perhaps most important is that I have come to love what I once loathed and to feel inspired that I have more to offer as a teacher of Political Science *AND* of writing. When I applied for tenure and promotion, my teaching statement had changed from when I'd applied for the job many years earlier. I still discussed active learning and student-led instruction, but I wrote my narrative about writing as a critical pedagogy and transformational activity in the classroom. I shared my student successes and my own transformation from resistant and even resentful of student writing to motivator and advocate for developing student writing in the political science classroom. My pedagogical changes were personal as much as professional and have helped inspire me to continue to be a better writer myself and to have more compassion and empathy for my students.

A Challenge for You

So, to conclude, here is my call to you, yes you the reader, a current or likely future teacher of undergraduates. My guess is if you've taught undergraduates you've felt the dread, despair and frustration from grading student writing. You may have felt like I did in my first few years of teaching—why should I teach basic writing skills? What is wrong with this generation? I didn't get my Ph.D. to do *this* in the classroom?

I challenge you to rethink how you approach writing. Don't just 'swallow your pride' and teach how to write a paragraph, but instead *inspire* pride in writing even if it means teaching or reteaching the basics. *Own* teaching writing as part of teaching excellence. Reflect on your own writing process and share your personal stories with writing—even the ugly ones, the ones that sound like failures and the ones that make you feel less-than. Think of teaching writing as one of the most important life-skills you can teach your students. Let's face it, it *is* more important than IR theory and more useful in our society. You might surprise yourself next time you go to grade a stack of papers or better yet, a short two paragraph online forum post. You might find that you didn't mind it as much as last time, and actually, those two students who were unreadable at the beginning of the semester actually now make perfect sense. You could find yourself beaming just a little as you post 'great work' as a response to them, and next class use their work as examples. The students will show surprise when their names come up on the screen in the front of the room—they've never been positive examples to a class before. On the way home you could realize you have just become a writing teacher even though you never meant to be one. If you are like me, this makes you feel extremely proud.

CHAPTER 14

Learning to Teach IR: An Active Learning Approach

Jennifer M. Ramos

Current institution: private liberal arts university
Typical classroom setting: seminars, small lectures
Typical pedagogical approach: active learning, engaged learning, student-centered, immersion courses, travel courses community-based learning
Disciplinary identity: international security, international norms, peacebuilding

When I first began teaching, I absolutely enjoyed it and it seemed pretty easy. Granted, I eased into it by working with students as a teaching assistant while still in graduate school. I naively thought that it would always be this way. The professor always made lecture look easy, grading was mountain high a few times a quarter but pretty straightforward, and discussion section was fun. I really liked students. I could relate to their struggles with the material and I enjoyed being the one to help them work through questions. Needless to say, when I went straight off to a liberal arts tenure-track job after crossing the graduation stage, I had a lot to

J. M. Ramos (✉)
Loyola Marymount University, Los Angeles, CA, USA
e-mail: Jennifer.Ramos@lmu.edu

J. Frueh (ed.), *Pedagogical Journeys through World Politics*,
Political Pedagogies, https://doi.org/10.1007/978-3-030-20305-4_14

learn. One of the most important things I had to figure out was who I am as a teacher; that is, what is my teaching style? How can I connect this big world problem out there with this student right here? For me, I found the answer in an active and engaged learning approach. This has made all the difference in truly enjoying teaching.

One of the few things I did know when I started teaching was that I really liked being with students. The best part of my day was and remains "going to class"—whether that be on or off campus. I would rather be with the students than anywhere else. Since so much of my formal education had been at large public universities, I assumed I would continue with the model of teaching I was most familiar with—the lecture. Faced now with my own classroom, the largest of which was only 30 students, I felt the challenge of creating engaging lectures for myself and my students. My dissertation advisor had made it look so natural and easy; my new mentor at my new job was a pro! But for me, the lecture style was just an uncomfortable straightjacket. It felt like this format cut me off from facilitating a deeper learning experience for the students and for me.

Certainly having a base of lectures to draw from helped immensely (thank you, mentors). There are so many new things to adjust to in a new job that a frame of reference for teaching is beyond helpful. But through those first semesters of teaching, when students are still taking your class because it's required and not because of your teaching or the course's reputation (if you are lucky enough to have that happen!), it can feel like a marathon to just get through a semester. Not only do you have to figure out which information is most important for the students to take away from the course, but then you also have to organize it and present it in an efficient, digestible manner. Moreover, I felt as if I had to be ready for literally any question, no matter how small. After all, hadn't I been to six years of graduate school? Shouldn't I know all this? It felt quite easy to psyche myself out over every lecture in "Introduction to International Relations." Trying to make sure I knew everything about World War I or every version of realism ever devised left me no time to consider course innovations.

Yet, I knew that there had to be another way. I came upon a fierce internal clash between what I thought was the proper, expert way to teach and the kind of student engagement I imagined in the classroom. By nature, I am a person who loves to experiment and try new things. When I cook a recipe, I hardly ever do it the same way twice. I love to learn, read, turn ideas upside down. It thus probably isn't a surprise in retrospect that I ended up in academia. I like to ask questions and suggest answers. How does that work? What if we did this? It became striking to me that I had really no idea about how to move forward in my teaching and suddenly the research aspect of my life was the easy part. Graduate school trained me really well for that.

Discovering Active Learning

I felt somewhat isolated with this frustration. I had planned for my research trajectory for the next lifetime! But I had not anticipated that I would need to spend serious time contemplating and "testing" different approaches to teaching, or even the possibility that I could! Thankfully, as a junior faculty member protected from service obligations, I had the time to attend events at our Center for Teaching Excellence to get schooled in pedagogy. I became a regular at those meetings, with a renewed appreciation for the hard work of teaching. I began to feel like I might find my authentic self in teaching as I started to learn about active learning approaches to engage students. Active learning involves students in their own learning rather than being passive receptors of knowledge. It engages students in activities that emphasize their higher order thinking skills while acquiring new information.[1]

This process of learning resonated with how I envisioned my courses. In class and in my syllabi, I talk to my students about my belief that we are a community in the classroom, a community in which we are all students and all teachers. Everyone (including me) will be required to actively participate in their own learning as well as each other's learning. I also review its pedagogical importance: cognitive psychology research shows that one of the best ways to understand material is to teach it to a peer,[2] students will learn more when they actively participate,[3] and active learning increases student performance.[4]

---

[1] See, for example, the seminal work: C. C. Bonwell, and, J.A. Eison. (1991). *Active learning: creating excitement in the classroom*. ASH#-ERIC Higher Education Report No. 1, Washington, D.C.: The George Washington University, School of Education and Human Development.

[2] Keith Topping and Stewart Ehly, *Peer-Assisted Learning*. Mahwah, NJ: Lawrence Erlbaum Associates, Inc., 1998.

[3] Judith Grunert. *The course syllabus: A learning-centered approach*. Bolton, MA: Anker Publishing Co, Inc, 1997.

[4] Scott Freeman, Sarah L. Eddy, Miles McDonough, Michelle K. Smith, Nnadozie Okoroafor, Hannah Jordt, and Mary Pat Wenderoth. 2014. "Active learning increases student performance in science, engineering and mathematics." *PNAS* 111 (23): 8410–8415.

As I ventured into the active learning arena, I started with simulations and debates in my classes, which really made the courses come alive for the students and myself.[5] Preparation is always key for these activities. For example, for the debates, I assign a debate paper as preparation for in-class debates. Each student is assigned one of two sides of the debate, such as for or against nuclear proliferation, and has to write a short paper, citing a certain number of scholarly sources. Over the course of three debates (and papers), I see steady improvement in their ability to make a written argument and their critical thinking skills.[6] As an instructor, I can also balance engaging classroom activities with grading sanity.

As I became more confident and saw the success of the active learning approach, I continued to look for other ways to improve upon it. This meant thinking outside of the box literally! The next step really solidified the active learning approach for me. I formed a partnership with our Center for Service and Action (CSA), which, as part of its extensive service work in the Los Angeles area, assists professors in creating community-based learning courses. Key to these courses is finding a match between community needs and the learning outcomes of a course so they are mutually beneficial relationships. Given that I teach in the field of international relations, I had to think creatively about how exactly to make this work for my set of courses. Little did I know how this would later evolve!

Since I was set to teach research methods courses (with an international spin), but could not wait to try the community-based learning approach, I dove right in. Prior to the start of the semester, I created a course focused on the theme of hunger, which would focus on the interconnections among the local, national, and global levels of this problem. After explaining my course learning goals to my CSA contact, she came up with a perfect match for our course. Our community partner was a local food bank, which needed data collected and analyzed that would help them to determine how to increase food donations. Together with our CSA staff, I met with one of the food bank's staff members to review the challenges the food bank had been encountering, develop a timeline, and set of expecta-

---

[5] ALIAS of ISA is a great resource for active learning resources.

[6] Yes, I have come to love the grading rubric. For this paper, I believe it allows the students to very specifically and clearly identify their weaknesses. Since they write the same type of paper multiple times, they know exactly what to address in the next paper.

tions for our survey, including a general idea of what kinds of questions should be asked and who should be surveyed. Beyond teaching the course, it began to dawn on me that I would also be responsible for a number of other things that I usually wasn't: obtaining IRB exemption, assuring students had transportation to survey food donors, maintaining communication with the food bank, organizing survey food donor student groups, and being ultimately responsible for an analysis that people were now counting on. I did wonder if I had taken on too much.

As the semester got started, it was easy to see how having students actively participate as researchers on a topic (hunger) that is so relevant in the city of Los Angeles made a difference to their motivations and mastery in the course. Many of them were from Los Angeles and had no idea that 16% of residents do not know where their next meal is coming from.[7] Moreover, students were used to volunteering but had not recognized that they could use their education to address community needs. Students immersed themselves at the local level by volunteering at the food bank as well as all aspects of the research process (with Human Subjects Protection Certification), from construction of the surveys to presenting the final analysis report. This active learning research project connected the students to their community and facilitated their own construction of research knowledge and critical thinking skills. Whereas previous courses provided students with datasets to learn about "independent variables" and "correlations" on distant subject pools, students in this course became invested in mastering the concepts in order to provide the food bank with the best analysis they could. In the process, we were able to achieve course goals and community goals. More to the point of this essay, however, is the fact that this hands on approach to teaching and learning made me yearn for more!

This initial experience was no doubt a ton of work beyond the usual course, but it yielded greater satisfaction for me because the work of the class that semester wasn't going to sit in my drawer; it was going to be useful for a real-world problem. The beginning certainly had some rough patches. Students had scheduling and motivational issues. Food donors or potential food donors would not fill out the surveys. But having the community learning project embedded in the course and thus required meant there was no turning back for any of us. All the students began to see that

---

[7] Los Angeles Regional Food Bank. "Hunger in L.A." https://www.lafoodbank.org/learn/hunger-in-l-a/

the food bank and the community were counting on us to get the survey and analysis done, and everyone had to do their part. Moreover, our university's mission is social justice, which students recognized, and I helped them to see that they were working for social justice, which requires work. In terms of the course, this work brought them to a deeper understanding of course material than if I used a traditional approach. For example, by the end of the course, they were very familiar with the pros and cons of qualitative versus qualitative measures of hunger because of their experiences with people at the food bank, conducting the survey, and working with the data.

I immediately recognized that I wanted to build on this active learning experience in my substantive courses. Many of my students were interested in visiting the United Nations, and it seemed a logical next step. It was relatively easy to build into the Global Human Rights course and I could test the waters of traveling with students short-term while remaining in country. Though the logistics proved to be very time-consuming, despite having the support of my administration, it still offered so much to students and myself in terms of learning outcomes and satisfaction. We traveled mid-semester to the United Nations in New York for a long-weekend (our fall break, 4 days, 3 nights). We partnered with a non-profit, Partnership for Global Justice, and created a program around our course themes, and incorporated a visit to the United Nations, in which the students participated in the celebration of the International Day of the Girl. Needless to say, this short-term, mid-semester immersion allowed us to reflect on and understand more deeply the real-world dynamics of human rights and have more open discussions because of the class bonding on the trip.

So I am hooked. These preliminary experiences led me to what I have now built as my signature program/course: an immersion research trip over spring break to Belfast, Northern Ireland embedded in a semester course, *Peace and Reconciliation*.[8] This short-term immersion course arose from my own travels to Northern Ireland where I realized that it was

[8] This trip is completely reliant on personal relationships. How this evolved over time is perhaps a subject for another paper. Needless to say, prior to the course, I had no connections to Northern Ireland! Also, to note, in the course, the issue of conflict tourism is discussed. I have written about the set-up of this course in more detail in "Windows and Mirrors in the Wall: Experiences in Experiential Learning." In *Conflict Zone, Comfort Zone: Ethics, Pedagogy, and Best Practices*, Susan Hirsch and Agnieszka Paczynska, eds. Ohio University Press, 2019.

an ideal place to study a fragile peace: it was safe, fairly easy to get to, English-speaking, has public archives for researchers, and accessible politicians. Overall costs are fairly reasonable as Belfast is still relatively cheaper than other European cities and we do not employ an outside tour operator to arrange the trip. To cover the costs of the trip, the course has an additional lab fee attached when students register for the course. However, students can apply for financial aid and we are fortunate that no student has ever been turned away from the course because of cost. It has been helpful that this has aligned with the university's desire to internationalize the curriculum and that we have had donors willing to support students in this way. The course has never had a problem filling, with an ideal number of 12 students. Initially, students were attracted to the course by their own Irish connections, their interest in peace and conflict, and/or their interest in travel. To delve deeper into this last point, it is important to note that for various reasons some students are not able to study abroad for a summer or a semester so the shorter term immersion courses may be their only option. These reasons, as well as hearing from past participants, continue to drive interest in the course.

Our travels to cold and rainy Belfast during the semester are transformative for students in their understanding of the complexities of reconciliation and building a sustainable peace. Few realize that over 90% of education is segregated still in Northern Ireland. The students' inclinations to make snap judgments about solutions melt away as they collect stories from ex-IRA members, ex-British soldiers, religions leaders, politicians, peace builders, and victims. I have now done this course/trip seven times with students. And true to my experimental nature, I have done this in various ways. The course has evolved its focus as I have gotten to develop relationships with the locals. I have taught it with a service-learning component, and as an interdisciplinary course with a psychology professor. Students conduct original research in Northern Ireland and write a comparative case study research paper. The course is not easy, but immersing students in the realities of Northern Ireland connects them in a very real way, personally, and academically. It ignites their motivation to write more complex, more nuanced papers. I believe that also meeting folks from all different backgrounds also reminds them that these are real people behind the statistics ("1 in 3 were affected by the Troubles") and who they are. Perhaps most importantly, students see themselves and their own community in new ways. It is difficult to pinpoint what I love most about this course, though this is not to say everything goes perfectly! I do adore the close mentoring relationships that evolve and linger after graduation. It really is something special that we share and now students across this course have found they share a kinship as well.

SOME OF WHAT I HAVE LEARNED ABOUT TEACHING IR

The *Peace and Reconciliation* course, in particular, has perhaps taught me the most about teaching international relations (and teaching generally) because it is an active learning course in the real world. My preference is *always* to take students out into the real world. Fortunately, there are many great ways to also do active learning in the classroom as well. In addition to this hands on approach being much more compatible with my own personal style, it makes the concepts of international relations more concrete. So much of what we teach can be abstract for students, but this course brings an experience that engages their intellect and their senses. For example, students will not only better understand the challenges of solving an intractable conflict, but also have a sense of what that *feels* like.

I've also learned that it is okay not to have all the answers, and even embrace this fact.[9] Teaching international relations can be overwhelming; do I really have to know everything about the world? Thank goodness, no! The course described above has allowed me to even welcome this. Because the situation on the ground is constantly changing in Northern Ireland and we continue to meet new folks on our visits, I am always learning new things. Indeed, I consider it a great opportunity to model for students how real research is conducted and to highlight the importance of asking the right kinds of questions. Developing the art of asking good questions is just as important as finding the answers, if not more so. Even though it is more work, I'm much more interested in students' questions; I've long given up assigning paper topics and questions. I remember early on someone advising me to give them a limited list of possible topics, which would be more efficient for me in terms of advising and grading. However, I would much rather read a paper that a student enjoyed writing than one with a forced topic. As they develop their research questions, students learn more about what I believe is the most important part of the

---

[9] I am cognizant of the gender implications of this.

research process, and helping them choose a topic also gives me a chance to have great conversations with them about their interests, how they see the world, and who they want to be in the world.

Related to this is my belief that the big picture matters more than the details.[10] I am more interested in students being able to understand how ideas and concepts fit together than whether they can memorize a bunch of terms and define them. When considering exam questions or how to weight items on a syllabus, I am always thinking about whether these are things that are building frameworks of knowledge or critical thinking skills—things they cannot google or find on a wiki. One of my more recent endeavors has been to try to focus on smaller, more frequent assignments in hopes of providing students with opportunities to grow in these areas. This offers them more chances for feedback with lower stakes.

While I have always believed that students are responsible for their own learning, I found that I could be asking more of them (and less of myself). For example, with preparation that includes meeting with me beforehand, students can lead excellent discussions. With the right incentives and structure, they can do great independent original research projects within a semester. The Northern Ireland course particularly demonstrated this. I did not want this to be a study tour; my goal was for this to be a research trip for the students. The students certainly have stepped up to the bar and become invested in their work. Thus, I have learned that if you provide the right experience, students can and will do more (most of the time!).

Finally, as the path toward active and engaged learning shows, I have learned to be more authentic in my teaching. It was not immediately clear when I first began how much, if any, of myself I should reveal to students. I think part of the answer just comes with time in the classroom, growing more comfortable with the actual teaching than with who one is in that role as teacher. As I mentioned earlier, I had really only thought about my development as a researcher as I began my academic career. My identity as a teacher was something that I had to grow into. Looking back, I would have told myself to trust my instincts more and that there are many ways to be an excellent teacher. Don't worry so much.

---

[10] This focus also helps with keeping the perspective of not having to "do it all."

So Why Do I Teach International Relations?

When I cannot take them out into the world for my courses, I try to bring the world to them through simulations, debates, and games. All of this requires hard work, creativity, and initiative. But the payoffs are worth it, both for the students and for me. And just like the students, I am constantly learning how to do things better. I continue to tweak my courses; I never have the exact same syllabus for the same course. The consistent thread throughout, though, is an active and engaged class.

For me, teaching international relations is not just about the theories and methods of international relations, but about reminding students about the connections we have to one another, across partisan mountains and sovereign borders. At its core, international relations is about people and relationships. This belief comes out of my own early experience living, working, and studying abroad—(all things that I encourage students to do; we'll figure out a way to make the finances work!). I was also deeply impacted by living in Manhattan during the terrorist attacks of 9/11. So, teaching international relations is a normative endeavor; it is about encouraging a mindset of global citizenship and empathy.

Moreover, international relations at its best is uniquely poised to take on the messy complex real-world issues that matter. IR, drawing on the wisdom of multiple disciplines, and through its own evolution, helps us better understand and contribute policy solutions for major phenomena like conflict and cooperation, global inequality, environmental injustice, among others. I believe that each of us as global citizens have a responsibility to use our education toward these ends; we all have a stake in the outcomes of the problems today. The knowledge, skills, and compassion for others gained through studying IR should motivate us to do better, be better.

IR as a discipline provides me a unique opportunity to share this journey with my students—seeing their worldviews change, shatter, rebuild; holding multiple conflicting thoughts in their heads; leaving with more questions than answers…hopefully feeding the flames of curiosity that will live on not only into a love for life-long learning, but also a desire to use that for the betterment of humanity.

REFERENCES

Bonwell, Charles C., and James A. Eison. 1991. *Active Learning: Creating Excitement in the Classroom*, ASHE-ERIC Higher Education Report 1. Washington, DC: School of Education and Human Development, George Washington University.

Freeman, S., S.L. Eddy, M. McDonough, M.K. Smith, N. Okoroafor, H. Jordt, and M.P. Wenderoth. 2014. Active Learning Increases Student Performance in Science, Engineering, and Mathematics. *Proceedings of the National Academy of Sciences* 111 (23): 8410–8415. https://doi.org/10.1073/pnas.1319030111.

Grunert, Judith. 1997. *The Course Syllabus: A Learning-Centered Approach*. Bolton: Anker Publishing Co, Inc.

Los Angeles Regional Food Bank. Hunger in L.A. https://www.lafoodbank.org/learn/hunger-in-l-a/

Ramos, Jennifer M. 2019. Windows and Mirrors in the Wall: Experiences in Experiential Learning. In *Conflict Zone, Comfort Zone: Ethics, Pedagogy, and Best Practices*, ed. Susan Hirsch and Agnieszka Paczynska. Ohio University Press.

Topping, Keith, and Ehly Stewart. 1998. *Peer-Assisted Learning*. Mahwah: Lawrence Erlbaum Associates, Inc.

CHAPTER 15

My Metamorphoses as an International Relations Teacher

Jacqui de Matos-Ala

Current institution: partially government-subsidized university
Typical classroom setting: large classes and seminar groups
Typical pedagogical approach: facilitating deep learning approaches; peer learning; reading and writing rich environments and critical engagement
Disciplinary identity: joint academic qualifications in IR and Higher Education pedagogy. Interests in decolonization of knowledge in IR in general and IR pedagogy in particular; gender and race perspectives for the Global South and teaching and learning practices in IR

Reflecting on my teaching career, it is quite apparent that I am rather passionate about teaching International Relations (IR), even though I have often been chastised to grow up and focus on the serious task of being a researcher. However, I could not think of a more serious task at a South African higher education institution than to be a great teacher, nor could I think of a better way to demonstrate my proficiency and mastery

J. de Matos-Ala (✉)
University of the Witwatersrand, Johannesburg, South Africa
e-mail: Jacqueline.DeMatosAla@wits.ac.za

© The Author(s) 2020
J. Frueh (ed.), *Pedagogical Journeys through World Politics*,
Political Pedagogies, https://doi.org/10.1007/978-3-030-20305-4_15

of international relations than by teaching it well. This is not to say that I think research is irrelevant or that good teaching takes place at the expense of research.

So by now you may think I am one of those crazy socialist idealists that turn underperforming, rebellious and societally marginalized students into top class students by abandoning the textbook curriculum and traditional chalk and talk pedagogy, instead choosing to teach them with them via popular culture references and slightly off-the-wall teaching methods, as depicted in numerous movies. Well maybe some of this is true. I believe that enticing students to adopt a deep approach in their engagement with the subject material demands innovation, both in how the course is constructed and how it is delivered. I have found a social cultural learning approach to be very effective in fostering this type of engagement, as learning is optimized when students are initially able to situate knowledge in a context that is familiar or relevant to them. This establishes a base upon which more unfamiliar contexts and abstract knowledge can be explored. So I often use popular culture and local or international events for this purpose—for example, I am a collector of politically based music and satire for a course I teach on protest and civic engagement.

My teaching philosophy has obviously evolved over my 20 years of being a teacher. My first formal teaching philosophy statement was written for promotion purposes. Until then my philosophy and what informed it existed solely in my head. The focus of this document was my desire to encourage and develop critical thinking in students, as well as an enthusiasm for the study of IR coupled with explanation of the methods I was using to achieve this. It is quite apparent when I read this document now that I was a novice teacher, as many of my approaches, and rationales for adopting them, were not fully conceptualized. It is further evident that I had very little knowledge of various learning theories, which meant that my teaching philosophy never explicitly drew from any of these. Instead, it was populated with pedagogical concepts such as constructive alignment, scaffolding, and teaching taxonomies, such as Biggs' (1996, 1999) structure of observed learning outcomes (SOLO). This is not necessarily a problem as these are excellent pedagogical tools for any academic to use, but what it demonstrates is that my approach to teaching was still that of a technician not a skilled, creative master. I was using sound methods to get my students engaged with IR but I did not understand the learning psychology that they were built on, which was the real reason for their effectiveness. It is only because I chose to study and focus on my teaching in more depth than is required by most higher education institutions that my understanding of learning has developed and concomitantly my ability to be more creative and effective in this role.

What has remained a consistent part of my teaching philosophy is that I have always found a strong resonance with Paulo Freire's perspective on the transformative nature of education (1970). Freire sees transformative learning as process through which not only individuals but entire communities can be remade and emancipated. My teaching philosophy has been strongly influenced by growing up under apartheid where racial inequality was reinforced through education and where the demand for equal education become a key component in mobilizing internal resistance against the government. Access to quality equal education for all has always been a fundamental goal for a post-apartheid South Africa. The right to education has always featured prominently in South African liberation movements' vision for a post-apartheid South Africa. It is a component present in the 1955 Freedom Charter, a statement of principles which would govern a post-apartheid society. Section 29 of the 1996 post-apartheid South Africa constitution enshrines the right to education for all citizens. My teaching philosophy has not deviated from a belief in the transformative nature of higher education. Moreover, the evolving societal and institutional academic environments in which I have been located have allowed me to give expression to this value in different ways, especially as my competency as a teacher has grown.

My Developmental Lifecycle from Novice to (Almost) an Expert Teacher

My academic teaching career began in the discipline of International Relations (IR) at the University of the Witwatersrand (Wits), South Africa in 1997 amidst post-apartheid euphoria. Both the new government and higher education institutions were focusing on ways to transform education in order to provide quality, equal education for all, as well as on ways in which to redress past educational inequalities. Meeting these goals involved creating access initiatives to assist people disadvantaged by apartheid education not only in gaining entrance to university but also in giving them the necessary academic support to allow them to succeed in their chosen degree program.

Academic development tutor posts were created within disciplines at universities and formed part of this redress initiative. I was appointed the university's IR academic development tutor. Unlike the normal academic lecturer track, this position necessitated both disciplinary and academic literacy expertise.[1] Our focus was on helping students pass their first year of study. These were very junior academic positions and seen as suitable for someone who wanted to start a career in academia. Often these academic development tutorship positions were seen as a way of marking time until a "real academic" position came along, but I chose to embrace this role as a "real academic position." The position was an extremely good fit for me as I was actually interested in pedagogical issues in higher education in addition to IR. However, there is a substantial gap between being interested in pedagogy because one wants to create transformative IR curricula and actually executing these ideals, especially when you have not been trained to be a teacher.

As a novice teacher I was keenly aware that although I possessed a good grasp of the IR content that constituted the first-year curriculum, I did not have the teaching expertise that this position demanded. This starkly highlighted a problematic element inherent in being a university lecturer that I still to this day find perplexing, namely, the assumption that mastery of disciplinary content is all that is required to teach in higher education. It seems to imply that teaching entails no specialist training, knowledge or practice—that anyone could stand up and do it. However, when I reflected on my experience as a student, it was patently clear that some of my lecturers were better at imparting knowledge and skills than others. Logically for me if school teachers had to learn how to teach before being allowed into a classroom, being knowledgeable and even passionate about your subject could only be one part of the equation for being an effective teacher. There must exist, I reasoned, things lecturers needed to know about the practice of teaching.

Fortunately, I was not left to my own devices in endeavoring to discover these skills through trial and error. Our Faculty of Humanities had hired three academic development advisors to assist academic development tutors from all disciplines in improving their teaching competencies. These advisors were qualified teachers and had expertise in teaching in a higher education environment. It was through my weekly interactions

---

[1] Academic literacy in this context would be defined as reading, lecture notetaking, research, writing, study and exams skills.

with them over a ten-year period as they assisted me in designing and teaching various IR curricula (starting with academic development curriculum) that I began my transition from a novice teacher to something approximating an expert. I cannot emphasize enough how much I learned about every aspect of teaching through interacting with these three academics and the communities of practices that they introduced me to.

However, learning how to teach involved me also having to assume agency for my development. Not only did I arrange to have continuous interaction with the academic development advisors, I also undertook to acquaint myself and engage with university teaching and learning policy and practice. I volunteered to sit on our Faculty Teaching and Learning Committee and did so for ten years. Further, I read books and journal articles, and I attended any seminar or course I felt might help me improve my teaching. Being located in South Africa, I further have benefitted from not only having access to the knowledge of world-renowned local academics, but also visiting foreign academics interested in the studying post-apartheid educational developments. Slowly as my knowledge built, I became more confident and started to initiate bigger teaching and learning initiatives in my own discipline. One of the most successful that I developed and led was the Foundation Course in International Relations, which ran from 1999 to 2006.

Learning While Doing: Creating and Developing the IR Foundation Course

The introduction of Foundation Course programs was the next devolution of redress initiatives as government and universities sought more efficacious ways of ameliorating the lingering effect of apartheid schooling at the tertiary level. The IR Foundation Course was an intensive extension program that covered essentially the same IR content as the mainstream first-year course. However, this content was covered in greater depth and had an extensive range of academic literacy skills integrated within it. The ability to execute such a rigorous curriculum was enabled by the fact that class sizes were small, no more than thirty-five to forty students. Moreover, the same staff members would teach the course for the entire year, allowing for the establishment of academic mentoring. The course ran parallel to the mainstream first-year IR program and students who passed the course were admitted into the second-year program.

In designing and teaching the foundation course, I was introduced to and started using John Biggs' (1996, 1999) model of Constructive Alignment, in conjunction with his Structure of the Observed Learning Outcomes taxonomy, as a tool to build a teaching environment conducive to the adoption of deep approaches to learning. Constructive Alignment demands the conceptualization of the curriculum as set of clear objectives that state the level of understanding expected of the students instead of merely being couched in the form of a list of topics that must be covered. We developed or utilized teaching methods that we believed would best realize our learning outcomes, and then we finally designed our assessments to verify whether students have indeed met the stated learning outcomes. This process allows students to learn subject matter through activities that have been designed for this purpose. The rationale behind this model is that students learn by doing and interacting with ideas, debates and course materials at a specific cognitive level that usually correlates with the year of study. It is through this process that they construct meaning from discipline content. Lecturers merely facilitate this journey. Their roles are to create learning structures that channel and focus students in ways that enable them to attain the learning outcomes set by the course. Thus, classes, activities and assessments would all be interwoven for the express purpose of achieving both the content and cognitive objectives.

Conceiving of the course in this way allowed the three of us who comprised the teaching team to develop innovative ways of allowing students to engage with knowledge as well as ways of assessing them. We specifically adopted a social cultural approach to learning in the introductory component of the course as we felt that learning would be expedited if we located the course within a familiar South African context and then framed introductory concepts, theories and debates within this context. Thus the course was constructed around the theme of the international dimensions of the struggle against apartheid using historical moments such as Harold Macmillan's 1960 "Winds of Change" speech and South African President HF Verwoerd's response thereto to investigate the issues relating to state sovereignty. We also used the United Nations sanctioning of South Africa to explore the emergence and utility of international organizations as well as the United States policy of disinvestment to consider bilateral interactions and the effectiveness of coercive measure versus co-option in modifying state behavior. For teaching international political economy (IPE), we employed a problem-based learning format in the form of a game. The class was grouped into different fictitious countries all having different economic and political profiles. Each week we devised a situation based on concepts covered in lecture to which each country had to draft a response that coalesced with their respective country profile. This was an effective method by which to get students to comprehend the effects of inequality in international systems; the implications the adoption of particular trade policies have for countries; the mechanisms and impact to using various protectionist measures; and the differentiated and evolving role played by Bretton Wood institutions in managing various aspects relating to international financial and monetary system.

In addition, we used portfolios to assess students' learning instead of formal sit-down examinations. The portfolios had both formative and summative functions. Students would submit their responses to each week's scenario. These were reviewed and returned to students with feedback for improvement. At the end of a course, students were required to choose what they believed to be their four best pieces of work that they had improved using the feedback received for submission as the summative component of the course. Another objective of the numerous assessment opportunities that we built into the foundation course was to create a writing intensive environment. This was premised on the belief that students improve their academic writing by being given numerous opportunities to write and receive feedback.

What was most exciting about the IR foundation course was that it was a space for developing, trying out and refining innovative teaching and assessment practices. This was again made possible by constant interaction with and feedback from the faculty teaching and learning advisors. We found that some of our ideas worked and others did not. Our IPE game worked exceptionally well, but we soon learned that we had to work out ways to deal with the problem of free-riders with respect to group activities or there would be fictitious state revolutions. Moreover, we quickly found out that writing intensive courses turned out to be extremely feedback intensive if you want to do them well, but as a means through which to improve student writing they were well worth effort. Frustratingly, students did not always engage with and develop their thinking and writing despite receiving intensive feedback. Some students were only interested in their final marks and nothing more. Often formative components not assigned marks were either not submitted for feedback or the feedback given was not reflected upon and integrated into the final submission. Thus, we learned that we had to assign marks to formative assessments if we wanted students to take these seriously. I also learned to be adaptable in my teaching in this course, as it is easier when interacting with a small group of learners to ascertain whether or not the way in which I was presenting, explaining or getting student to engage with material was producing learning. The course won the 2001 Vice-Chancellor's award teaching excellence by a teaching team. This gave the team an enormous sense of achievement, as we were all junior academics each with less than five years of teaching experience, as well as validation for the work that we were doing.

Unfortunately, in late 2004, a shift in university management policies and priorities resulted ultimately in the closure of all Wits' Foundation Courses. Management argued that by this stage enough resources had been devoted to educational access and redress initiatives and that it was now time to deploy these resources elsewhere. This was the first time I really grasped the limitations of my agency as a teacher within the university as management ultimately held the discretion regarding an educational initiatives' value, irrespective of its teaching and learning benefits and results. I would be lying if I didn't admit to be deeply hurt by the decision. However, this taught me that there are different seasons within a teaching career and although some do not occur due to your agency, they are nonetheless opportunities to grow, mature and reinvent yourself. I found myself taking over and being allowed to re-imagine the introductory first-year IR course. Even though this was a move to large-class teaching, I found that I could adapt teaching practices that worked well in a small class context to work just as well in a large-class context. I developed an academic literacy program extending from third- to fourth-year (honors) IR to assist students in learning to become academics. I started this initiative because these were skills that I was never explicitly taught, despite them being essential competencies for academic writing. However, it is in my class on gender that I have had the greatest opportunity to create an environment conducive to transformative learning.

Experimenting with Shifting IR Ontological Perspectives and Learning Agency: Teaching Gender and International Relations

My gender course is predominantly comprised of fourth-year or honors students and is taught by way of seminars. However as the course progresses, agency regarding the course content is transferred from me to the students. In the last eight weeks of the course, peer learning takes place, with each student getting a turn to choose that week's topic, the readings and facilitate the discussion. For the first eight weeks, I provide an introduction to the study of gender in IR. I have expressly designed my component of the course to challenge and transform students' perspectives or preconceived notions on gender.

The course interprets the term "gender" broadly in order to be as inclusive as possible. Thus, we do not just focus on women, but men and Lesbian, Gay, Bisexual, Transsexual and Intersex (LGBTI) people as well. I introduced race into that course seven years ago to add additional nuance and context. The first class sets out to arrive at an agreed upon definition of the term gender. This necessitates a discussion on the differences between sex and gender as well as the socially constructed stereotypes that are attached to gender. It usually transpires that the majority of the class have never thought deeply about these issues. Instead, they have just accepted the roles assigned to them by their respective social environments. I present my narrative of how culture and class have shaped my perception of my gender and the implications that they can have in determining the agency I am able to have over my own life and the place I occupy in society. I then ask students to talk about their gender narratives. It quickly emerges that there are a plethora of different experiences and understanding of the concept just in our class and that is in a large way reflective of South Africa's multicultural society. We then consider how race, culture and class further impact gender identity and the societal norms that they are connected to. The aim of the class is for students to comprehend gender as a malleable social construct that is most often used as a mechanism to entrench specific power dynamics within a specific social context, and that a social construct establishing universal truths about its composition and function is not possible. Consequently, we cannot formulate homogenous ways of disrupting gender-based discrimination. It is important to note that incorporating personal narratives at the start of the course immediately grounds it in an African context with which students can identify, expediting their ability to move from concrete to abstract thinking. The course does obviously investigate the issue of gender in a global context, but having grasped the complexities related to the concept, students learn to adopt a nuanced investigative approach.

Establishing the importance of a nuanced approach to the subject has proved to be exceptionally productive in generating intense deep discussion and debates on issues that have expanded students' thinking and perception, as well as my own. In considering how gender stereotypes limit people's freedoms and choices, the discussion expands beyond women and LGBTI categories to interrogate problems with male stereotypes. Stereotyping men as aggressive has been used to co-opt or coerce men into different forms of military service. However, if killing came naturally to all men, military services would not need to devote so much time to exercises that are designed to get men to overcome their reluctance to kill. We also considered how different genders experience conflict (specifically conflicts in Africa)—what they have in common and what is different. In later classes, students examine the need for gender awareness in policy making regarding peacekeeping, humanitarian interventions and post-conflict reconstruction. Students at the end of these lessons often reflect on how they had never realized that stereotypes can be disempowering for all genders and why it is important to be aware of these. Race is then added as an additional stereotype on top of those prescribed by gender. There have also been many debates regarding the extent to which we can label certain gender practices as discriminatory or wrong, who has the right to make these judgments, who is allowed to speak on behalf of people deemed to oppressed, how best to engage and transform societies to become more gender equitable and whether we should strive for equality or equity.

I have also incorporated some provocative texts regarding gender and international relations written by prominent IR scholars. One article in particular argues that gender is biologically predetermined and not a social construct. Thus, the author believes that society, cultural and race have little effect on the behavior of men and women. However, in the previous class we have established that gender was most definitely social constructed. This was further enforced by looking at and discussing our individual experience. But now a prominent academic, in a prominent IR journal disputes this. What do we do with conflicting stances? Well, we unpack this article, using our knowledge and experiences for the previous class as tools. Students are quick to notice that the article deals with the concept of gender very superficially—even biological aspects of gender are more complicated than presented. Lastly, the author seemed only to include examples of leaders that support his point of view. The class usually quickly comes up with many cases that disprove his points. Students find the exercise uncomfortable, but on reflection they realize they developed academic agency by choosing to interrogate and challenge another academic's positions to see whether they could stand up to scrutiny. Further, due to the interpretivist nature of the field of gender, these types of exercises help students realize that just because scholars having divergent opinions on various issues does not automatically render one valid and the other invalid as long as they can adequately justify their position. Hence, social science is able to accommodate ambiguity. It also teaches students that interacting with scholarship that does not align with their own understanding and knowledge can be beneficial as it spurs us to interrogate our own views and strengthen our own arguments, modify or change our perspectives as well as open ourselves to new knowledge. Developing this epistemic virtue allows students to expand their opportunities to engage in transformative learning.

What is exciting about this class is that students consistently tell me that the course has changed their lives. When I have probed deeper, it seems that the course does not simply provide students with new and interesting knowledge. What students like about the course is that it has developed their capacity to discover or figure things out for themselves. They have also expanded their ability to critically engage with knowledge. Finally, they have been allowed to develop and exercise agency as young academics and members of society. Further, many of the students have become gender activists in the public, private and civil society sectors. However, what I find most interesting about every time I teach the course is that the interaction between each unique cohort of students and the subject matter also changes me.

Formalizing My Teaching Knowledge in Higher Education

Much has changed over the time period that I have been a teacher at Wits. I have evolved and so has my institution. The classes that I teach are substantially larger at both the undergraduate level and postgraduate level than when I started teaching. The South African public schooling system as a whole has not realized the objective of providing quality education to all. As a result, many students are still underprepared for the rigors of university and I have had to find ways of adapting my teaching to these new realities. Further, I am now a senior member of staff and have large administrative and research responsibilities that now necessitate immaculate time management so that I can give my teaching the attention that it deserves.

What has simplified my life regarding the academic job triad of teaching, research and administration is that I have made teaching IR my main research focus. The benefits of this are that my research strengthens my teaching. To improve my ability to research and publish on pedagogical issues, in 2015 I enrolled in Wits' newly offered postgraduate diploma in Higher Education and then in a Masters in Higher Education program. This has again transformed my abilities as a teacher and opened up an exciting new world of scholarship and practice. Although the primary purpose of offering these degrees on the part of my university was to develop staff's intellectual understanding of learning rather than their teaching practice, I now teach with a greater understanding of how the methodology and methods I employ precipitate learning. I am also able to effectively communicate these explanations to students so they understand what they are doing. This is not only done through discussing course expectations, but also by setting these out in various forms of written criteria. This strategy is a new component of my teaching philosophy, namely to afford students more agency in their learning. As previously mentioned, I allow students to have input regarding course content, teaching format and exam questions. I am also endeavoring to introduce activities to get students to self-reflect on their learning as well as the quality of the work they produce. I hope that will develop students' capacity to evaluate how effectively they are engaging with and mastering the knowledge and skills contained within the course, as well as their ability to demonstrate this in the work they produce. Learning the skill of evaluation enables learners to effectively manage and take agency for their learning. Evaluating and reflecting on the extent to which their work aligns with set criteria further allows for the development of strategies to improve its quality.

Ultimately, my objective for studying higher education if to find answers for questions on why most IR curricula, even in the Global South, are populated with knowledge derived predominantly from the Western scholarship. Even though there has been a substantial increase in publications from the Global South, this scholarship has this not permeated curricula. In this regard, both the diploma course and the MEd have introduced me to new scholarship that has allowed me to reconceptualize Freire's notion of the transformative potential of education. For example, the work of Bernstein (2000), Hountondji (1983), de Sousa Santos (2015) and Mignolo (2009) is useful in understanding the reasons for and implications of the dominance that Western knowledge structures and knowledge in IR, as well as how to rebalance the knowledge equation. The objective of this research is to investigate how to construct and utilize knowledge-plural curricula that would expose my students to a myriad of different realities and ways of thinking and knowing. Theoretically, this should expand their repertoire of intellectual instruments that can be used to understand not only their immediate reality but also the world beyond. This potentially gives students' agency not only to engage with and reshape their individual reality but to reconceptualize and challenge the social reality that they are part of. A key component of this project is the incorporation into my curricula of more knowledge generated in Africa, particularly Southern African knowledge that is applicable to the study of IR. However, this process is complex, as it involves more than just adding African examples or case studies or substituting folk stories (usually recorded by Western anthropologists) for African philosophy (Hountondji 1983). Indigenous knowledge needs to be formalized through intellectual engagement on the part of scholars to ensure that it is properly repre-sented, conceptualized and developed. In other words, it has to be brought into the academic canon through research and disseminated among the broader intellectual or academic community. Only then is it suitable for incorporation in curricula. Hence, the ability to deliver the decolonized IR curriculum demanded by my government, university and students requires a lot more thought and skill than meets the eye.

I Am More Than What I Was, but I Am Still Becoming

My development as an international relations teacher has been most pro-foundly influenced by the people who have mentored me and provided me with the knowledge to improve my practice. This was crucial as universi-ties do not usually have formalized programs to induct academic staff into the teaching component of the job. By providing teaching and learning advisors that I could consult with regularly, my university assisted in mak-ing me a better teacher. I benefitted from the continuous interaction with these academics far more than I would have from intermittently held teaching seminars. The reason for this is that I got constant feedback and input on my teaching. If I encountered something problematic, it could be dealt with timeously. If I wanted to try a new approach, I could bounce ideas off people who could give me informed input on how to execute these ideas effectively. It also provided an environment where I could reflect on my teaching and whether I was achieving what I intended in each of my courses. In this sense, my development was akin to an appren-ticeship with me being informally inculcated into a community of practice. Like most apprenticeships, as you become increasingly more competent, your role shifts from mentee to mentor to a new member of the community. I believe that if a university is serious about staff development then they must institute initiatives that focus on learning how to teach. To re-emphasize an earlier point—being competent in researching one's own discipline does not automatically make you a competent teacher of it. Moreover, to be effective these types of initiatives need to engage staff on an ongoing basis. You cannot effectively give a staff member a good foundation in teaching in a few seminars. To earn a primary or secondary level teaching diploma takes on average four years of study just to be deemed adequate to stand in front of a class. Yet we require and provide much less training for academics. The catch with this model is that it requires a fair amount of resources in terms of time and money. Firstly, specialist teaching units or positions need to be budgeted for. Secondly, staff need to devote time in order to derive the maximum benefit from teaching development initiatives, and this time should be factored into academic workload allocation. Allocating mentors to assist in teaching development, and establishing communities of teaching practice are further effective measures to improve pedagogy but again they require time commitments to be effective. However, these are effective ways of developing your teaching. For me, teaching seems to be an activity of always becoming. It strongly embodies Chinese and Japanese philosophies on lifelong learning where one is always in a process of learning and perfecting ones practice irrespective of your years of experience.

References

Bernstein, Basil B. 2000. *Pedagogy, Symbolic Control, and Identity: Theory, Research, Critique*, Critical Perspectives Series. Rev. ed. Lanham: Rowman & Littlefield Publishers.

Biggs, J.B. 1996. Enhancing Teaching Through Constructive Alignment. *Higher Education*. 32: 347–364.

———. 1999. What the Student Does: Teaching for Enhanced Learning. *Higher Education Research & Development*. 18 (1): 57–75.

de Sousa Santos, B. 2015. *Epistemologies of the South: Justice against Epistemicide*. London: Routledge.

Freire, Paulo. 1970. *Pedagogy of the Oppressed*. London: Penguin Random House, UK.

Hountondji, Paulin J. 1983. *African Philosophy: Myth and Reality*, African Systems of Thought. Bloomington: Indiana University Press.

Mignolo, Walter D. 2009. Epistemic Disobedience, Independent Thought and Decolonial Freedom. *Theory, Culture & Society* 26 (7–8): 159–181. https://doi.org/10.1177/0263276409349275.

Oh Yeah, There's Always Community College

Julie Mueller

Current institution: community college
Typical classroom setting: small lecture (<30)
Typical pedagogical approach: active learning, case studies, lectures
Disciplinary identity: all fields of political science

"What Is One Thing You Thought You Knew but Later Found Out You Were Wrong About?"

This is a question posed by reporters to each of their guests on one of my favorite podcasts.[1] I actually have several answers to this (the list grows as I get older!). And it's a brilliant question for reminding me that we should always be re-examining and questioning our understanding of the world. While this may be the main object of academia, academics are much more likely to do this in our research than in our approach to teaching.

---

[1] Make Me Smart with Kai and Molly https://www.marketplace.org/topics/make-me-smart

---

J. Mueller (✉)
Southern Maine Community College, South Portland, ME, USA
e-mail: jmueller@smccme.edu

© The Author(s) 2020
J. Frueh (ed.), *Pedagogical Journeys through World Politics*,
Political Pedagogies, https://doi.org/10.1007/978-3-030-20305-4_16

185

My personal trajectory in academia did not go quite as originally expected, so I'm happy to share two important facts that I once thought I knew about teaching, but later found out I was wrong about. The first incorrect belief is that education at community college is inferior to that at four-year schools. The second is that teaching is primarily about the teacher.

How Did I Get Here??

When I chose to go to grad school, teaching was my ultimate career goal. While I enjoy doing research, what I like most about it is sharing what I find with others. So upon beginning my job search, I was more interested in schools that focused on teaching, rather than scholarship, however, I never even considered community college. There was a joke in grad school that, when interviewing on the job market, if a school asked if you could teach ____ (e.g. Dog Psychology), your reply should be, "I would love to teach (Dog Psychology)!" We laughed about it at the time, but throughout my career I have taught a total of 16 different courses (most more than once), including American Government, history, and technical writing, and I may have gotten my first full-time job in part by devising the idea for a course on "Music and Politics – Protest and Persuasion" on the fly.[2] Being flexible and multidisciplinary is definitely an asset. But my main field has always been International Relations.

That being said, while in graduate school, I taught several classes at the local community college, all to auto mechanics, and none concerned International Relations (IR). I taught them macroeconomics, technical writing, and American government. The fact that I had never actually taken a class in any of these subjects may have led to my misperceptions about community college education. These classes were small, and I got to know my students well, unlike the enormous lectures I also taught at my graduate institution. Obviously, I was not really an expert in the subjects I was teaching, and I had some of those annoying habits that new public speakers tend to have—namely, I said "ok?" after almost every point I made. The automotive students cured me of that! Apparently, they kept track of how many times I said it during a lecture and took bets on the number. Once I found this out, I quickly checked myself.

Meanwhile, I was also teaching Intro to IR classes as an adjunct at my grad school. Although I know a lot more about this subject, I probably was

---

[2] I never did get to teach this course.

pretty terrible at it at first. While I didn't write out my whole lecture, I was very attached to my notes. And I was probably way too academic about the subject. My fellow grad students and I loved to sit around at conferences and have deep discussions about IR theory, but most of my students really didn't care. They were not going into academia, and most were simply taking the class to fulfill a general education requirement. I had the added disadvantage of being a young woman, not much older than the college students, so I struggled to establish my authority in the classroom. I also taught large sections of American government as a grad student. I approached these huge lecture classes (250+ students) just looking to survive. I tended to write out my lectures, didn't know the material as well as I should have, and was tempted to fudge the answers to questions I didn't know.

My first full-time job was a very different situation. It was a small, private school with little diversity among the students. I taught a 3-3 load every year, with three distinct preps, including a history class each semester. Despite this large teaching load, there were also very high research expectations for tenure. During my time there, I developed eight new classes, including a Model UN program. I taught a total of 11 different classes. On top of this, I had two small children and a husband who traveled a lot. Needless to say, my research suffered.

Perhaps the most difficult aspect of my teaching at this school was the mix of interest and abilities in each class. This school wanted nonmajors to be able to take upper level political science classes, and so they would not allow prerequisites for these classes. The result was that there were numerous students in something like a 400-level international political economy class who had never taken IR or economics. Therefore, I was forced to teach the basics of both before I could get to the more advanced concepts. Unfortunately, there were also political science majors in the class who were bored by the refresher. One strategy I used to deal with this was to turn the majors into the teachers for the other students. I put them in groups, mixing the more experienced students with the less experienced students, and had them discuss the day's readings together. The experienced students benefitted from teaching the material they already knew and the inexperienced students got up to speed in a nonthreatening environment.

The lack of diversity among these students also made it difficult to get interesting discussions going. They tended to agree with one another, or the one student in class who had a different viewpoint would feel marginalized and unwilling to speak up. There were a couple of strategies that I tried to introduce more diversity, including playing "devil's advocate" and bringing in speakers. Unfortunately, the chair of my department was not very supportive of the speakers if they presented a conservative view, which was sorely lacking in most classes in this department.

When I failed to get tenure at this school, I was forced to go back on the job market. Unfortunately, tenure-track jobs are few and far between for "experienced" professors, and my family had no interest in moving. I was extremely lucky that a full-time position became available that spring at my local community college. The previous instructor was retiring after several decades in that position. But I was hesitant to apply because of the stigma associated with community college teaching. At no point during graduate school was I encouraged to apply to teaching positions at community colleges, and my adjunct position there was something I did not talk about much. The focus of my training was on a research and teaching position. So, honestly, if my advisor had suggested community college jobs, I would have taken that to mean my research was terrible. I was already feeling like a failure, and applying to a community college seemed like I was admitting that I may never teach at a four-year institution again.

However, I did apply, at the urging of a good friend, and luckily I got the job. I *was* lucky because one thing I thought I knew, but now know I was wrong about, is that education at community college is substandard. I am very glad that the editor of this volume decided to include an essay by someone who teaches at a community college. The fact is that just over a third of students entering college this fall will be going to a two-year school. This means just over a third of college teaching jobs will be teaching those students. Given the dearth of tenure-track jobs at four-year institutions, this may be your future, and it is one you should not fear. My own prejudice against community college almost led me to miss what has become an amazing and unexpected career change. Teaching at community college has been both rewarding and frustrating, so I'm happy to share what I've learned about this experience.

CONFRONTING THE MYTHS ABOUT COMMUNITY COLLEGE TEACHING

Prior to teaching at community college, my impression was that most instructors there were unqualified and did not have advanced degrees in political science. Also, I thought that the students would generally be low performing and uninterested in learning. Both assumptions, I am happy to say, have turned out to be completely false. I wondered where this prejudice came from? Some brief interactions with a professor (let's call her Professor Smith) at a local state university gave me one possible answer—fear of competition and the need to feel superior about their own academic positions lead some professors at four-year schools to denigrate community college professors. While trying to help a student who was transferring from my school to hers, Professor Smith's interactions with me were rude and condescending. She and I had never met, and as far as I know, she knew nothing about me. Yet she assumed that, because I was teaching at a community college, my classes were sub-par. She had not seen my syllabus or even met any of my students, since I had just recently started teaching there. However, our schools are in a consortium where students can take classes at either school. Since I teach the same subject as she does, at a vastly reduced cost, she had a justifiable fear that she might lose students.

I would like to try to change this erroneous impression held by my colleagues at four-year schools. To begin with, every full-time professor in my department (social sciences) has a Ph.D. It is not a requirement, but it is a fact. Many of our adjuncts do as well, and all adjuncts have at least a Master's degree. Of the full-time faculty, most of us have published in our disciplines, and some continue to do research. Our adjuncts tend to fall into two categories. The first are older, more experienced people, who want to teach because they love teaching. Many of them are retired from other full-time jobs and are teaching really for the fun of it. The other category comprises young, unemployed graduate or postgrad students who have yet to find their first full-time job. The former are great teachers but may struggle with the technology or the latest pedagogy. The latter are great with the technology and keeping current but need to polish their teaching skills. Both offer benefits for our students. I realized from my first interview at this school that my fear of working with colleagues who lacked my expertise was grossly unfounded! Instead, I would need to keep on my toes to keep up with them!

Also, professors at four-year schools should start to see community colleges as their allies, not their competition. Most of my students want to transfer to a four-year school eventually. Many will probably go to that local state school, due to convenience and cost. Those professors denigrating community colleges should be trying to attract my students and to work with me to ensure my students are well-prepared during their first two years. We have made some progress in that direction thanks to an articulation agreement,[3] but we still have some work to do. Community college students still start at these schools with a stigma attached.

I saw a similar stigma regarding community college students when sending interns out to work in legislative offices. One local office had never had an intern from my school before I took over the program, and the staff member I met with was skeptical about taking one on. However, the student I placed in her office was among our best—a nontraditional male who was going back to school for a teaching degree. He impressed them enough that they offered him a full-time job at the end of his internship (which he turned down to pursue his teaching career). I was happy to upend their expectations but sad that one of our top legislators had that bias to begin with.

I should not have been surprised, however, as I came to this job with my own biases. Fortunately, the students I encountered here were vastly different from my expectations. Oh yes, they did struggle with some basic academic issues, as Professor Smith had been quick to point out. I learned my first semester that I would need to adjust both my reading and writing requirements—not because these students were incapable, but because many of them had never been taught the skills I assumed they had learned in high school. For this reason, I now incorporate critical thinking skills, writing skills, and test-taking skills into my classes.

There are many reasons that people go to community college, but I find that most students fall into three broad categories. The first are the traditional college students, looking to get an inexpensive start. While they do have the basic academic skills, and could have gone to a four-year school, they may lack the resources and/or may be the first generation in their family to go to college. Some of them had done poorly in high school and so need to get back on track in order to get into the four-year school of their dreams. The challenge with these students is to keep them from getting bored with the class material.

The second type of student I have are multinational students. They are refugees and immigrants; many have English as a second (or third or fourth) language. They have experienced trauma and loss, but now are hopeful that they will begin a new chapter of their lives. These students

---

[3]Articulation agreements help students transfer as seamlessly as possible to a four-year school. My department has several with the local four-year colleges, and they spell out clearly for students what courses will transfer at each school and what courses they will still need to take to complete their major.

have many barriers to success. Some struggle with English, some must take care of other family members, and most of them work full-time in addition to going to school. Some are incredibly shy. But for those willing to speak about their experiences, they are an invaluable resource in class. To have a member of the class who has witnessed a civil war first-hand makes the issue so much more real for the other students (and for me). They provide a perspective that I cannot.

The third type of student I tend to see are those studying the trades, for whom their Associate in Applied Science degree or a certificate may be a terminal degree. These students are hard-working and practical-minded. And some see little point in studying American government or international relations. But knowing that they need my class to fulfill their general education requirements, they are generally good sports about it. The challenge with these students is to maintain their interest in the class throughout the semester.

Learning to Teach Differently

So what do I do differently, teaching at community college? One change I have made to all of my classes is to have some kind of assignment relevant to the reading due in class every week. This serves two general purposes— it encourages the students to actually complete the reading, and it helps me see if students are understanding it. Getting students to read is one of the fundamental challenges of teaching college. If there is no graded assignment attached to it, the majority of them will not do it. These assignments can also serve as a jumping off point for discussions. Students who have something written down will be more comfortable participating, and student input to the discussions will be more thoughtful. Having an assignment due every week in every one of my five classes has created a massive amount of grading for me, but it has definitely benefitted my students.

Also, despite the low cost of my school, student retention is a continual problem, as it is for most schools. One activity I've used to combat this is a photo scavenger hunt, done in groups. They have a list of items to take pictures of, on campus and in the nearby community, and the students are randomly placed in groups. They get some class time to do this, but mostly it must be done outside of class. And they have most of the semester to do it. There are several benefits to this assignment: they learn where resources are located on campus, they get to know a little about what the departments of the federal government do, but, most importantly, they make connections with classmates. They have multiple contacts they can ask if they need notes, an assignment, or just do not understand something. Also, some groups have gotten to know each other well enough that they check up on each other when someone misses class. I will confess that this is a group bonding activity I stole from my daughter's volleyball coach (thanks!), but it has generally worked well. Even though it has a fairly low point value, students still take it seriously and it has the desired effect.

Here's the key point I have learned about teaching in general: it's not about me, it's about the students. This realization has come to me only through a great deal of experience and some maturity. I needed to learn to focus more on the students' needs than on being an "amazing professor." For example, it is possible to know too much about a topic to be good at translating it into an understandable lecture. Personally, I have a really hard time teaching students about the International Monetary Fund (IMF)—not because I don't understand it, but because I understand it too well. So for me, *everything* about the IMF is important! Distilling all that information down into what the students actually need to know and can digest is very difficult. On the other hand, it is OK not to know everything, as long as you admit it. Learning from experience, I do not try to fake answers when I don't know something. Students know when you're faking it! Instead, I start every semester with the confession to students that I am not omniscient. But I do promise that if they ask a question I don't know the answer to, I will research it and get back to them, and then I follow up on this promise.

This understanding about the role of a professor also helped me figure out how to deal with challenging students. I often have students who are bright and understand the material, but who fail the class anyway, usually because they don't turn in assignments. I used to take this personally, assuming they disliked me or the class and were refusing to do work out of protest. After many conversations with these students, I came to realize that their reasons for not completing classwork are many and varied, and almost never have anything to do with me. They have family problems, health issues, or mental illness. They usually want to do well, but feel like issues beyond their control are leading them to failure.

When I encounter a student like this, it is a good reminder for me that teachers need to focus on the student rather than themselves. When a student is hostile, angry, or upset during class, it is more likely a personal issue for them, rather than something the instructor has done. For this reason, our graduate training would be more complete if it included some training in counseling. If a student is disengaged in class, I no longer take it as a personal affront but instead try to find out what problem the student is struggling within their own life and direct them to the proper resources.

This realization has also been helpful in focusing on the content of my classes. Most of my students don't care that much about IR, so it's important to find a hook that interests them. As much as I love the IMF and talking about monetary policy, the fact is that most of my students don't love it. Yes, I can try to teach it in a way that they understand and can relate to, but they are much more interested in cybersecurity, global warming, and refugees. I have definitely seen a change in students' awareness of global issues over the past twenty years. For example, when I was teaching in the late 1990s, I used a case study about the illegal trade in endangered species. I just couldn't get a good conversation going about the issue, and it finally dawned on me that the students just didn't care about elephant extinction! They saw no connection between this and their own lives. Today, however, students have been inundated with information about the environment from an early age, so they are clearly able to articulate why we should care about this. They are much more aware of global politics, even if they aren't super knowledgeable about the historical context. Therefore, I have been able to shift away from trying to explain the relevance of IR in the first couple weeks of class to talking about details of current issues. They may not always be the issues I am personally most interested in, but the students will be energized and excited.

We all know that active learning works best for students and that we should try to lecture at them as little as possible, but sometimes it's hard to break out of the lecture mold. The day I knew I had really become a seasoned professor was the day I made up a simulation activity literally on my way to class. As I walked across campus, I suddenly thought to myself, "I cannot bear to do a lecture today! I'm bored and the students will be bored! What if we do a trade simulation instead?" When I got to class, I broke them into three groups. Each group represented a fictitious country. I wrote the country characteristics on the board. Country A was an advanced capitalist economy that created new technology. Country B was a large, low-income country with a large workforce. Country C was a small, impoverished country with control of a strategic resource. Despite literally making it up on the fly, the simulation went smoothly and took the entire class period (and could have taken more). From this, they learned several key points about trade:

- Negotiations are complex, and issues with one country are dependent on negotiations with other countries
- There are different types of power in the international system and states are interdependent
- Factors that seem unrelated to trade may play a role
- The structure of the negotiations makes a difference
- Bombing another country is unrealistic

I continue to use this simulation in class, and while I have written out the country characteristics, I have changed very little from the first time I did this. And it continues to be one of the most valuable, and entertaining, learning experiences in my classes.

Another point I wish I had known was how important it is to study and understand history in order to teach what is happening today. I'm sure I probably knew this intellectually, but I just didn't have time to learn the history that would benefit me. Fortunately, at my first full-time job, we were required to teach world history every semester. In the fall semester, we taught ancient history and in the spring was modern history. We were given some latitude to design these classes, so I chose to teach this course as a politics and religion class. The intersection of these two always interested me, but I didn't have much time to research it. By teaching it I was forced to learn it, and my understanding of IR today is much richer because of this.

Conclusion

Teaching is a fulfilling career. I do have to remind myself of that sometimes—when I have a giant stack of papers to grade, numerous students unloading their personal problems on me, and administrators reminding me to complete the paperwork they sent me. And you must love teaching to be at a community college. I regularly teach six classes per semester. I am only required to teach five, but I offer an internship class every semester for any student who wants to take it as well. I don't say this to get sympathy from my four-year school colleagues, who I know are also overworked in different ways, but to give readers realistic expectations about what this career involves. I do love my students, and I personally find it very rewarding to teach them. They are very appreciative of my efforts. It was my great privilege to speak at our graduation a couple of years ago, and here is one excerpt from my speech that encapsulates my experience:

The faculty of [our college] have committed to teaching community college because they believe strongly in our mission – we inspire *all* to learn, succeed and lead. And although our mission is to inspire *you*, please know that you actually inspire us on a daily basis. You have overcome disabilities; escaped civil war in a distant land; cared for relatives and friends; and fought for our country in places other Americans can't find on a map. Your stories are diverse – both difficult and heartwarming. And as much as we hope that [our college] has changed you and made your life better, please know that you have also left an imprint on [our college].

So to answer my original question—two things I thought I knew but was wrong about were that community colleges provide substandard education and that teaching is all about the professor. Both of these were proven wrong through my experiences as a teacher, and I'm happy to say that I'm probably a better teacher today because of this realization. And a happier person!

REFERENCE

Ryssdal, Kai, and Molly Wood. Make Me Smart with Kai and Molly. *Podcast.*
https://www.marketplace.org/topics/make-me-smart

CHAPTER 17

An Individual Odyssey in Teaching International Relations

Paul F. Diehl

Current institution: large public Research I university
Typical classroom setting: small (10–20) seminars, medium (25) lecture discussion, large (100) lecture
Typical pedagogical approach: lecture with a wide variety of active learning strategies
Disciplinary identity: War and Peace

Early Experiences

Early experiences as teaching assistants have a formative effect on the ways that instructors teach at least early in a career and in some cases in a path-dependent fashion for many years thereafter. Ideally, exceptional instructors in international relations (IR) classes serve as role models for those who work under them and graduate assistants adopt what they see as best practices when the time comes to be independent instructors. Similarly, guidance in conducting recitation sections and grading not only improve the learning experiences of the students but allow assistants to hone their

P. F. Diehl (✉)
University of Texas-Dallas, Richardson, TX, USA
e-mail: pdiehl@utdallas.edu

© The Author(s) 2020
J. Frueh (ed.), *Pedagogical Journeys through World Politics*,
Political Pedagogies, https://doi.org/10.1007/978-3-030-20305-4_17

skills in leading discussions and carrying out classroom exercises. Unfortunately, my formative experiences had neither of these elements.

As a teaching assistant for the first time to an introductory International Relations (IR) course in the early 1980s, I was assigned to a senior professor who taught the course pretty much as he had for decades. A "sage on the stage" in front of 200 students, he frequently taught outdated materials ("The UN is only a tool of the superpowers") in an entertaining, but traditional, lecture format that largely mirrored his own research. Assistants leading discussion sections were left to their own devices in terms of what to do in the once a week meetings and were given freedom, but no direction, in designing assignments and associated grading that went beyond the objective tests that the class as a whole took. Although I subsequently worked for better instructors in other subfields of political science, I was still left largely to "learn by doing" with all the accompanying problems and benefits that went with this trial and error process.

To the extent that I was able to stretch myself beyond lectures (yes, I did these even in a discussion section), it was interactions with other teaching assistants that led to innovative experimentation. Several of us with past Model United Nations experience had a fascination with simulations, and we designed (and even published some short articles) on role-playing exercises for students. International Relations offers a number of scenarios for this in structured (e.g., United Nations) and unstructured (e.g., crises) environments and students responded well to these. I can't say that all the pedagogical outcomes were carefully planned or assessed, but this was an early attempt at making students see the viewpoints of others and recognize differences, something that would take on increasing importance later in my career.

Without any mentoring, I found myself relying on traditional fallbacks for organizing and conducting international relations classes. The topical organization of my classes on introductory international relations, international conflict, and international organizations, were determined primarily by the textbooks that I chose for the courses. There were some preconceived notions on my part about the key topics to cover and the sequences in which they were covered as I perused different textbook options. Nevertheless, the book options were always suboptimal, even the ones ultimately selected. I was reluctant to include emerging topics at the time (e.g., human rights, environment) if there were no corresponding textbook chapter on the subject. Still true today, at least in the North American market, textbooks tend to be more similar than not and thus there was not much room for innovation outside of the canon of subjects (e.g., power, conflict, and actors in introductory textbooks) addressed in textbooks.

From the earliest days of my teaching, one of my respites from the "tyranny of the textbooks" was the adoption of "readers" that included selected articles or essays that roughly corresponded to the chapter outlines of the textbooks. Nevertheless, I always shied away from two kinds of supplements. One is supplemental readings that are designed to provide students with contrasting viewpoints on controversial topics or questions of the day. These could be self-assembled or contained in books of readings that contained the words "Debates" or "Controversies" in their titles. Although these chapters provided the contemporary relevance that students craved and I thought to be important, most of the essays had a short shelf-life and did not encourage the development of analytical skills and generalizations that would allow students to assess future policy problems. At the other extreme, I have generally eschewed readings drawn from scholarly journals. Students find these difficult to read (especially articles with quantitative content) and do not necessarily take away the key points from them. Indeed, those students who tend not do the reading are even more so disinclined with such articles. I suppose that an alternative is to have class time centered on a discussion of readings (much as graduate courses are), but this would give such articles a prominence that overshadows the textbook and lectures and a role that was not consistent with their designed supplemental purpose. This is not to say that I ignored the research findings in such articles, but rather have integrated them into lectures where the conclusions were presented in a more digestible fashion, including with examples. I have tended to assign readers that have works that are scholarly in the sense that they contained broad principles, analytical schemes, and ideas, but are also approachable for an undergraduate audience. Over time, I began to assemble my own collections of such articles and indeed published readers myself based on those collections in the fields of international organization and international law respectively. A concern for the cost to students and the ability to access many of the same materials online led me to abandon the use of formal readers.

My teaching in the classroom was also conventional in the early years, with the modal format being instructor-centered with a heavy reliance on lectures and instructor-prompted questioning. This was a time when active learning techniques were just beginning to take off; lectures were far more common than today, even if they remain the most used teaching technique. The primary deviation from lectures and questions was the use of small group games and simulations, largely of my own construction or adaption on subjects ranging from arms races to treaty negotiations. I retain many of those today, albeit with a number of tweaks and much greater attention to tying these to various learning objectives.

MAJOR CHANGES IN CONTENT AND STRATEGIES

Over the past 25–30 years, my international relations teaching has evolved in an incremental fashion and there has not been a single "aha!" moment. Nevertheless, and somewhat paradoxically, my teaching strategies were modified significantly only *after* I won several undergraduate teaching awards. I recall one of my colleagues saying that it was only after he had won one of the national Carnegie awards for instruction that he thought more carefully about what he did in the classroom and beyond, and only then became a good teacher. That inspired me to be reflective of my own practices. Helped along with this was that I became the director of a college teaching and faculty development program. This was my introduction to the scholarship of teaching and learning. I discovered not only that I was already using a number of what pedagogical research has determined to be best practices, but more importantly that there were many other innovations in active learning and use of technology that had a solid empirical basis for student learning and could be adapted to teach IR.

Looking back, there were five major changes that were made over time and reflect my current pedagogical strategies.

TEACHING THEORY BY NOT TEACHING THEORY

The first change is that I no longer explicitly teach or cover IR theories. Presenting the tenets of realism and liberalism, and more recently constructivism and feminism, is a staple at the outset of introductory IR courses and for some upper-division courses as well. Yet students did not understand what theory was nor how it was to be used. Even when I directly explained it, for some reason students still thought that theory was some kind of tool that leaders used to make decisions rather than ways for analysts to explain those decisions. Does this mean that I don't think that theory is important? Certainly not! Rather, I found that there are better ways to achieve the goals of theoretical thinking than going over the "isms." I have labeled this approach "sneaky theoretical."

The question "why?" has become central to class discussions as well as exam and paper assignments. I try to force students to offer reasons for why states provide aid to rebel groups in neighboring states or why China exhibits reluctance to crack down on North Korea. Most useful is asking students to account for actions that are counter-intuitive, such as imposing tariffs when a state knows these will be met with retaliation leaving all sides worse off. Students are not allowed merely to offer broad opinions about what happened, but must provide some underlying rationale or logic to accompany their explanation. They are also encouraged to consider alternative explanations, and finally to consider what evidence would be convincing for the explanations to be considered correct. In effect, rather than be taught about theories, students are theorizing themselves, albeit on a scale much smaller than grand theory. My strategy is consistent with the "learning by doing" approach, but as a practical matter, I think that the skills and thought processes acquired in sneaky theorizing are more likely to have long-term consequences for citizenship and decision-making than memorizing the key elements of grand theory. I have doubts that years later students will say to themselves: "what does realism or constructivism have to say about this?" Much less likely is that they will be able to answer practical questions with reference to those theories.

IR AND CURRENT EVENTS

A second shift concerns how I deal with current events, both a blessing and a curse for international relations instructors in contrast to those who teach ancient history. There probably are not many international relations instructors who believe that it is our primary duty to teach contemporary political events to our students, even if that is sometimes the public perception of what we do. At the same time, most of us want our students to have the tools to analyze what is in the news today and make informed political opinions. Students crave relevance in university classes, and among their common complaints is that they do not see the utility of what they learned in the classroom for their everyday lives. I had long used examples "ripped from today's headlines" (apologies to fans of the *CSI* TV series). Furthermore, my exams often contained plausible, real-world scenarios for students to analyze; one notable question asked students to assess the legality of a US raid in Pakistan to capture Osama bin Laden, a prescient item on my international law exam that appeared several years before the actual event. These were useful, but I still wanted to do something more to focus on sneaky theoretical analysis, while increasing the relevance of what was unfolding before them in the news.

My solution was to require students to submit five news reports (with five more available for extra credit during the semester). I'd like to say that this was an original idea, but actually, it was the result of co-teaching a course on peacekeeping with a doctoral student who had successfully used the assignment in other courses. These were not merely summaries of news articles, but rather the assignment required some analysis—Why did the event occur? What are the implications? How does the event relate to the things that are covered in the course? This forces the students to read the news and hunt for stories that are directly relevant to the course (e.g., ethnic conflict, peace, war). They are also required to interpret the events rather than be passive receptacles of information. Students are provided with a list of suggested news sources for stories and although many of these include the standard *New York Times* and *Washington Post* outlets, I include other media outside the US (e.g., *BBC*, *Al Jazeera*) to encourage broader perspectives. Several suggested outlets are in languages other than English. There are limits to this in that today's students will only look at news sources that are easily available on the internet, and this necessarily excludes a number of publications in the Global South, although increasingly less so over time.

With all the controversy over "fake news" in recent years, I have also posted a list of fake news sites and as yet no student has submitted a report from such disreputable sources. That said, I assigned the honors students in my Approaches to Peace class to find false information or claims about peace on the internet. The results were disappointing, especially so given the universally high quality of students in the course. They proved unable to distinguish between stories or claims that were biased, misleading, and outright false, respectively. This is likely to be a continuing problem for instructors, and one not confined to international relations teaching.

So Little Time, So Much to Cover

A third shift in my international relations teaching over three decades has involved the content or topics covered in international relations courses. In general, I decided not to succumb any longer to the "tyranny of coverage," that is the perceived need to cover as much material as possible rather than worry about whether students actually learned it. Indeed, it became clear to me that I was relying on the assumption—"If I covered it, they must have learned it." Each successive year I seemed to cover fewer ideas, with the most noticeable indicator being the number and length of my PowerPoint slides that accompany each class topic (whether there are lectures or not). I have made a strategic decision that depth was more important than breadth and covering less meant that there was more room for discussion and introducing contemporary examples.

Even as I have covered less material in the course, changes in the world and the international relations discipline have led to a number of substantive changes in the IR courses that I teach. For an introductory course, this means giving much greater attention to international political economy (IPE) issues. IPE, except in its Marxist variations, was a nascent field at best in the mid-1980s, but has gradually become as a major subfield in IR. The rise of the European Union (EU) and the importance of trade and international financial cooperation have forced the subject matter to be part of the core of the international relations curriculum. What once was a course that was Cold War oriented has evolved to focus as much on cooperation as conflict.

Other substantive alterations have been more reflective of changes in world politics. Topics such as human rights and the environment are now part of the substantive focus in my introductory course. I recognize that to some extent this is constructing courses that "chase headlines," but such decisions do reflect scholarship in the discipline, increase the relevance of the course, and are favorably received by students.

Advanced courses in international relations also reflect changes in the world and accompanying scholarship. Most notably, I incorporated conflict management issues (e.g., mediation, peacekeeping) into my upper-division conflict courses. More conflict scholars turned to examine these approaches; the rise of regional organizations and the explosion of conflict management efforts (in cases such as meditation, the frequency was tenfold greater than in earlier eras) demanded attention. The increase in civil wars and the decline of interstate wars also meant adjustments in conflict courses, lest these appear to be abstract and historical exercises about wars that occurred before most of the students were born. The importance of these phenomena, and increasingly how they could not be accommodated under existing frameworks, has spawned new courses in my repertoire of offerings. I now actually can and do teach a broader set of courses than at the outset of my academic career; these include specialized courses on peacekeeping, conflict management, and civil war.

One more change in teaching comes from a different source: my own research agenda. It is not unusual for a research agenda to evolve over the course of one's career. I have had colleagues take this to the extreme, moving from being a specialist on American politics to doing research on the Middle East, and from international political economy to national environmental policy respectively. My own transformation has been less dramatic and most relevant to my teaching has been a partial shift in focus from the study of war to peace, with the latter defined as more than merely the absence of war. I always hated the idea of courses, especially at the undergraduate level, that were defined narrowly according to the book project of the instructor at the moment; thus, courses such as the politics of international environmental treaties or civil wars in Africa are created to serve the interests of the instructor rather than necessarily the students. On the one hand, it might not matter for undergraduates in that any course that gets them to think in different ways is a good thing. On the other hand, do we do students a disservice in defining phenomena so narrowly so as to suggest that topic areas or regions are completely unique? Accordingly, for my new courses on peace, I have adopted a survey approach that covers the phenomena broadly and addresses many of the same subjects as some traditional security (e.g., deterrence) and international organization (e.g., peacekeeping) courses, but through the lenses of the peace concept rather than from the perspective of merely preventing war.

CONTENT AND THE BIGGER PICTURE

The fourth change is an ever-evolving one, and more a function of the extant curriculum than pedagogical approach. One key question is how does one fit a course you teach into the curriculum offered by your program or department? That is, how should one adjust the content of a given course according to what is covered in courses by other faculty members? The concerns are complementarity and duplication respectively. Generally, if the subject matter (e.g., the World Trade Organization or WTO) is covered in another course, should you give it the same level of detail and cover some of the same readings and ideas in your course (e.g., international law)? At the graduate level, this was an easier decision for me. Most graduate students will take the same set of courses in international relations in preparation for exams and a dissertation. With that in mind, I would add or delete some topics from certain courses according to how my colleagues taught companion courses. For example, the extent to which the European Union (EU) was addressed in a graduate course in international organizations would depend on its coverage in IPE or a specialized course on the EU. At the micro level, having a section on transitional justice was unnecessary if there was a week on that in a course on civil war. This approach insures that graduate students don't do the same readings across courses as it is based on the assumption that they need less reinforcement or it will come during the process of studying for qualifying exams.

The complementarity-duplication tradeoff is less clear for an undergraduate curriculum. There, students are far less likely to enroll in the full range of courses in a program or department, even if they are majors. From experience, I also know that nonmajors might take one of my courses and never take another in political science, much less international relations. Thus, in a heterogeneous class, some students will experience redundancy whereas others will be introduced to the subject matter for the first time. Undergraduates are not harmed by reinforcement of material, and most often I am asking them to meet different (usually higher order) learning objectives. Furthermore, there is no clear coordination or transparency on the courses that I and others offer, such that the courses of my colleagues are not fully planned out when I need to make decisions on syllabi and assignments. In an ideal world, there would be meetings of faculty members who jointly decide what is covered and in what course. Realistically, and leaving aside concerns of academic freedom, this rarely happens except perhaps with respect to the content of different sections of the introductory course.

Teaching Millennials

Last, but not least, are the adjustments made to what are perceived as generational and other differences of the cohort of students in my classes at any given time. Seminal research from decades ago suggested that students had attention spans of approximately 15 minutes and therefore instructors needed to shift presentations, topics, and approaches in order to reset the attention clock. Much has been made of millennials and their differences with earlier generations, and I strongly suspect that the 15-minute window has shrunk. Furthermore, students read conventional text less than older cohorts and rely more on visual media for information. Rather than kvetching about these turn of events, I have tried to adapt my courses accordingly with the goal of promoting student learning in ways most conducive to that process for the students involved. Thus, I don't necessarily assign fewer readings than previously, but they are shorter pieces and of a different type than what I did years before. Faculty members are not necessarily different than their students. Indeed, there has a been a trend over the last decade plus in academia toward shorter works; note that books have fewer pages and journals increasingly impose word limits even as those journals are increasingly online and without the page and cost constraints of earlier issues. It is more likely that students will read and understand shorter works that convey important ideas than extended ones that force students to discern key points amidst a host of other information. The best illustration comes from my course in international law. Rather than having students read law review articles, which are inordinately long and obsessively footnoted, I rely on the short, policy-relevant, but theory-informed essays provided by the American Society of International Law: *ASIL Insights*. These are only a few pages in length, are written for a general audience, and address legal questions related to contemporary concerns (e.g., the legality of Israeli settlements).

I confess to still using PowerPoint slides for class (in the old days it was outlines on a blackboard), but pedagogical research has convinced me that outlines of material are sufficient for allowing the students to understand how different topics are connected and sequenced. At the same time, the slides are not very detailed, leaving students to process the material and fill in the notes themselves, something that research also indicates enhances learning. Last, I now employ videos and movies far more than I ever did. Fortunately, International Relations, in contrast to a discipline such as chemistry, offers a host of different options and many of these come from different cultures, thereby exposing students to events and ideas not found in mainstream Western media. This has led me to reduce or eliminate the number of exams I give (which eat up class sessions) and substitute assignments such movie "reviews" in which students must choose their own films on the subject (student choice is also associated with learning in some studies) and apply concepts from the course to what they see. For example, the influence of instrumentalist leaders is more salient to students when they see illustrations in films on ethnic conflict than when they must complete an exam essay on the subject.

FINAL THOUGHTS AND OVERARCHING GOALS

In my fourth decade as a faculty member, I find that I retain many of the overarching goals that I always had, but I have significantly changed the targets and strategies for my instruction. A good portion of the motivation for these changes stemmed from surveys of my students, which revealed that many were not political science or international studies majors, and those planning on going to graduate school in these fields were rare. Fundamentally, I still have two primary and interrelated goals that cut across all levels and topics of my courses. The first is to contribute to the civic education of my students. Most or all of my students will not continue with the study of international relations beyond their undergraduate years (perhaps not even beyond my class). In one form or another, however, all will participate in discussions, make political decisions, and be affected by international events in their lives. As the world becomes more globalized, these will only increase. This is a basic responsibility for anyone who teaches international studies and from which I have never wavered.

Second, I have put greater emphasis on having students develop critical thinking and writing skills, not only as a way to promote the first goal above but also as an end in itself. Most students don't have the ability to analyze a problem critically, and by that I mean reach a judgment or position that is not merely what they have been told or that which merely justifies prior beliefs. In political science and international studies, this is complicated by political or cultural biases that often cloud their judgments. I try to get my students to look at problems with a fresh attitude, specifically to have them recognize the subtle gray aspects of political behavior rather than being drawn to its perceived black and white components. Every "ying" has some "yang," and every argument or policy position has some limitations.

One of the keys to being an effective instructor is a willingness to reflect on teaching and periodically reinvent ourselves in the classroom. The enjoyment of teaching comes from this renewal, and international relations instructors are fortunate in that the world changes quickly and there are always new and exciting things to analyze and share with our students. I must admit that changing the ways and what we teach faces some stiff headwinds. It is difficult not to be weighed down by the sunk costs that went into all of the preparation the first time that we taught a course. Furthermore, time pressures have increased on faculty members, especially with respect to research and grant getting; indeed, these are demands that instructors now face at all colleges and universities, even those once designated as "teaching institutions." Nevertheless, at the end of a career, few will likely lament that they didn't publish another article or book chapter (that no one was likely to read). Rather, it is the missed opportunities to impact student lives that will be the sources of regret, and it is that realization that keeps me going and willing to make changes even at what might be the twilight of my academic career.

CHAPTER 18

Disciplinary Dungeon Master

Marcelo M. Valença

Current institution: state military academy
Classroom settings: large classes; introductory classes;
Pedagogical approach: active learning; storytelling
Disciplinary ID: Political Science, International Relations;
International Politics

I never thought I would end up being a professor. During high school, I wanted to be a music journalist. My plans lasted for about three weeks after I started college, when I decided to change my major and become an attorney specialized in cyberlaw. Two semesters later, my plans changed again; my goal became to work with human rights. And then it changed again a few years later, as I applied for grad school in a completely different area.

   Like other authors in this book, this chapter is autobiographical. My narrative reflects the many positive (and the not-so-positive) experiences I have had in more than ten years as a professor. It reflects the choices I made and the challenges I faced while navigating that path from grad school to a professorship. You won't hear me complaining about not getting formal training in teaching or how teaching plays a marginal role in tenure evaluations or funding—but these are facts, especially for adjunct and junior faculty.

M. M. Valença (✉)
Brazilian Naval War College, Rio de Janeiro, Brazil

© The Author(s) 2020   209
J. Frueh (ed.), *Pedagogical Journeys through World Politics*,
Political Pedagogies, https://doi.org/10.1007/978-3-030-20305-4_18

Although I am writing from Brazil, I believe my experience applies to other academic cultures. I was an adjunct faculty member in private colleges for several years. I got tenured in a research university and moved to a military school in a new tenure-track position and new research topics. Now my research and teaching include maritime studies side by side with international law and international politics.

A lot has changed since I started lecturing. I always had plans to guide my choices, but none of those plans were fully executed, and I am totally fine with that. I hope this chapter somehow helps graduate students and junior faculty feel better about choices, strategies, and decisions made with the intent of securing a more fulfilling career.

A WARM WELCOME

Graduate school was not part of my plans until my senior year. When I was about to get my J.D., I landed a couple of job offers from law firms and the United Nations High Commissioner for Refugees (UNHCR) office in Rio. However, I was not sure I wanted to be an attorney. I had some OK internship experiences, but I was not very fond of corporative environments.

While I was writing my undergraduate final paper, my advisor suggested that I apply for graduate school. He insisted a bit, explaining the possibilities, challenges, and what to expect from pursuing an academic career. After some reflection, I decided to apply to the International Relations (IR) program at another department, ranked among the top three in the country. It was a long shot, but I decided to try.

I wasn't a complete stranger to IR. My final paper discussed the tension between solidarists and pluralists on human rights. During undergrad I took some courses on IR theory and international politics that I really enjoyed. Brazil was a rising player in international politics and there were future opportunities for IR specialists. The job market was expanding due to the boom in IR undergraduate courses, so teaching jobs were plentiful at that time. Moreover, and being quite frank, I felt comfortable staying in school for a few more years. My acceptance letter came in a few weeks and I was scheduled to start in the following year.

My first experience teaching was probably the same as most of grad students. I was a teaching assistant (TA) in an introductory course on Peace and Conflict Studies for freshmen. The professor responsible for the course was finishing his Ph.D. We had chatted a few times so he could brief me on my responsibilities and on the expectations students had of me when he said something that still echoes in the back of my mind. It was something like "no matter what happens in class, don't be afraid to say, 'I don't know. Can I look it up and get back to you next class?'" Can you imagine a professor saying that to his students? At the time, I couldn't.

His premise was that students have to trust you. And the best way to get someone's trust is to be honest with them and with yourself. He explained that by knowing and recognizing your limitations, you will feel more comfortable in class. Your lectures will sound more plausible and students will be more tolerant, no matter which teaching strategy you adopt, even the less orthodox ones.

This was both a relief and a shock. "OK," I thought, "I am ok with the idea that I don't have to know everything, but should the students know that?" My experience in college was that most of my professors dodged or simply ignored challenging questions. Most were prosecutors, judges, or renowned lawyers who wanted to have some college affiliation just to beef up their résumés. Being a faculty member in a top school would grant them prestige. They didn't want to show weakness or any flaw that would impact their reputations. Even the few full-time professors were not as honest as this Ph.D. candidate.

At one point in the semester, I was responsible for some of the sessions. I still remember a particular class about humanitarian law, a familiar topic, as I had studied it in college. I took some days to reread my books and notes. I was going to be so prepared nothing wrong would happen, but you can guess what happened in real life.

When the class started, I completely froze in front of forty-something students. I did not remember a line of the material and I was not able to speak for several minutes. OK, maybe it was only a few seconds, but it seemed like forever. I may or may not have spoken some random sentences and I probably looked like I was planning to run through the door. Students were starting to laugh when that *a-ha moment* came up.

I sat on the desk, looked at the students, fixed the sleeves of my shirt, and started talking: "There was this episode of 'The Simpsons' when…". And then I started describing what happened in a given episode that somehow correlated to our class. I don't recall which episode I mentioned or the situation I described, but it worked. As I spoke, I felt more comfortable and relaxed. The students sat there in a mix of shock and awe.

I talked for a little more than an hour that day. I was able to go through all the topics by mixing it up with some references to pop culture as I somehow created a narrative full of twists and cliffhangers that resembled the Dungeons and Dragons (D&D) campaigns I played with my friends a few years earlier. I went through the details of the reading material and I even made some funny jokes. I left the room at the end of the class thinking that I did an OK job. By the end of the semester, I had lectured a few more times in the same fashion and I felt good about the choices I made and happy about the evaluations students provided at the end of the course.

As I go through these evaluations to write this piece, I see students saying they had never had a professor lecturing the way I did. They wrote that most TAs were eager to show they were knowledgeable and fit for the job. I, on the other hand, looked so authentic they were more open to the ideas I was suggesting. They appreciated the efforts I made to create connections between concepts and reality (or the reality constructed by movies and cartoons) and praised me for easing their study sessions.

This experience helped me feel more comfortable and created a positive learning environment in class. I was hired a year later to offer that same course. When I was planning my course, I was not sure which path I should follow. However, I knew I should look for strategies that worked for both the students and me. I was just 26 and my students were only a few years younger, so they knew I was still learning how to teach. I decided that my best shot was to be as honest and open as I could be, choosing strategies and topics I felt comfortable with. A little more than a decade later, I guess it worked.

On the Door Step

As with many grad students, I had no experience at all when I began teaching. I could go on by saying I did not have any formal training during grad school, but we all know the drill: programs don't train grad students to teach so we have to learn on the job while we try to publish to get more attractive to land a teaching position.

My first positions were as an adjunct faculty member at private colleges. I was a Ph.D. candidate at the time and juggled multiple courses at these schools with my studies and publications. I had both no incentive or time to innovate in teaching, as adjunct faculty were hired as bodies to perform the tasks senior faculty were not willing to do, that is, teaching and advising undergrad students.

A few colleagues were willing to help me during my first months as a teacher, advising me on how to perform better in the classroom. However, it didn't work very well. Their focus was on easing the class workload; they had the tips and shortcuts to replicate the same class in different courses. They didn't want to become better teachers, just to decrease the time spent preparing classes. Their advice sounded like it would produce my average college course—monotonic lectures based on a prewritten script that followed the table of contents of the adopted books. These classes were uninteresting and didn't excite me. I didn't know what I was going to do, but I knew I didn't want to be like them, so I kindly ignored their advice. I didn't want to sound as boring as many of the professors I had.

Don't get me wrong. I was not planning to be Robin Williams in Dead Poets Society. But I did not want to replicate what they did. If I was going to spend four hours every week with a group of students in class, at least I should try to make the best of our time. Maybe even try to score some good evaluations to add to my résumé. Not an easy task, I know.

Despite being the most reasonable option, I wasn't comfortable doing something that would make me unhappy if I were in my students' shoes. I had little time to prepare lectures from scratch, so I focused on bringing my own abilities and the good experiences I had while in college to the table. I also asked myself a simple, but revealing question: if I were a student in that class, what I would like my teacher to do?

I am the type of person that needs to relate to something in order to understand: ideas need to make sense by correlating to everyday events, even the most ordinary ones. I decided to refer to something I had already read about, applied sometimes during undergrad, and that was reasonably successful. I decided that using active learning strategies to structure my courses would be the way to go.[1] As it helped me to study, I hoped it should contribute somehow to my teaching.

Active learning consists, by and large, of using pedagogical techniques to engage students in the discovery of knowledge (Lantis et al. 2018). One of the premises of active learning strategies is that we are more able to learn and retain knowledge by engaging critically with the subject and exploring several cognitive processes (Valiente 2008). Active learning

[1] At that time I did not know that the strategies I focused on my courses were described as active learning. The strategies I chose to develop were means that I frequently referred to in order to understand some specific aspects of what I was studying. The first time I attended an ISA conference, in 2007, I was introduced to a group of scholars studying pedagogical techniques to improve how students learnt. They called it active learning and it involved many strategies and class activities that I already did in class but without any structural planning.

strategies place students as active participants in the generation of knowledge (Kille et al. 2008: 412), leading to a meaningful connection with the subject. Moreover, studies show that we are able to retain more knowledge when we create meaningful connections between what we study and real-life examples (Cherney 2008; Valença and Inoue 2017). By using these strategies, active learning promotes collaborative work between students and teachers, as well as a conscious pursuit of long-term pedagogical goals, such as the creation of conceptual linkages between theories and real-world examples, better learning and retention, and adding meaning to what is studied (Cherney 2008; Kember et al. 2008; Powner and Allendoerfer 2008; Kille et al. 2010).

Incorporating active learning strategies increased my teaching skills. I became more involved in this discussion and included cognitive studies and pedagogical approaches in my research agenda. I realized I could become a more dynamic professor without neglecting my substantive research.

At first, it did increase my workload to prepare classes. That's a natural outcome as I was getting used to new approaches, questions, and other structural formalities. The workload, however, gradually decreased, as I discovered efficiencies in class. Depending on the topic, the number of students, or the expected outcomes, I managed to create different pedagogical environments in class without much effort. I was able to pick from a variety of activities to use in class. In some, I ran simulations and played quick games. In others, I opted to use case studies or structured debates. But one thing was common to all of them. In every class, I structured the reading material within a story, as if I was a Dungeon Master (DM) in a D&D campaign. It sounded like a solid strategy to communicate with my students, as well as to engage them on the topics in the lecture.

I gradually increased my ability to connect theory and practice and transmit it to my students. My classes were getting more crowded and I landed a few job offers before graduating. As IR was becoming a popular major in Brazil, private colleges were looking for new faculty. My reputation of being a good lecturer spread and helped me to get a better, yet still temporary, position.

INSIDE INFORMATION

My teaching methods and philosophy reflect the difficulties I had as a student and the strategies I developed to overcome them. I adopted two main approaches to my classes that eventually became my style of teaching, as well as helped me to overcome my discomfort of public speaking: telling a story as a way to engage students and using pop culture references to illustrate the contents. These two aspects characterize my classes and students know beforehand what they will face when they sign up for one of my courses.

I have always struggled with theory. As I have said, abstract concepts rarely made sense to me without adding some context to them. Beginning in high school, I learned that I need to connect what I am studying to applied situations, either referring to the real world or to the not-so-real-but-still-relatable fantasy world. When I started teaching, I tried to replicate these strategies for my students, using my experience as a DM to create learning narratives. I spent a lot of time playing D&D during high school. I always liked to be the DM to control the destiny of the players and tweak the rules according to my will and humor. And, man, I was good at that.

A noticeable quality of my courses is that they are structured as a long narrative. I like to call it "story-telling teaching." Since the first time I lectured, back when I was a TA, I realized any session could be structured as a part of a campaign. The audience is looking for a narrative that will catch their attention. In the same fashion, students are willing to be entertained, to experience different emotions. The power to do so rests on the hands of the narrator, the lecturer, the DM. Instead of describing elves, dwarves, and dragons, I play with concepts such as deterrence, peace, and security dilemma. These concepts play a key role in my courses and they should be treated accordingly: their legends (i.e., their description and their role in the discipline) were told to the folks and they battled other concepts and ideas for glory (or perhaps dominance in a rival debate).

Teachers, as well as DMs, are in charge of the whole experience. Both teaching and DMing develop your ability to grip an audience and keep them involved with your story. You learn how to mix the ideas, elements, and descriptions available for a class/game session and turn it into a coherent narrative in real time. Being a DM helped me to identify quickly which structures benefit my story and what does not work with my players, I mean, students.

It may sound nerdy,[2] but it helps students to get involved with the course contents. They create expectations on the topics and become more open to new ideas. They even try to guess what is coming up next. Young students, especially freshmen, are not used to the vocabulary or the demands of college courses. By creating a narrative and telling stories in class, I am able to ease the transition from high school to college while I introduce more complex discussions and get them prepared for advanced courses.

Please don't get me wrong. I don't consider "making students feel good about themselves and bringing joy to the world" to be a part of my job description. I do consider, however, that, as much as entertainers do, lecturers need to engage students and keep them with you while you walk them through your narrative—or the contents of your course. Teaching is a job that demands empathy and professors should be able to establish a relationship with their students in class. That explains my choice to be a DM in the discipline.

Much like a D&D campaign, every class is structured as a story, either real or invented. I first introduce students to the main aspect of a given topic—"the plot." The underlying goal in presenting students with the plot is to describe the main topics and concepts of a given session as characters. This part of the class is structured as a regular lecture, when I highlight the background of our heroes as a way to create a context where the characters will perform. It takes around 15–20 minutes to create the right atmosphere and then I move to the next part of the class.

The next step is to give life and agency to the characters. This is done by creating a side story for these characters based on people students know or even friends of mine. All my stories are either true or inserted from a pop culture reference, which helps students create meaningful connections with the situation described. Students get involved with the narratives to the degree that they can relate to the stories. That is why I like to add references to pop culture. The use of songs, cartoons, and movies do impact how students comprehend and translate the definitions and ideas of the class into operational concepts they may apply to real-life situations—or something close to it.

I use storytelling to try to explore students' perceptions and emotions. Sometimes the narrative involves humor; many times I keep them

---

[2] I must confess I named the sections of this chapter after the chapters of Tolkien's *The Hobbit*. Is this nerdy enough?

interested by creating an environment that resembles a thriller movie. Most of the time, students are anxious to find out what is going to happen next. In some cases, I add a plot twist to the narrative, something that creates an uncomfortable situation and leads them to question the validity or the relevance of what they are studying.

The conclusion of the lecture coincides with the end of the story. I offer the tools and resources to create that "a-ha moment": they connect the dots and find out the definition of a given idea or the state of a given topic. During the debrief, when they are asked to recall the details they consider most interesting, students usually bring some key aspects that helped them to construct the concept or definition. They do seem to be truly involved with the lecture, especially younger students.

This strategy works as a pedagogical tool in two different ways. First, it provides a break from the intense debates and theoretical approaches. It helps me to take some moments to mentally review how the class is going and what I should do next. Students feel more involved in the discussion and can easily refer to the idea we are discussing. Secondly, it refers to something students can relate to in order to show them that the idea/event is not that distant or abstract. Students realize that it is possible to learn and to build knowledge in any situation.

THE LAST STAGE

"Things should be made as simple as possible—not simpler" (Jackson 2011: p. xii). This principle is frequently neglected based on our expectations of what a scholar should be or represent. But that is exactly what we, as teachers, should aim for. Many early career scholars do not think about a teaching philosophy unless they are writing a piece for a job application. By and large, we teach as we are told to or as we are used to.

The advice I got when I was a TA led me to focus on what I teach and how I teach. It made me realize that I could do a lot more if I were able to understand how I learn in order to help others learn. As a result, I got involved with and developed my way of storytelling teaching. It helped me to be a better teacher and to enjoy what I do a lot more. Even if this method does not fit everyone's profile, the experience of developing your own strategies based on who you are may be beneficial to early career scholars.

REFERENCES

Cherney, Isabelle D. 2008. The Effects of Active Learning on Students' Memories for Course Content. *Active Learning in Higher Education* 9 (2): 152–171. https://doi.org/10.1177/1469787408090841.

Jackson, Patrick Thaddeus. 2011. *The Conduct of Inquiry in International Relations: Philosophy of Science and Its Implications for the Study of World Politics*, The New International Relations. London/New York: Routledge.

Kember, David, Amber Ho, and Celina Hong. 2008. The Importance of Establishing Relevance in Motivating Student Learning. *Active Learning in Higher Education* 9 (3): 249–263. https://doi.org/10.1177/1469787408095849.

Kille, Kent J., Matthew Krain, and Jeffrey S. Lantis. 2008. Active Learning across Borders: Lessons from an Interactive Workshop in Brazil. *International Studies Perspectives* 9 (4): 411–429. https://doi.org/10.1111/j.1528-3585.2008.00345.x.

———. 2010. The State of the Active Teaching and Learning Literature. In *The International Studies Encyclopedia*, ed. Robert A. Denemark, 1–18. Malden: Blackwell Publishing. https://doi.org/10.1093/acrefore/9780190846626.013.427.

Lantis, Jeffrey S., Kent J. Kille, and Matthew Krain. 2018. *The State of the Active Teaching and Learning Literature*. Vol. 1. Oxford University Press. https://doi.org/10.1093/acrefore/9780190846626.013.427.

Powner, Leanne C., and Michelle G. Allendoerfer. 2008. Evaluating Hypotheses about Active Learning. *International Studies Perspectives* 9 (1): 75–89. https://doi.org/10.1111/j.1528-3585.2007.00317.x.

Valença, Marcelo M., and Cristina Yumie Aoki Inoue. 2017. Contribuições do Aprendizado Ativo ao Estudo das Relações Internacionais nas Universidades Brasileiras. *Meridiano 47 - Journal of Global Studies* 18: 1–15. https://doi.org/10.20889/M47e18008.

Valiente, Carolina. 2008. Are Students Using the 'Wrong' Style of Learning?: A Multicultural Scrutiny for Helping Teachers to Appreciate Differences. *Active Learning in Higher Education* 9 (1): 73–91. https://doi.org/10.1177/1469787407086746.

Swimming, Not Sinking: Pedagogical Creativity and the Road to Becoming an Effective IR Teacher

Gigi Gokcek

Current institution: small private comprehensive university
Typical classroom setting: small lecture classes (25–30 students), with some smaller seminars of 10 or fewer
Typical pedagogical approach: combination of lecture and interactive learning (discussion, activities and other engaged learning techniques).
Disciplinary identity: primarily IR, with some comparative politics, but very interdisciplinary/international studies

The Accidental Professor

As an undergraduate majoring in Political Science and Spanish, the last thing I could have ever predicted is that someday I would become a college professor. At the time, my university did not have an international relations (IR) major. But my passion for it was always present because as a child immigrant, I was fascinated with comparative political systems and

G. Gokcek (✉)
Dominican University of California, San Rafael, CA, USA
e-mail: gigi.gokcek@dominican.edu

© The Author(s) 2020
J. Frueh (ed.), *Pedagogical Journeys through World Politics*,
Political Pedagogies, https://doi.org/10.1007/978-3-030-20305-4_19

foreign relations between countries. I thrived in my major courses and selected cocurricular experiences that reflected my love for IR. While I respected and admired all of my professors, I never imagined as an 18–22-year-old that I could join their ranks. Instead, I set upon a path to pursue a career in the foreign policy bureaucracy. I earned a master's degree in international policy studies and secured a graduate fellowship in the intelligence community, which eventually led to a job offer. Yet, I did not believe that a career in intelligence alone could fulfill my quest for greater knowledge. To satisfy my curiosity, I enrolled in a doctoral program in Political Science.

My doctoral program, like most, was designed to help graduate students become productive scholars and secure tenure-track appointments. Initially, this aspect of a doctoral program did not resonate with me because my plan after earning the Ph.D. was to return to the intelligence community with all the knowledge I had acquired. Three weeks into my program, I realized it was unlikely that I would return. Academia spoke to my constant need to learn. Granted, graduate school was not a cakewalk, as I spent many sleepless nights writing papers and preparing for comprehensive exams. In addition to coursework, my program included monthly professional skills fora, with the aim of helping graduates prepare for the academic profession. Most of the tips we acquired were geared toward research, not teaching. As a result, I did not think much about the role teaching plays in the profession. I was intellectually aware that teaching was part of a faculty member's workload, but the message I received was that without publications, there would not be any academic job or tenure. Throughout the years, I remained focused on this notion that it was research that was going to help me land the coveted tenure-track job and earn tenure later on. If I had been on a path to seek employment at a research university this would have been the case certainly. It was not my path though, and once I realized I would not return to the federal government, I decided to pursue a job at a small liberal arts college or private comprehensive university.

In retrospect, I should have realized sooner that a job at a liberal arts college or private university meant that teaching would be the primary focus to secure employment and tenure. Fortunately, I enjoyed teaching very much. The first time I stepped into a classroom, I did so without any experience. It was the beginning of my second year in the doctoral program. I had been assigned as a teaching assistant (TA) for an upper level US Foreign Policy course. The course had approximately 80–100 students, which was considered small. I was one of only two TA's assigned to the course. Whereas this was my first time, the other TA was a more seasoned teacher. My lack of experience was evident during lecture. While the other TA sat in the back and hardly wrote down anything, I was always in the front row with all of the other eager undergraduates taking copious notes. I did not want to miss anything in case the students in my discussion sections would ask me a question that I would have to answer. So my own journey into teaching IR began like a newborn baby being thrown into a swimming pool. As the proverbial saying goes, I had to "sink or swim" to survive.

Today, I am a confident professor with 20 years of teaching experience behind me. In this essay, I share the rest of my journey, from that first time I stepped into a classroom to becoming *Teacher of the Year* prior to tenure. As I narrate my experience, I discuss the lessons I learned that helped transform me into the experienced teacher that I am today. The first section describes the early years in the classroom, including my transition from a TA in graduate school to entering the academic job market. In this section, I provide the teaching philosophy I developed and relied upon while on the job market. The second section focuses on carrying out that teaching philosophy while adjusting to a new role as an assistant professor in a tenure-track position. On-the-job training paved the way for me to become a more secure teacher of international politics. However, as I write in the third section, it was not until I gained tenure that I became more critical of my teaching and I began embarking on a more out-of-the-box thinking in the classroom. Relying on my passion for movies, I discovered an innovative pedagogical technique to teach IR. The success I found with this technique inspired me to communicate it to others through pedagogical scholarship. Twenty years into my career, I view my teaching philosophy through an entirely different lens, built on the many mistakes and victories I gained over time. I have adopted ideas borrowed not only from my professors while I was in college, but the colleagues who I have come to know across multiple disciplines and institutions. I close out the essay with some tips for those just starting out in the classroom as well others who are looking for ways to invigorate their IR courses during the latter phase of their academic career.

TEACHING WITHOUT TRAINING: FORMULA FOR SUCCESS?

Many doctoral students who step into a university/college classroom for the first time do so with little training. Doctoral programs educate graduate students with the aim that they will become employable and make significant contributions to the body of knowledge in the discipline. Yet Ph.D.'s are expected to be excellent teacher-scholars, upon entry into the job market and throughout their academic careers. Based on my own experience as an undergraduate, I assumed that a good teacher, or rather college professor, was someone who lectured to 500+ students in a large auditorium for an hour. This was my experience and I did not have much else to compare it to. I had one professor in a large introductory course in Political Science of several hundred students who deviated from the norm. He would run up and down the auditorium with the microphone (like talk show host Phil Donahue) posing questions and interacting with as many students in the class as possible. His pedagogical technique seemed effective because no one could hide or show up unprepared for fear of being called upon in front of everyone. Thus, my only gauge for successful non-lecture teaching was this one unique example from college.

Many years later when I stepped into the classroom with zero teaching experience, I could not emulate what I considered teaching success because my section had only 20 students, not hundreds. I recall looking behind me to find someone more senior who could help guide me. Of course, realizing that there was no one else and that I was "it" made that first experience surreal. With all eyes staring at me, I could not grasp immediately that the undergraduates in the room were depending on me to provide some knowledge. In the early days, I would often think to myself, "How am I standing here right now? Why me? What do I know?" What comforted me was the very compelling advice I received from a more senior TA. My lead TA said to all of us newcomers, "No matter how much you think you don't know, you still know more than anyone else in the classroom." I relied on this advice every day teaching and still do. Of course, it also helped that before walking into each class I would tell myself, "Today in the role of professor is Gigi Gokcek." For the one hour or so that I had to be in front of a classroom, I pretended that I was acting as professor and could not turn it off until I exited the room. This mindset seemed to work throughout my first term teaching and the years that followed. I earned high teaching evaluations and was even nominated a few times for best TA. While I did not win any awards, I assumed I was doing well as a teacher because year after year all of my sections fully enrolled, including those at 8 am.

Needless to say, I had no real understanding of pedagogy or learning outcomes as a graduate student. All of that would come much later after I had become an assistant professor. As TA's we knew how to grade large quantities of work and run our sections. No one ever conducted a peer-observation of our teaching. I suppose high teaching evaluation scores were considered an adequate indicator of our abilities as teachers to guarantee future assignments. Given that there was very little instruction or training, I relied on my own instincts to guide me in the classroom. I knew from my experience as an undergraduate to engage with as many students as much as possible. I was organized and prepared as a TA. I would start out each class with a "question of the day" as a way to warm up the students before delving into the substantive material I had to review for that week. I ran my discussion sections replicating the content covered in lectures. I would outline the most important points that I believed the course professor wanted to convey to the students by using the large board behind me. Students seemed to appreciate the interactive format of my sections. I would clarify and review information that might have been too complex for students to easily absorb during lecture. I believed my approach to teaching was the formula for success. The evidence of success was based on the repeat customers I had each term, as well as every new course I was assigned to TA.

The first negative comment I received came early on when a student wrote in one of my teaching evaluations that I seemed to lack confidence. This was one of the first comments to sting because I was unaware that students could see through my own inexperience as a teacher. From then on, I told myself never to let on if I felt uncertain about anything and always act as though I knew what I am talking about. But I also had this constant reoccurring nightmare that I would have an unruly class that I could not gain control of because the students perceived me as an instructor lacking confidence.

Fortunately, aside from the occasional bad dream or complaint over a grade, I rarely encountered much negativity in the classroom and in my teaching evaluations. However, as a female TA, I faced some unique challenges that my male counterparts did not encounter. Sometimes students would comment on my appearance during class or in the evaluations, instead of focusing on the content/organization of the course and my ability to teach. I assumed it was because I was young and approachable. Yet it concerned me too, because I wondered if the students did not perceive me as a serious teacher and future academic. I struggled to find a balance between appearing serious yet approachable as I continued to develop my teaching philosophy. My teaching philosophy at the time was based on five principles that I believed accurately captured my attitude toward students and learning.

- *A boundless intellectual curiosity;*
- *Strong enthusiasm for teaching;*
- *A passion for motivating students inside and outside of the classroom;*
- *A desire to offer well structured, rigorous, substantive and innovative courses; and*
- *A belief that any student can rise to a challenge with hard work and positive encouragement.*

When I revisit my teaching philosophy today, I am humored by it because it seems somewhat naïve. My reaction does not take away from these five principles that still hold true for me today. I have intellectual curiosity, especially for global politics. Otherwise I would not be a professor of IR. Indeed, I am still very enthusiastic about teaching IR. In fact, I often tell students "this is my favorite course, even if I won the lottery, I would volunteer my time to teach IR to anyone who is interested." I am passionate about motivating students, or I could not have maintained a 14-year career at predominantly teaching- and student-centered academic institutions. I believe all of my courses throughout the years have been structured, rigorous, substantive and at times even innovative. For a few years, I even had a reputation for being a "tough" professor. Last but not least, I have never abandoned this idea that all students can rise to a challenge through hard work and positive encouragement. I witnessed students with lower grade point averages in high school secure graduate program admission in IR-related fields at elite universities. Thus, my early teaching philosophy remained salient throughout my career. What it did not take into account was some of the challenges that were to come once in academia. The next section delves further into these.

Learning to Teach IR on the Job

Prior to securing a tenure-track job, I had never taught my own course. Somehow, all the years working as a conscientious TA with a sensible teaching philosophy enabled me to land two tenure-track appointments, the first of which was at a university's School of International Studies. On-campus interviews not only involved job talks, but also teaching demonstrations. I was surprised to learn that teaching demos were required because at my doctoral institution this was not the norm for academic job candidates.

Now that I have been in the profession for 14 years at a teaching-centered institution, I am surprised this did not occur to me as a graduate student because it is the norm at most colleges and universities across the United States. I spent more time preparing for the teaching demos instead of my own research talk. I was quite familiar with my doctoral dissertation and comfortable presenting on it. But the teaching demos varied from foreign policy to the European Union to Middle East politics. So I had to make adjustments for each campus. I approached each teaching demonstration in the same way I had treated my sections as a TA. I was organized, thoughtful and determined to engage with students. Although my approach was purely instinctual, having sat on several search committees, I can now state those elements are key. But doing a one-off teaching demonstration is not the same as teaching one's own semester-long course.

Prior to entering the job market, I had developed sample course syllabi modeled on my own professors' courses. I was inspired by different styles and managed to put together a syllabus that my dissertation chair deemed "excellent" after reviewing it.

Another faculty mentor said to me, "This syllabus and course organization is better than what I have seen from some of my colleagues do around here." With that kind of encouragement, I felt confident as a teacher on the job market. Once I landed the job and had to teach my own courses in international studies, I knew I had to replicate the sample syllabi I had used in my applications. Each course syllabus took time and effort. As a TA this was not something I had to worry about because the professor provided the syllabus. I searched other IR syllabi to determine how to organize the course, the selection of readings to assign, and the tools I would need to use to evaluate student academic performance. But no one told me that one class session could take up eight hours of preparation or that I had to include learning outcomes in a syllabus. Suddenly, I was faced with a new problem, "What is a learning outcome?"

Through trial and error, and by mimicking the ways of my professors I supported as a teaching assistant, I began my academic career. Initially it was all about getting through the material ahead of the students to make sure I covered everything in class I had indicated on the syllabus. The syllabus is the contract with the students, so I felt obligated to deliver on it. Yet, at times, the burden of having to deliver on it got in the way of my creativity in the classroom. My professors relied on overhead projectors, and PowerPoint. This was by far the "fanciest" teaching technique I had observed in the IR classroom. Up until that point, the most innovative teaching I had observed took place within the context of foreign language courses where students watched movies, sang songs, interviewed their peers or delivered presentations. When appropriate, and especially with smaller IR classes, I would adapt what I had observed in my foreign language classes. I felt good about my teaching style because most of the student feedback was positive. Once in a while, I would still receive the rare negative comment about "going off on tangents" or "spending too much time telling students to do better" or "assigning too much reading." The year after I won *Teacher of the Year* at my university, and earned tenure, one student wrote in my evaluations, "She does not know how to teach, she needs to be trained." This comment was not only a surprise, and slightly amusing given the years of experience I had behind me, but it also stung again. As an associate professor, I did not anticipate this type of comment. While some colleagues told me to shrug it off, remarking, "It is just one comment among so many...," it still resonated because I kept asking myself, "what did I do in the course that made a student write what s/he did?" I wondered if I had become arrogant post-tenure and was not as thoughtful or sensitive to student needs? Had I become stale? Was I not being creative enough? Did the old techniques no longer work for a new generation? It was apparent to me that teaching about IR theory in an organized manner, covering the readings carefully, explaining complex ideas thoughtfully, and grading papers/exams promptly was no longer enough to be considered a good teacher. I had to find another way to convey knowledge to undergraduates of the digital age in order to achieve teaching excellence. I found the answer in my second passion: big popcorn movies.

IR AT THE MOVIES: A NEW PEDAGOGICAL APPROACH

During my second year teaching international relations, one day I found myself struggling to convey the dangers of nuclear proliferation to a generation of post-Cold War undergraduates. I could not come up with a recent real-world example that could resonate in the same way it had for my generation. In my quest to explain why arming every country in the world with nuclear weapons was a bad idea, suddenly I recalled a line out of one of my favorite movies, *Crimson Tide* (1995). The movie takes place on a nuclear submarine when the first officer, Lieutenant Commander Hunter (played by Denzel Washington) engages in a mutiny in an effort to stop the Captain (played by Gene Hackman) from launching missiles before confirming his orders. In one scene Hunter and Captain Ramsay engage in a debate about the meaning of war à la Carl von Clausewitz. The highly intellectual Hunter says to Ramsay, "In the nuclear world, the true enemy is war itself." The students seemed fascinated by Hunter's quote and asked if they could view the movie since they were all too young to have seen it. I made an impromptu decision to show the movie in the next class. What followed foreshadowed a new pedagogical approach to teaching IR.

Teaching IR with movies is not a new idea. Many others have recommended it over the years (Engert and Spencer 2009; Gerner 1988; Gregg 1998, 1999; Kuzma and Haney 2001; Lieberfeld 2007; Lindley 2001; Simpson and Kaussler 2009; Sunderland et al. 2009; Swimelar 2013; Weber 2001). However, I turned the application of movies in the classroom on its head. Instead of relying on the movie to teach, I required students to identify the scenes that emulated the IR theories and concepts. Consulting more pedagogically knowledgeable colleagues at my institution, I drew on Bloom's taxonomy to develop an active learning technique (Bloom et al. 1956). One might assume that relying on movies is a lazy approach to teaching. But as I quickly found out that it actually entails a significant amount of preparation. Prior to finalizing the course syllabus, I had to determine the most appropriate time in the semester to show the movie. In IR, my goal is to teach students the ability to apply theory to different scenarios. I had to decide whether to show the movie after covering all of the theoretical approaches (realism, liberalism, constructivism, feminism, Marxism, etc.), or toward the end of the semester when students had learned the application of theory to contemporary world issues like nuclear proliferation, human rights, climate change, terrorism, etc.? While the timing varied, depending upon the course, for IR the movie-viewing activity took place toward the end of the term. Often, I selected unconventional movies, big popcorn flicks that one would not automatically associate with an educational setting. For example, I selected movies from the *Fast and the Furious*, Marvel and DC comic books, *Star Trek*, and *Star Wars* franchises, to name a few. My choice of movie deviated from the norm because these were not the traditional IR films (like *Dr. Strangelove*). Through observation, I learned that students had an easier time applying IR theory to movies that they enjoyed. Since the students were *not* told in advance which scenes illustrated particular theories, this encouraged them to think more critically. I designed worksheets that they could rely on while viewing the movie. Before starting the movie, I would engage the entire class in a discussion to review course content and after, I would break them up into smaller groups to share the scenes they identified that illustrated a particular theory or concept.

For many years now, this is the pedagogical technique that epitomizes my approach to teaching. Just as I stumbled into an academic career, I also did so with this innovative technique using unconventional movies to teach IR. I have written about it in several venues (Gokcek 2016; Gokcek and Howard 2013) and presented it at professional meetings. Students anticipate and anxiously await the revelation of the movie for a particular course each semester. Alumni have written to me many years later to say, "I recall prisoner's dilemma because of the ferry scene in *The Dark Knight*." According to Halpern and Hakel (2003), "the purpose of formal education is transfer." In essence, educators constantly need to keep in mind that they "are teaching toward sometime in the future" when students are no longer in their classrooms. How and what professors teach has to enable students to transfer what they learned from their teachers to the unpredictable real-world "tests" that they will encounter (Halpern and Hakel). In order to optimize their learning potential to achieve student success, professors must build interaction into the classroom after laying down "a solid foundation of skills and concepts" through lectures, selected readings and other assignments (Hoover 2008). I believe one way to achieve this is through the use of unconventional movies as pedagogical tools. Yet movies alone are not the only option, as I point out in the final section.

THE CONFIDENT PROFESSOR

Fourteen years into my career and with 20 years of teaching under my belt, I have a renewed philosophy. The five core principles that made up my teaching philosophy early on still hold true. However, now I can add more based on the lessons I have learned. Today I believe teaching excellence entails all of the following:

1. Organization before, during, and after the term
2. Innovation, creativity, imagination and fearlessness in the classroom
3. Interdisciplinary teaching and collaboration with colleagues across campus
4. Clear and constant communication with students throughout the course
5. Openness to adapting the latest technology and multimedia source
6. Interaction with the community to maximize student civic learning
7. Incorporating pop culture to increase classroom engagement
8. Finding effective learning strategies to reach mixed level students

For veteran teachers all of the above will look very familiar. It is less obvious for doctoral students entering academia, especially those who may be seeking tenure-track appointments at teaching/student-centered academic institutions. At institutions like mine, faculty may be asked to teach courses outside of their discipline. Given that promotion and tenure is impossible without teaching excellence, professors strive to achieve these eight standards and more, while balancing scholarship and service. There are a variety of professional development opportunities on and off-campus for faculty yearning to become more effective teachers throughout their careers. These include ALIAS, the Active Learning in International Affairs Section of the International Studies Association, which facilitates interaction among teachers of IR through conference presentations and workshops. The American Political Science Association, annually host a Teaching and Learning Conference and provides opportunities for academics to publish pedagogy articles in *PS: Political Science and Politics*, and *Journal of Political Science Education*. There are many other places one can find resources for college teachers, including on-line at *Active Learning in Political Science* (activelearningps.com), or through the Association of American Colleges & Universities. The point is that no matter the stage in one's career, there are countless ways to learn to become an excellent teacher. After all, teachers of IR do not merely talk about current events in the classroom. We are productive teachers motivated not only by our own passion for global politics, but also by our own students who will someday be the actors in that world.

REFERENCES

Active Learning in Political Science. Blog. http://activelearningps.com/
Bloom, Benjamin S. (Ed.), M.D. Englhart, E.J. Furst, W.H. Hill, and D.R. Krathwohol. 1956. *Taxonomy of Educational Objectives: Handbook I: Cognitive Domain.* New York: David McKay.
Engert, Stephan, and Alexander Spencer. 2009. International Relations at the Movies: Teaching and Learning about International Politics Through Film. *Perspectives: Central European Review of International Affairs* 17 (1): 83–104.
Gerner, Deborah. 1988. Films and the Teaching of Foreign Policy. *Foreign Policy Analysis Notes* 15 (3): 3–6.
Gokcek, Gigi. 2016. Unconventional Movies as Conventional Pedagogical Tools: The Dark Knight. *Active Learning in Political Science*, September 9.
Gokcek, Gigi, and Alison Howard. 2013. Movies to the Rescue: Keeping the Cold War Relevant for Twenty-First-Century Students. *Journal of Political Science Education* 9 (4): 436–452. https://doi.org/10.1080/15512169.2013.835561.
Gregg, Robert W. 1998. *International Relations on Film.* Boulder: Lynne Rienner Publishers.
———. 1999. The Ten Best Films About International Relations. *World Policy Journal* 16 (2): 129–124.
Halpern, Diane F., and Milton D. Hakel. July 2003. Applying the Science of Learning to the University and Beyond: Teaching for Long-Term Retention and Transfer. *Change: The Magazine of Higher Learning* 35 (4): 36–41. https://doi.org/10.1080/00091380309604109.
Hoover, Linda. 2008. Thoughts on Higher Education. *PRO* 25 (2): 1–2.
Kuzma, Lynn M., and Patrick J. Haney. 2001. And . . . Action! Using Film to Learn about Foreign Policy. *International Studies Perspectives* 2 (1): 33–50. https://doi.org/10.1111/1528-3577.00036.
Lieberfeld, Daniel. 2007. Teaching about War Through Film and Literature. *PS: Political Science & Politics* 40 (03): 571–574. https://doi.org/10.1017/S1049096507070837.
Lindley, Dan. 2001. What I Learned Since I Stopped Worrying and Studied the Movie: A Teaching Guide to Stanley Kubrick's Dr. Strangelove. *Political Science & Politics* 34 (03): 663–667. https://doi.org/10.1017/S1049096501001068.
Scott, Tony. 1995. *Crimson Tide.* Hollywood: Hollywood Pictures.

Simpson, Archie W., and Bernd Kaussler. 2009. IR Teaching Reloaded: Using Films and Simulations in the Teaching of International Relations. *International Studies Perspectives* 10 (4): 413–427. https://doi.org/10.1111/j.1528-3585.2009.00386.x.

Sunderland, Sheri, Jonathan C. Rothermel, and Adam Lusk. 2009. Making Movies Active: Lessons from Simulations. *PS: Political Science & Politics* 42 (03): 543–547. https://doi.org/10.1017/S1049096509090878.

Swimelar, Safia. 2013. Visualizing International Relations: Assessing Student Learning Through Film. *International Studies Perspectives* 14 (1): 14–38. https://doi.org/10.1111/j.1528-3585.2012.00467.x.

Weber, Cynthia. 2001. The Highs and Lows of Teaching IR Theory: Using Popular Films for Theoretical Critique. *International Studies Perspectives* 2 (3): 281–287. https://doi.org/10.1111/1528-3577.00058.

Strategies of a Boring Teacher

J. Samuel Barkin

Current institution: large public research university
Typical classroom setting: classes ranging from 6 to 300
Typical pedagogical approach: pedagogical approaches vary with class sizes, levels, and topics
Disciplinary identity: International Relations Theory, International Organization, Environmental Politics

I'm not a natural teacher. I don't have the sort of natural charisma that will hold people's attention, and I can't exude the sort of infectious enthusiasm that will bring a room full of people along. I am the sort of person who often self-selects as an academic; I'm drawn to the material because I find it to be intrinsically interesting. Furthermore, I'm by nature a theorist, interested in the concepts we use for international politics as much as (or more than) the day-to-day minutia of those politics. I have no problem teaching people like me, people who don't need to be convinced that international relations (IR) theory is useful and are drawn to it by the material itself rather than the presentation. Unfortunately, people like me are a tiny proportion of most undergraduate audiences. I came into teaching woefully unequipped to teach everyone else.

J. S. Barkin (✉)
University of Massachusetts Boston, Boston, MA, USA
e-mail: Samuel.Barkin@umb.edu

© The Author(s) 2020
J. Frueh (ed.), *Pedagogical Journeys through World Politics*,
Political Pedagogies, https://doi.org/10.1007/978-3-030-20305-4_20

233

My undergraduate experience was at a large public university, where pedagogy was not at a premium. So my introduction to undergraduate teaching involved being lectured at in rooms with hundreds of other students. The professors that made the biggest impression on me at the time were the charismatic ones, but I can't replicate that. Graduate school was, of course, different, but the techniques of teaching and learning that work in small graduate seminars do not translate directly to undergraduate teaching, with classes that are generally larger and students who are not necessarily as committed to a disciplinary education. In other words, I had no viable model or template on which to base a successful undergraduate teaching style once I started in the classroom.

This became clear to me fairly quickly. Students didn't think I was a terrible teacher, they just thought I was boring. And they were quite comfortable expressing this opinion in teaching evaluations. How to make my teaching more interesting? By making it less centered on me. There are a few easy ways to do this, such as showing films, or getting students arguing about the politics of the day. But the risk with these sorts of activities is that they take the students away from what I find interesting in the material, and from what I feel I should be teaching them. Having students watch films is easy, but teaching those films, connecting them to general concepts, is hard. Getting students to argue about the politics of the day is easy, but connecting those discussions to general concepts is, again, hard.

This points to a tension that has motivated my thinking about teaching international relations for the past two decades, the tension between the interest in current events that brings a majority of undergraduates into international relations classes and the conceptual tools of international relations theory that I feel it is my job to teach them. Phrased in other terms, this is the tension between lecturing (lots of focus on conceptual tools, but boring) and discussion (more engaging, but hard to keep focused on conceptual tools). Charismatic lecturers can deal with this tension by making their lectures engaging enough to hold students interest. Teachers who are really good at Socratic engagement with students can keep the focus on conceptual tools by keeping control of discussions (in suitably small classes). I'm not particularly adept at either. So how then to address the tension?

The solutions I've found came to me through conversations with other academics, both those more senior and those more naturally gifted at teaching than I, and through processes of trial and error. I cannot stress enough the benefits of these conversations (which continue to this day) to my teaching. Find a few people in your field with whom you are comfortable talking about teaching, and talk to them on a regular basis. Bounce your ideas off them, and in turn be a sounding board for their ideas; you will benefit from both directions of the conversation. These should not be one-off conversations. They should span careers, because even after one has found one's style, one can still continue to improve one's teaching. The profession is not set up to encourage such conversations, however. You have to make the effort to find your pedagogical community.

SMALL GROUPS

One answer to the question of how to teach that works for me is small groups. By small I mean groups of anywhere from two to five students, depending on the exercise and circumstances. Groups can be assigned randomly, or can be constructed by the instructor for particular purposes (e.g. putting the quieter students together in a group so that they actually get a chance to talk, or making sure that all groups have a range of skill levels represented to increase the chances that the weaker students learn from the stronger ones). Particular groups can be left intact over a range of exercises, so that students develop a comfort level within their group, or can be changed around for different exercises, so that students are exposed up close to as wide a range of views as possible. Getting these decisions about group composition right requires a combination of careful thinking about what the goal of each exercise is, and experience with what has worked in the past.

Small-group work has two key advantages over bigger classroom discussions. The first is that the students are talking directly to each other, not to (or through) the instructor, and not to the bigger audience of the class as a whole. Students are generally more willing to participate openly and thoughtfully in a small group of peers, where they do not feel they are performing to an audience and do not fear making fools of themselves in front of the instructor. Students in groups of up to five, in my experience, will all participate if both the goal of the exercise and their role in it are clear. Any larger and conversation in the groups risks being hijacked by the talkative students who inevitably dominate large-group discussions. In other words, in (well-designed) small-group exercises, each student is having an active learning experience, interactively engaging with the material, rather than passively absorbing inputs from the instructor (via lecture, film, etc.), or other, more vocal students. Finally, many small-group exercises scale well; they can work almost as well with 50 groups of 5 students in a class of 250 as with 5 groups in a class of 25.

The second advantage of small-group work over bigger classroom discussions is that they can be designed quite specifically to highlight individual concepts. Lectures, of course, can highlight individual concepts, but in lectures students are being told about the concept, rather than developing a sense of it through practice. Bigger group discussions can be useful in drawing out concepts, but are more difficult to focus as precisely. Longer-term exercises involving the class as a whole, such as negotiation simulations in which each member of the class has a different role, can be effective pedagogical tools, but require major commitments not only of instructor effort, but of class time—this sort of simulation is something that the entire course is often built around. But small-group exercises can be short and to the point. An effective targeted exercise can take as little as 15 minutes of class time, meaning that one can have a number of exercises, along with significant lecture time to contextualize and connect the concepts that the exercises highlight, in one class meeting. This allows the instructor to highlight particular concepts and mix methods of instruction without too great a commitment to any one exercise or pedagogical tool.

In this second advantage lies an effective way to address the tension between current events and IR concepts. The small-group exercises can be used to highlight concepts, lectures can be used to contextualize those concepts, and large-group, class-wide discussions can be used to explore the application of those concepts to the events of the day. (Small-group exercises can also be used to apply concepts to events, but I find this to be pedagogically effective only if the exercise is structured around a clear answer or set of answers—small-group meetings that allow students to argue about current events without instructor supervision and without a clear end-point generally lose sight of the relevant concepts that they are supposed to be focusing on fairly quickly.) Having students develop through practice a feeling of ownership of IR concepts generally makes them more willing to think about current events through the lenses of those concepts.

When I say IR concepts, I am referring to a wide range of ideas that can be used to explain international relations and that can be meaningfully isolated, distilled, and simplified for a short, stylized exercise. Such concepts could include the difference between absolute and relative gains, the relationship between economic core and periphery countries, the meaning of a commons, the gender assumptions implicit in specific international treaties, and deterrence, to pick an unrepresentative (and somewhat random) sample. The instructor needs to keep in mind in designing exercises what the core analytical point of the exercise is, and then needs to find a stylized mechanism through which to make that point. Often the point can be reinforced by rewarding students within groups who do the exercise most effectively, either by identifying them as winners, or by giving them material rewards (chocolate always works well), or by setting up competition between groups to come up with the most efficient solutions, depending on the particular exercise.

Designing exercises of this kind takes practice, and even with experience doing so, new exercises do not always work well, or as intended, on the first try. However, each exercise is only a small commitment of class time and student attention. If one 15-minute, or even half an hour, exercise falls flat, the instructor can still salvage the class. Furthermore, the experience is not wasted, because exercises are reusable. Figure out what failed to work, fix it, and use the exercise again next year. After a few years, one finds oneself with an expanding set of exercises that are tested and perfected (or at least improved), that one can draw on, mix and match, and incorporate into class plans with fairly little effort. So although designing and honing exercises is an up-front investment of time (granted that investment is early in one's teaching career, when one often does not have the time), it is an investment that pays off in the medium term.

To this point, I have been talking about a particular kind of class exercise, one that is short, generally contained within one or two class meetings, and breaks up students into small groups that each tend to do the same exercise at the same time. I am arguing that such exercises are useful, particularly for bridging the gap between analytic concepts and current events, and particularly for teachers who, for whatever reason, find that making themselves the center of attention in the classroom is not pedagogically effective. I am not, however, arguing that such exercises are the only useful technique, or that they should be used exclusively. I noted above that they work best when interspersed with whole-class activities. But they also work well when combined with a variety of other techniques for involving students in class.

Two such techniques, both alluded to earlier in this chapter, are group projects and large-scale simulations. By group projects, I mean exercises that span a significant portion of the semester, and which result in a graded product. In the context of teaching IR, I find that these kinds of projects work best when explicitly policy-related, and when the group structure accurately reflects how policy is made. Such projects can work well when they are structured enough that groups can't go too far off track (e.g. by having pieces of the project due in stages) and when students are given the chance to comment on their role and the roles of their colleagues within the group.

By large-scale simulations, I mean exercises that either take up entire classes or are spread out across the semester, and which involve the entire class as one group. These can be quite pedagogically effective, but represent a major commitment both of class time and of instructor effort. I find they work best in classes that are focused on specific issues or institutions that can be effectively simulated, such as climate change negotiations or the Security Council, rather than more generalized classes such as Introduction to IR or International Political Economy.

There are two other techniques I use frequently that I also find to be reliably effective. The first is assigning each student responsibility for being the expert in something specific. In a foreign policy class each student can be assigned a country; in a class on international organizations (IOs) each student can be assigned an IO. When specific organizational characteristics come up in class, each student is expected to be able to fit their organization into the characteristic, whether it is the responsiveness of their country's foreign policy to nongovernmental organization pressure or the structure of their IO's budget. This technique does not necessarily scale well, however. It works well in seminars and lecture classes that are small enough that everyone's input can be canvassed, but not in larger lecture classes when getting answers from each student would be unwieldy.

The other technique is to ask students to send me two or three questions about the week's readings before class and have them compare and contrast their questions in small-group discussions. Each small group then collectively decides which of their questions they would like the class as a whole to discuss. This technique works best in great-works type courses, in which the focus of the class is on particular readings themselves rather than on the issues that those readings highlight. It also works best in seminar-sized classes, in which the whole group can usefully discuss the questions brought forward. In these contexts, when the students collectively decide via a clear process what it is about the readings they want to discuss, they often feel greater ownership of the discussion. The technique has the added advantage of giving the instructor advanced knowledge of what each particular group of students finds most interesting about the readings.

Negotiating Water Pollution

Having discussed small-group-targeted exercises as a general category, the time has come to illustrate it with a specific example. This example, which I co-developed with Elizabeth DeSombre, is designed to highlight the difference between international cooperation over common issues and over directional issues. It is potentially useful in a range of classes, including introductions to international relations, international organization, and international environmental politics. Because it is designed primarily to highlight the negotiating advantage of upstream countries, and the potential political effects of this advantage, it is rigged to make cooperation over commons issues a little easier than is realistic, and cooperation over directional issues more difficult (one can use other exercises to examine the difficulties of commons cooperation).

The exercise is for groups of five students, and has two rounds. In the first part, five countries all border a lake from which they draw their fresh water and into which they dump their pollution. All five countries are of similar size, with similar economies and levels of development. The lake is becoming sufficiently polluted that the costs of pollution (primarily in health effects) are beginning to outweigh the cost of cleaning the effluent flowing into it. This is a classic collective action problem, but it is an iterated game, since countries can monitor the pollution coming out of their neighbors. The solution is straightforward—each country commits to an equivalent level of pollution reduction, with a system of monitoring. In this round, the students can usually negotiate a version of this agreement in 10 minutes or so. Note that this exercise comes with specific numbers for the costs of pollution and pollution mitigation, for the size of the national economies, etc., so that students are negotiating specific commitments, not general principles. But they will do so more quickly if the exercise is designed so that the ideal point of cooperation is a nice round number.

The second round of the exercise is organized around a river rather than a lake. Most of the details of this round, such as the cost of pollution and its mitigation, and the similar economies across countries, remain the same. But the five countries are arrayed on the river from upstream to downstream. So the uppermost country can pollute all it wants without suffering any of the effects on its water, while the country situated where the river meets the sea suffers all the other countries' pollution, without polluting any of them in turn. The three countries in the middle have varying degrees to which they are polluted by upstream countries and pollute downstream.

There is an economically efficient solution to this round (in the Coasian sense), much as there was in the first round. In this solution, downstream states pay the costs of pollution mitigation. Some small groups come to this solution, but most do not. Downstream states often argue in terms of fairness for equal cost-sharing, and upstream states often try to hold downstream states hostage to their ability to pollute. There are threats from upstream states to make the water undrinkable if downstream states don't pay up, and threats from downstream states of economic blockade or war (and the occasional inquiry about nuclear weapons; in this exercise the answer is no). In round one, most groups within a class come to similar results. In round two, the outcome is all over the place, and groups that generate an actual agreement are in the minority.

The final element of the exercise is bringing the results of both rounds back to a discussion of the class as a whole. Each small group is asked to describe their results in both rounds, and, if they failed to come to an agreement, why. This generally opens up a broader discussion of issues like fairness and power in international negotiation. Students who, when told of the difficulties of international cooperation, might have responded that negotiators should have done some seemingly obvious thing (be it cooperation or power projection), are more likely to appreciate the difficulties of navigating national power and international benefit having tried, and often failed, themselves.

In Lieu of a Teaching Philosophy

The sort of technique-based teaching that this exercise is an example of requires some investment in planning. Even more so, it requires careful thinking about what key concepts you as a teacher are trying to get across, and how those concepts might best be learned. Ideally it also involves talking through both teaching goals and techniques with peers; having to explain what you're trying to do to a peer makes you think it through more carefully, before you can embarrass yourself in front of your students. It's a worthwhile investment, though. Designing exercises, once one gets the hang of it, is fun, and turns class preparation from a chore into an intellectual endeavor. In other words, teaching well is hard work, but it is also sufficiently rewarding that it is worth the effort.

That last sentence doesn't sound like much of a teaching philosophy, but it's actually a good start. I can't say much, in general, about how to teach well, beyond the observation that each teacher has different strengths and weaknesses, and in order to teach well a teacher needs to put the effort into finding out what those strengths and weaknesses are, and how to build on the former and ameliorate the latter. In my case, it took several years to figure this out. Still, sometimes I get lazy, and go to class knowing that I can give a pretty-well organized lecture off the cuff about whatever is on the syllabus for that day, and that it will be adequate. And it is generally adequate, but no more. Teaching well means putting in the effort every course, and every class.

In talking about my teaching, I try to avoid platitudes. It is difficult to talk convincingly about one's teaching in general terms, because everyone agrees on those general terms (I have yet to see a teaching statement in a job application that speaks of the need to prevent student engagement in class, for example). Talking about putting in the effort is similarly unconvincing. The way to demonstrate an interest in and commitment to pedagogy in talking about one's teaching is by giving specific examples of what you have done, and would like to do, in class. Describe an exercise, a simulation, an assignment, a mode of class discussion, and its pedagogical background and purpose. In other words, do not talk, in general, about how to teach; talk specifically about how you teach.

As a final note, very little of the discussion in this chapter is specific to international relations per se. IR is an excellent focus for teaching critical thinking, because it brings together such a broad range of social science thinking (and because I find it interesting I can teach it more engagingly), but the pedagogy discussed in this chapter can be applied equally well across the social sciences. Measured over the course of my career, a majority of my teaching has been in IR narrowly defined, but not a large majority; I have also taught environmental politics and policy, political economy, and social science epistemology, among other things. Each has its own challenges, but by and large I bring the same pedagogical approach to each; decide on a specific set of concepts or analytic tools I want the students to take out of the class, and design a set of classroom experiences around it.

CHAPTER 21

The Unexpected Gift: "Oh, and You'll be Responsible for the Model UN Program"

Carolyn M. Shaw

Current institution: large public research university
Typical classroom setting: mid-sized classes, mostly upper division
Typical pedagogical approach: active learning, skills development
Disciplinary identity: International Organization, Conflict Resolution, Human Rights

INTRODUCTION

I remember well my campus interview at the institution where I got my first job. I had given my research talk, met with all the faculty members and some students, and was on my way to the airport with the department chair when he told me, almost as an afterthought, that the position would include serving as the faculty advisor for the Model UN program on campus. As many other job candidates do, I readily agreed that I would be able to meet this expectation should I get the job offer. The truth was, however, that I had never participated in, nor even observed a Model UN conference before. When the job offer came several weeks later, my com-

C. M. Shaw (✉)
Wichita State University, Wichita, KS, USA
e-mail: carolyn.shaw@wichita.edu

© The Author(s) 2020
J. Frueh (ed.), *Pedagogical Journeys through World Politics*,
Political Pedagogies, https://doi.org/10.1007/978-3-030-20305-4_21

mitment to running a Model UN program suddenly became much more real. Looking back today, after nearly two decades of leading the Model UN program on campus, it is hard to believe how much I have gained from this experience. I didn't realize at the time when I was hired how many opportunities and benefits would come from serving as a Model UN faculty advisor. It really has been an unexpected gift.

PLUNGING IN

After my campus interview, and thanks to some sound advice from a mentor, I had the foresight to ask for some support with taking on the Model UN program when I negotiated my job contract. A graduate student at the university who had participated for several years would be my assistant during my first year serving as the faculty advisor. This was tremendously helpful and allowed the program to transition more smoothly to new leadership. My assistant answered innumerable questions as I learned how Model UN worked, and served as a sounding board for my own new ideas about preparing our students for their Model UN conference.

We spent the fall semester recruiting students and training them, and then attended a regional conference in the spring. I sat in the back of the ballroom at the conference and observed the proceedings, taking copious notes and also asking lots of questions of the veteran faculty advisors who were there. It was a bit overwhelming, but also stimulating. All of the rules and procedures that hadn't made sense to me at first suddenly clicked. I was filled with ideas for how I wanted to improve our training process now that I understood what the end goal was. It was a steep learning curve, but it also gave me a greater appreciation for the struggle that new student participants face every year when they join the program. I have further been reminded of this perspective over the years as other new faculty advisors have sought me out for advice as they begin their programs. It is a good reminder for me of how challenging it is to teach any class for the first time, and how important it is to seek input from others as you develop new content and new approaches to instruction.

CURRICULAR DEVELOPMENTS

During my first year as the faculty advisor for the Model UN, I basically adopted the framework that my graduate assistant had used the previous year, recognizing that this was what students were familiar with and having no specific improvements of my own in mind. My second year, I began to make some modifications to the curriculum, requiring revisions to positions papers, not just a submission of a final draft (some of which had not been very polished the previous year). I arranged one-on-one meetings with the students to help them with their research preparations and required them to prepare and deliver ambassadorial speeches prior to attending the conference. While these modifications were improvements, they did not produce the kind of excellence I was hoping for, so I began to think about more robust revisions to the curriculum.

What I came to realize was that most of the student preparations were individualized assignments, whereas the work that they would engage in at the Model UN conferences was all highly interactive with other student delegates. They knew a lot about their research topics, but were not very good at working with other delegates to address global problems collectively. I began to design new, small group activities for each class that would develop a particular skill that the students would use at the conferences (analysis/problem solving, resolution writing, applying rules, and procedures). For example, they would be given a problem on campus (parking, food options at the union, etc.) and asked to identify why it was a problem, what the consequences were to not addressing it, what had been done to resolve it in the past, and what their proposed solution was. This did not require any extensive knowledge on their part, and they got to work creatively with their classmates to address the given problems. The following week, they would be assigned to groups based on the topics they were researching for the conference and asked to do the same kind of analysis. First, they became comfortable analyzing a familiar campus topic, then they used those budding analytical skills and applied them to a global issue. I took the same approach with regard to writing resolutions. Students would first try to draft resolutions on campus topics (upgrading technology in the classrooms, improving library resources, etc.), and would then draft resolutions on their conference committee topics. Writing with multiple participants is a much different process from writing individually, so this group work was quite effective in helping them build the skills they would need to be successful at the conference. Each of the group assignments built upon the previous one, with the culmination being several committee simulations to help the students become comfortable with using the appropriate procedural rules. An added benefit of all of the group activities in class is that there is a lot of group accountability. Students get to see the efforts that their peers are putting into their work and can encourage and mentor each other. The variability in performance also reflects the future reality of colleagues in the workplace, and I think provides a good environment for students to figure out how to work with people who may have greater or lesser skills than they do.

For my first five years, I continued to revise the curriculum, making it gradually more rigorous each year. I thought at one point that I would eventually reach a "perfect" training plan for the delegates, but I have since realized this will never be the case. Each year, I adapt the curriculum, changing the focus or emphasis. Where I might have once seen this as a burden, I now see it as an opportunity. By regularly asking for delegate feedback regarding the most effective exercises and assignments, I'm able to respond to the changing nature of our students over time. Some of these changes in the student body are pretty obvious. With students today being much more adept at finding information on the internet than their predecessors were, I don't need to hold their hand and teach them where to look for good information online. Other changes are related, but less obvious. Since students can look up information with the tap of their phone, they don't spend as much time getting a solid foundational knowledge about many global issues, so it's harder to get them to think about crafting *better* solutions to problems when they are not familiar with failed *past* efforts. This has required spending more time on nuanced analytical skills. They have a lot of information but are not always good at figuring out what it *means.*

My curriculum has also evolved because my own perceptions about the value of Model UN have changed over time. Whereas I once saw the primary benefit as an increased exposure to and knowledge of the larger world (as opposed to a narrow, US-centric perspective), I now view the skills-based components to be critically important to our students. The skills they learn in researching, writing, public speaking, and particularly in consensus building are applicable in nearly any profession they choose to pursue. While a broader worldview is still important, I think the students are looking for ways to market themselves to employers, and the skills-based focus helps them articulate their own marketable strengths. All of these adaptions over the years have helped me stay energized and engaged.

Bureaucratic Hurdles

While I anticipated the academic challenge of figuring out how to prepare my students to be effective Model UN delegates, I was not expecting the bureaucratic hurdles that came from traveling with students. Whereas I had good support from my assistant as well as other faculty advisors at the

Model UN conference, my institution provided very little instruction regarding how to complete the required travel paperwork. I faced the rude discovery that the university only provided reimbursement for travel, not advanced payment. This meant that I had to pay for my own hotel room, as well as my students' rooms, on my own credit card and then file paperwork to get reimbursed. This was a bit nerve-wracking, hoping that my check would come before my credit card payment was due. Further rules about travel in university vans and student waiver forms created an even more daunting environment for a new faculty member to navigate. Although these administrative hurdles have not eased over the years, I have become more familiar with the necessary routines. I see these simply as an annoyance that has to be tolerated in order to achieve the more rewarding goal of allowing students' to attend Model UN conferences.

Program Growth

After surviving my first year as new faculty advisor and learning so much about Model UN, I was determined to see the program grow and thrive. It had been several years since the group had had any faculty advisor and there was lots of room for improvements. The first challenge was to recruit more students to participate. Although the program had been in existence for over 40 years, the current student body was largely unaware of its existence or the benefits of participating as a delegate. I endeavored to learn more about student organizations on campus and signed up to participate in the Welcomefest and other recruitment events. This was modestly successful, but I learned over the years that students are the best recruiters for their peers, so I eventually left these efforts to the returning members of the group. They did a great job telling their friends about their positive Model UN experiences and inviting them to participate.

As the program began to grow, I suddenly had to rethink our travel budget. Whereas all of the delegates had always been able to attend two conferences in the past, a growing number of participants meant a tough decision was needed. Should the program numbers be capped, or should I limit the number of students who could attend the second conference? I requested more funds from student government, but eventually I decided to take everyone to *one* conference, but only a select group to a second conference. This was a hard thing to do because I did not want to create hard feelings in the group, and I really wanted everyone to have the opportunity to attend two conferences. It is still a hard choice today, but it does bring out the best in students who are determined to be part of the select group.

SETBACKS

As with nearly all endeavors, there are times when we face setbacks. This was true with my leadership of the Model UN program as well. About five years after taking over, the student government, which provided 100% of our funding, decided to completely defund us. There was no particular reason for this, just a quirky decision by the current student body president. Fortunately, the student fees budget process allowed for an appeal process and all of my students went into high gear, contacting each of the student senators and asking them to reverse this decision.

This incident also sparked some outreach by me to our many alumni of the Model UN program. I had a list of previous participants dating back about ten years but had never had any reason to put together a more comprehensive list. The defunding episode inspired me to contact the alumni association and put together a full list of past Model UN'ers. I sent out a letter to them regarding the defunding issue and asked them to write to me about the value of their Model UN experience while they were in school in order to make a case to the student government. The letters I got in response completely blew me away. I already believed that Model UN was beneficial to our students, but these letters stated unequivocally that Model UN was one of the best experiences they had had at the university and fundamentally prepared them for their various professional careers. Several had powerful stories to tell about how putting Model UN on their resume led to specific questions in their job interview that allowed them talk about their unique qualifications. In the end, given the lobbying efforts of the current students and the testimonials of alumni, the student government reversed their decision and restored about 80% of our funding. This was a transformative moment for me, reaffirming the impact of Model UN on my students, and the importance of maintaining ties with my alumni. That same year I decided to start putting out an annual Model UN newsletter to alumni, and have done so ever since. The replies I get from alumni continue to inspire me and renew my commitment to the program.

One additional insight that came from this defunding incident was the recognition that I needed to have rhetorical and financial support from the university administration for the Model UN program. I approached the Dean with a request for additional regular funding for Model UN, noting that I could not run an effective program with the uncertainty of funding from student government. He supported this request, and this support has continued even through a change in college leadership, due in part to deliberate public relations efforts regarding Model UN. I never miss an opportunity to share photos, conference awards, etc. in press releases. Not only are students developing research, writing, speaking, and consensus building skills, they have the opportunity to meet with real diplomats for mission briefings at our national and international conferences, and they get to interact with students from around the world, exposing them to many different global perspectives. My efforts to highlight all of these benefits have helped give Model UN a much higher profile on campus and consequently a very positive image. I never realized when I first took over leadership of the Model UN that such PR efforts would be an integral part of the job, but learning how to advocate effectively for my program has definitely paid off in the end.

CONTINUING OPPORTUNITIES

After a decade of growth in the program, and successfully overcoming some setbacks, one might easily be tempted toward complacency. Due to a variety of circumstances, however, a whole series of new opportunities began to present themselves related to the Model UN program. One of these stemmed from my outreach efforts to alumni. I decided it would be a good idea to try to establish an endowed scholarship specifically for a Model UN student. I began to include information about this effort in the annual Model UN newsletters and received a handful of small contributions over several years. This was a bit disheartening, but then the Development Office contacted me and said they had a prospective donor who was a former Model UN participant. We talked with him and he eventually decided he wanted to single-handedly provide the remainder of the funds for the scholarship and name it. This was something he was passionate about and he was pleased to be able to help current students in the program. I learned some new skills through this experience of partnering with the Development Office, and it reaffirmed my belief in the value of the program. It's hard to become unenthusiastic about a program when you continue to see the attachment alumni demonstrate through their generosity.

Several years later, I had the opportunity to build on this relationship with the scholarship donor when a colleague asked me if I would be interested in hosting a UN Day Dinner to celebrate the anniversary of the founding of the UN. The idea was to provide a dinner for students and invite a speaker from the UN in New York. Given the expense of catering and limited student budgets, the dinner would need a sponsor. I approached our donor and he was pleased to contribute to this new endeavor. The first year he was unable to attend, but the second year he joined the dinner and was seated with four of his previous scholarship recipients. Being able to provide an opportunity for alumni and current students to connect was very satisfying. It was a great celebration in so many ways.

Another opportunity came at the invitation of a friend who taught at a local high school. He had asked me for several years to consider sponsoring a high school Model UN conference. I had regularly declined, until one year my college students heard me talking about this and jumped on the idea. I figured if this was something they were excited about, I could help make it happen, but it would be theirs to run. They did an amazing job staffing the conference and the high school teachers were pleased as well. Thus began a new tradition. I provided careful instructions about the rules and coached them on how to interact confidently with the high school students, focusing on the goal of making it a positive learning experience for all. My students were given the freedom to determine any adjustments that needed to be made in their committees for them to run smoothly, and they came away from the experience totally empowered. Over the next several years, the conference more than quadrupled in size, and eventually, I had some freshmen in my college group who had participated as high school students. The Admissions Office has been pleased at this new campus recruitment activity and my program gets the added benefit of experienced "new" delegates joining the group.

As the creation of the high school conference suggests, Model UN can lead to different service opportunities locally and nationally. As faculty, we can use our expertise to provide advising to not only our students, but also to those in the community. One opportunity I have had was the invitation to serve on a regional Model UN Board of Directors. This was an unexpected honor and gave me insights into the strategic direction of the conference as well as the leadership training for the staff. I was able to provide insights on the Board from a faculty perspective and help shape future planning. My service also increased the profile of my institution and was well received by my Dean. Overall, this was a worthwhile service commitment.

One final experience that has provided a growth opportunity for me has been choosing new Model UN conferences to attend. As some of the more experienced delegates realized that there were international Model UN conferences, they began to ask about the possibility of attending one of these conferences. I looked into this and decided to take the plunge and try something totally new. This was a real stretch for me because I like to have a lot of control over my classroom and student activities. I was very familiar with the conferences that we usually attended, and could predictably prepare students to do well at those conferences. The idea of going to a totally new conference was unsettling, but we decided to try it. We have a now attended four different international conferences and have had some great experiences. Not all are organized as I would desire, but the students have learned a lot at each of them. I've learned to be more flexible, and I've worked to set realistic expectations for my students so they have positive experiences.

As I look back at each of the different opportunities that have arisen, I'm so glad that I chose to pursue these instead of resting contentedly on my laurels. I did not actively seek them out but was able to respond when the opportunities presented themselves. I recognize that I could not have been successful in all these endeavors if I had tried to do them all at the start of my career. It was important for me to focus on the basics first, and then look for new opportunities once I had the basics mastered. This has helped me develop new skills and new connections, and brought new energy to my work.

FINAL REFLECTIONS

Reflecting back on nearly two decades of serving as a faculty advisor for the Model UN program, I can really appreciate all of the benefits that have come from this experience. It has been so much more than a career shaping "add on" to the job I thought I was taking when I was hired. One benefit has been the networking connections with other faculty advisors. When I first started attending Model UN conferences, other faculty welcomed and mentored me. Those professional connections have continued to develop, resulting in coauthoring relationships, panel and workshop collaborations, and external review letters. Another benefit has been increased professional recognition within my institution for my students, for the program, and for my own professional leadership. Colleagues in many departments recognize that some of their best students are Model UN participants and support these students in their work. Administrative offices across campus ranging from Admissions to Development and

Alumni Relations appreciate the work I have done to build connections in the community. All of this has contributed to my successful professional advancement.

When you begin a new job, you never know what unexpected assignment might open all sorts of new doors; that has been the case with my role as Model UN faculty advisor. I've found so many ways to build onto the basic job of preparing students to participate in a Model UN conference each year. It's been a foundation to stretch and grow. It is the one aspect of my job that I have always looked forward to. It has kept me energized and excited even when other responsibilities have been less inspiring. It's a pleasure to devote my energy to an endeavor that I know the students will remember and appreciate for the rest of their lives. My contacts with alumni constantly reinforce what a transformative experience Model UN is for the students. These are the students I am closest to and know best—the ones that I write letters of recommendations for, and receive wedding invitations and birth announcements from years after graduation. I've come to think of myself as a coach, pushing everyone to give me their very best, knowing that some have less to give than others, but all are worthy of the effort. Students will often tell me at graduation how much they appreciate that I believed in them, even when they didn't believe in themselves. Model UN not only brings out the best in my students, it brings out the best in me. I'm very thankful for this unexpected gift that I received when I first began teaching.

CHAPTER 22

Better Than Before: My Pedagogical Journey

Marc J. O'Reilly

Current institution: small private liberal arts university
Typical classroom setting: small classroom lecture/seminar
Typical pedagogical approach: Socratic method
Disciplinary identity: IR

Having earned degrees at large research universities, I knew nothing about small liberal arts institutions that emphasize innovative teaching and mentoring when I started as an Assistant Professor of Political Science at Heidelberg College (now Heidelberg University) in the fall semester of 2001. In my early years, I invested in teaching. Yet I taught global politics courses rather conventionally, mostly emulating my professors. I lectured a lot, gave mid-term and final exams, and had my students write and present semester research papers. I insisted on drafting, which only a few of my graduate school professors had asked of me, and conferencing. While I became known for drafting, which I referred to as the "process," many of my students struggled to develop the analytical skills necessary to understand global politics. My self-designed class evaluations confirmed that my Model United Nations (MUN) course, with its emphasis on experiential learning, proved an exception.

M. J. O'Reilly (✉)
Heidelberg University, Tiffin, OH, USA
e-mail: moreilly@heidelberg.edu

© The Author(s) 2020
J. Frueh (ed.), *Pedagogical Journeys through World Politics*,
Political Pedagogies, https://doi.org/10.1007/978-3-030-20305-4_22

253

As I gained classroom experience, I modified my teaching. I started to lecture less, have students author brief reflections every week on readings, and have small groups discuss material before partaking in-class discussion. Likewise, I experimented with unconventional assignments, such as portfolios, blogs, and campus advocacy events. Teaching interdisciplinary Honors seminars and First-Year Experience courses helped me be more creative in the classroom and with assignments, as did team teaching with talented colleagues. Organizing and leading student groups on international trips and to Washington, D.C., also made me a better teacher and advisor, as did taking select groups of high achieving undergraduates to local, regional, and international conferences. My administrative responsibilities (as the Director of International & Multicultural Academic Programs, as a department chair, and as the chair of an interdisciplinary program) similarly contributed to improvements in the classroom and other facets of teaching and advising.

Pondering over my 17 years as a teacher-scholar at a small university that spotlights teaching, I realize that my pedagogy has significantly evolved. As a mid-career professional with tenure and full professor rank, I can chuckle and cringe, reflecting on the many teaching mistakes I have made over the years, without worrying that I have jeopardized promotion and all its attendant financial and other benefits. While my teaching will always be a work in progress, my many modifications, which I discuss in this chapter, have made me a more effective professor.

My Education and Professors

In this pedagogical era of "flipped" classrooms, experiential learning, PowerPoint and Prezi, internet research, smart phones, social media, and blogging, I boggle the minds of my students whenever I describe my elementary and high school education. Given some of their reactions, you would think I had been born in 1869, rather than 1969, and in some wretched backwater of the world, not in Canada. Like my parents and grandparents, I learned cursive, diagrammed sentences, memorized multiplication tables and poetry, and recited French, English, and Latin vocabulary. I read dictionaries, encyclopedia, and printed books—several of which I checked out from a library, others my mother had used in her studies. If I did not handwrite my assignments, one of my father's law office assistants typed them for me...on a typewriter. As I developed an interest in global affairs in the early 1980s, I read printed Canadian newspapers (in English and French) and started reading Time Magazine, to which my parents subscribed. I watched episodes of M*A*S*H, CBS Sunday Morning with Charles Kuralt, and the Lebanese civil war on NBC Nightly News.

After graduating from a well-known French-Canadian high school/prep school with a so-called classical education, I matriculated at McGill University in my hometown of Montréal in the fall of 1988. Majoring in Political Science, I specialized in International Relations (IR). Given McGill's emphasis on undergraduate instruction, I took courses with some world-class IR professors, such as Patrick James and Michael Brecher. I also benefited from Charles Taylor's excellent teaching. The famous political philosopher delivered the most memorable lecture I have ever witnessed—on Aristotelian teleology. All of my Political Science education, save one course, followed the traditional lecture model. The exception occurred the year I studied abroad in the United States, at the University of Connecticut. During the spring semester, Mark Boyer taught an international negotiation course whose central assignment was a foreign-policy simulation (known as the International Communication & Negotiation Simulations Project) developed by the University of Maryland, Dr. Boyer's Ph.D. alma mater. I very much enjoyed my initial exposure to active learning. It served me well when I joined McGill's Model United Nations (MUN) team in fall 1991. MUN conferences at Smith College and Princeton University that academic year made me appreciate the value and importance of experiential learning.

Two other experiences likewise had a profound impact on me. In 1990–91, I took a team-taught all-year political theory course. Having four instructors, instead of just one, opened my eyes and mind to an exciting and quite different form of intellectual inquiry. The course format called for one professor to lecture for two or so weeks on an iconic thinker (e.g., Aristotle, Rousseau, Kant, Machiavelli, Marx, and Arendt). The other instructors would then offer their analysis and interpretation of the same theorist. This prompted the kind of engaging debate between learned scholars that I found fascinating. It provided me with my first example of compelling intellectual exchange. I have never forgotten it. My other remarkable undergraduate experience occurred in spring 1991, in an upper-level team-taught course on war and deterrence theory. Not only did multiple McGill professors provide content and analysis, several were from disciplines other than Political Science—for example, History, Law, Medicine, and Philosophy. My classmates and I listened to lectures on the history of warfare, the international laws of war, the physiological effects of nuclear warfare, and Kant's notion of perpetual peace. The multidisciplinarity of the course and cumulation of knowledge made the learning heterodox yet noteworthy. It was the most challenging class I took as an undergraduate. Several of the readings were difficult, as was the semester written assignment—a five-page paper that required every student to write precisely and insightfully, a task that required drafting, which I had only done minimally until that semester. These highlights from my undergraduate education would inform my own teaching a decade later.

As a graduate student from 1993 until 2001, I became familiar with the seminar. This format required much better preparation than a lecture, held me far more accountable for the readings and demanded participation from every student. The noted Cold-War historian John Lewis Gaddis initiated me to the expectations and exigencies of this type of education while I was a student of his at Ohio University's Contemporary History Institute. His rigorous, daunting seminars challenged and stretched my thinking. His willingness to draw from all manner of academic disciplines (e.g., paleontology, geology, literature, and IR theory) was simultaneously surprising, relevant and captivating. Gaddis' thinking knew no disciplinary boundaries even as he promoted History as the model field of inquiry. Not content to open and expand minds, he stressed quality prose like no other professor. He harped on writing at every opportunity and insisted on drafting and revisions. To underscore his point, he even gave his students multipage writing guidelines. I use them with my own students to this day. As someone studying both Political Science and Contemporary History, I was able to marry the methodological strengths of both disciplines while learning to write as a professional academic. Since political scientists typically privilege research design and method over prose, I was glad to polish my writing while a Master's student. It is a lesson I continue to impart upon my own students: without quality prose, your work will not impress, no matter how dazzling your research design and method(s).

As a Ph.D. student in Political Science at the University of Connecticut, with fields in IR, Comparative Politics, and U.S. Diplomatic History, I became well versed in the qualitative and quantitative methods favored by political scientists, particularly IR specialists. I mostly enjoyed my seminars and appreciated the quality of my professors. Mark Boyer taught me once more, as did a few others, including my wonderful advisor, Garry Clifford, a historian who remained skeptical of Political Science methods despite an appointment in the Political Science Department. One UConn professor,

Jennifer Sterling-Folker, who had not been in Storrs when I had studied abroad, made a favorable impression on me despite being overly enthralled, in my opinion, with Realist theory. From a pedagogical standpoint, my most worthwhile experience stemmed from serving as a teaching assistant of Dr. Boyer's for multiple semesters. Initially, I helped him with the international negotiation simulation course I had taken with him a few years earlier. More interestingly, I served as a moderator for the Connecticut Project in International Negotiation simulation he had created for high schoolers.

Although I remain fond and appreciative of the education I received at UConn, and I am grateful as I was able to teach several courses as the instructor of record, I did not gain much pedagogical knowledge while pursuing my Ph.D. My peers and I were not required to take a course or attend workshops on teaching. Whenever we asked for brownbag discussion on this subject, our well-meaning professors told us publishing was what mattered. Publications, not teaching, would earn us jobs at R1 institutions, and research would be the key to tenure and promotion. Classmates and I tried to point out that, statistically, we were more likely to work at a teaching institution, but to no avail. Hence, I started at Heidelberg having taught a lot as a graduate student, while knowing little about the profession and various techniques I could use in the classroom.

HEIDELBERG: THE EARLY DAYS

Upon arriving at Heidelberg in August 2001, with a one-year contract and three new preps (one in the fall semester, two in the spring), I did not dwell on my pedagogical deficiencies. Instead, I worked feverishly to learn the content of my fall European Union (EU) course—I also taught an introductory Global Politics course, identical to the one I had offered repeatedly while at UConn. I had not taken a European Politics course since my first year at McGill, when the EU did not even exist. Fortunately, at one of my campus interviews (I was not offered the position), I met an expert on the EU, someone who had authored textbooks on the subject. He recommended one for my introductory course. Lacking familiarity with the subject, I spent that semester hewing to the textbook.

To preclude critical, if not awful, evaluations, I informed my students on the first day that I had never taught the material. The seminar format allowed me to rely on them, some of the time at least, for information and analysis. I emphasized the semester research paper, which required drafting and conferencing with me, a presentation of their draft, and revisions.

They also had to write a take-home, cumulative final exam, which I thought demanding. As luck would have it, I dealt with my first plagiarism case in that class. A smart, articulate student submitted a draft that read like a journal article. Even though I conveyed my suspicion when we conferenced, he denied any wrong doing. At first, despite using the internet, I did not uncover any evidence of plagiarism. At the end of the semester, however, Heidelberg's academic dean informed all faculty that they could henceforth use a website called turnitin.com to search for plagiarized work. After uploading the suspect paper, I quickly received a report informing me that the work was, indeed, mostly copied and pasted from a European journal article. Apparently, graduate school had taught me a certain type of intuition when it came to student papers! Documenting the plagiarism proved tedious, however, a tutorial in college protocol—there will always be paperwork.

The most interesting lesson I learned that inaugural year came courtesy of a campus forum on September 12, 2001. I had been on the job less than a month when the 9/11 attacks transpired. In response, a colleague in Philosophy, also my faculty mentor, invited me to an all-campus event, which she would moderate. A select group of professors (one from Anthropology, one from Philosophy, one from Psychology, and me) would answer student questions. Since I had written my dissertation on post-World War II US policy vis-à-vis the Middle East, I was deemed a 9/11 expert!

At one point during the forum, a young woman asked about the Palestinians she had seen on television celebrating in the aftermath of the attacks. She wanted to know why they were behaving that way. Given my expertise, I provided her with an explanation. I prefaced by saying that I did not condone the joyous Palestinians. I informed her, and everyone else assembled, that, in my opinion, the Palestinians were pleased because, for once in their lives, they or their brethren had not died—typically due to Israeli weapons supplied by the US government. This time, Americans (and other Westerners) had died. Now, Americans who survived knew the pain and suffering that Palestinians had endured on multiple occasions. In response to my answer, the student was livid. She thought the Palestinian celebration sickening. Soon after, presumably overcome with emotion, she exited the room. As she did, I whispered to one of my colleagues: "There's a student who will never take class with me." While I surely could have been more tactful in my reply to a student obviously stricken with grief, I do not regret my dispassionate explication. My job as a teacher, as a scholar, was to educate her and the audience, which I did. Had 9/11 happened during my second, third, or fourth year at Heidelberg, I might have known the student who asked the question or known someone near her. Familiarity with the audience, and the latter with me, would likely have allowed me initially to provide comfort and reassurance, before giving a clinical explanation of a disturbing, for most Americans, television visual. For example, I might have asked an adjacent student to give her/his classmate a hug or hold her hand. I might have said her name and offered some kind of encouragement. Or I might have acknowledged her pain before delving into professor mode. Instead, I lacked the necessary emotional intelligence to proceed in both a humanistic and a social scientific manner.

As I familiarized myself with the "other duties as assigned" part of my contract, such as attending monthly faculty meetings (initially, I found them intimidating; nowadays, I think them mostly insufferable), I regularly turned to various mentors for advice regarding every facet of my job. I asked my designated campus mentor for insight about my new colleagues—who they were, their reputations, etc. As Heidelberg's most beloved professor (the student body repeatedly selected her as the Faculty of the Year), I keenly observed, and tried to emulate, how she interacted with students both inside and outside the classroom. Watching her teach philosophy was a delight. She masterfully conveyed content, while continuously engaging her students, especially those reluctant to participate. Socrates would have been proud!

My department mentor, a 25-year veteran of Heidelberg, helped me better understand my chair, who sometimes treated me as if I was one of his young adult sons. In my first semester, he asked me to chaperon his Cities and Society class on its November three-day sojourn to Chicago, a legendary annual trek. On my maiden off-campus trip as a faculty member, I roomed with Heidelberg's visiting Chinese scholar, a wonderful man who had survived a labor camp during Mao's Cultural Revolution. That weekend also taught me about logistics, various undergraduate behaviors, and the value of experiential learning. And, courtesy of an excellent museum visit, it introduced me to Mexican Day of the Dead traditions. For many years, in my International Studies Capstone course, I have assigned Eduardo Galeano's fascinating Upside Down, a polemical work on globalization, in part due to its memorable Day of the Dead artwork.

A genial German professor served as another Heidelberg mentor. At our frequent lunches at the cafeteria, he answered my many pedagogical and other questions, taught me school history, and dispensed useful advice. The venue allowed me to converse with students beyond the classroom. I enjoyed these conversations, which humanized me and gave me insight into student lives.

Beyond Heidelberg, I continued to rely on the wisdom of former professors, particularly Patrick James, Betty Hanson, and Garry Clifford, my Ph.D. advisor. I also turned to Marijke Breuning, whom I met at my initial International Studies Association (ISA) conference (in 1997 in Toronto). We were presenters on the same panel. Mark Boyer recommended I speak to her. I will always be thankful for his recommendation. As a nervous graduate student attending my first major conference, I was so grateful Marijke, who was a junior professor at Truman State University, took time to meet with me. She even agreed to read my paper, which was a condensed version of my Master's thesis. For years afterward, we met for breakfast at the ISA convention. As I started my Heidelberg career, she provided all manner of advice and encouragement—she also taught at a liberal arts institution. That continues to this day, although she is now a full professor at the University of North Texas, an R1 school.

Having reapplied for and kept my position, I completed my initial year at Heidelberg with two seminal off-campus experiences. In April 2002, I led a group of approximately eight students to San Francisco, where they participated in the annual Model United Nations of the Far West (MUNFW) conference. I knew nothing of the event beforehand, but immediately liked the size and feel of the conference. As veteran Model UN advisors know, you have to choose a venue compatible with the caliber of students you have. As someone who mostly takes Model UN rookies, I need a conference tailored to inexperienced delegates. That precludes attending Harvard or Nationals in New York City, two of the most competitive MUN conferences. At such events, the quality of the average delegate is impressive. And with individual awards given out, many participants roleplay zealously in an effort to secure much sought after prizes. For me, that can often warp the simulation, as delegates play out of character. They inflate the role and influence of their country. At Model UN Far West, organizers minimize competition by only giving delegation awards for preconference work. I like that emphasis, and so happily have taken a group to the conference every year since. I also learned that year that I could not adequately teach a course that simultaneously spotlighted International Organization, the United Nations, and Model UN.

By my second year, I modified the course so that I dwelled on the UN and conference preparation. Since that proved manageable, I have kept that general template. This year will be my 17th taking a group to MUNFW. Heidelberg has become sufficiently prominent and well regarded at the conference that it regularly serves as the organizing/host school—next year will be our fourth time since 2011. This honor has allowed several of my students to serve as members of the Secretariat and as committee chairs.

Unlike some Model UN advisors, I entrust my head delegates (i.e., permanent representatives) with a lot of responsibility for preparing their delegations for conference participation. In the first half of the class, I provide the necessary basic information and analysis on the United Nations as an intergovernmental organization as well as convey a profile for each country that Heidelberg students will represent. Simultaneously, my permanent representatives work with their delegates on the preconference materials—the country profile, policy statements, and draft resolutions. I only help edit the profile. I want my students to earn a certificate of achievement, rather than have me win it for them. In the second half of the course, I introduce negotiation theory, discuss diplomatic protocol, and oversee in-class mock Model UN sessions, complete with chairs and placards. Meanwhile, head delegates devise delegation and committee goals and prepare their conference binders. Throughout the semester and at conference, delegations communicate via their GroupMe, a texting app. I am included in each delegation's GroupMe, so at all times I know what each delegation is doing and thinking.

Conference occurs late in the spring semester, an added bonus. Having a near full semester to prepare a group is much less stressful than having mere weeks, should the conference be held early in the semester or midway. And a novel textbook by MUNFW colleague Brian Dille, who teaches at Mesa Community College, makes preparation easier than ever. Given my experiences at Model UN Far West, I highly recommend this conference, particularly if your students have not previously participated in such a simulation. Be aware, however, that, like me, you may have to devote many hours to raising the necessary funds for attending a conference a good distance from your campus. While I could register for one near my school, the extra benefit from traveling to California, whose campus and societal culture differs markedly from that of my midwest university, is well worth the additional expense. Having support from Heidelberg's president, Rob Huntington, who has attended the conference, makes it much easier to justify the lengthy travel.

In July 2002, three months after attending my initial MUN Far West, I taught an interdisciplinary summer course at Oxford University with my Heidelberg faculty mentor and a colleague from the English Department. The course compared British politics, philosophy, and culture to that of America. My spouse, then a Ph.D. student, and my brother, about to start his undergraduate studies, joined the Heidelberg contingent on this amazing academic, intercultural, and travel experience. Spending a month working with two of Heidelberg's most gifted educators significantly improved every component of my teaching (preparation, delivery, assignments, grading, and assessment) and gave me confidence in my own pedagogical ability. Seeing students thrive in that environment further convinced me of the value of experiential learning.

OFF-CAMPUS EXPERIENCES

Given the success of that initial abroad experience, I subsequently took several other groups on visits to various countries. On three occasions (2004, 2007, and 2011), my group went to Canada, my homeland. In 2006, 2009, 2012, and 2015, trips to various European and Muslim countries (Italy, Greece, France, Monaco, Turkey, Spain, and Morocco) ensued. All journeys served as experiential addenda to an Honors course I was teaching or had taught that semester. With respect to the Canada trips, I had taught an interdisciplinary course on my home province of Québec, which is majority French speaking. As for the European and Muslim country ones, I was teaching or had taught my multidisciplinary Empires course.

Eager to take students on other off-campus trips and immerse them in academia, I started taking several of my best students to conferences. At first, we attended a state conference (the Ohio Association of Economists and Political Scientists—coincidentally, where I first presented, while pursuing my Master's degree). We graduated to a regional conference (ISA-Midwest) and eventually to a national/international one (ISA). I also started taking students to the Walsh University Political Science/ International Relations Undergraduate Research conference, a well-run event expertly organized by Koop Berry. My students have substantially benefited from presenting their own work at this type of student friendly gathering. And I have enjoyed serving as a chair/discussant on a number of panels over the years. Note that Heidelberg has its own annual Student Research Conference, at which many of my students present.

Making Changes

While I have always given my highest achieving students various presentation opportunities, believing that most would continue their education in graduate and law school, I have significantly evolved my assignments to better accommodate the academic and professional needs of all my students, most of whom will not pursue a Master's or Ph.D. degree in Political Science, never mind International Relations. Hence, whereas I started my teaching career by asking for, in most of my courses, a semester research paper, often a rather lengthy one in an upper-level class, I now privilege a variety of written assignments (quizzes, exams, memos, blogs, journals, papers, and portfolios). As an undergraduate, I never took a quiz, wrote a memo, blogged, kept a journal, or submitted a portfolio of any kind. Attending a school, even a prestigious one, of many thousands in the late 1980s–early 1990s, the course format rarely varied from the typical mid-term exam, semester research paper, and final exam. An advanced course on the U.S. presidency substituted a group presentation for the mid-term. If you lacked exam taking and research paper skills, you could not excel in IR or any other subfield of Political Science. Note that I hand wrote every one of my undergraduate exams.

As someone cursed with barely legible handwriting when having to write quickly, I had to proceed deliberately, so graders could make out my words, a handicap when taking timed essay exams that required a lot of information and analysis. Thankfully, as a graduate student, I wrote few in-class exams and typed my Ph.D. comprehensive exams. With that in mind, I have purposely assigned typewritten take-home final exams in most of my courses. Since, in this World-Wide-Web era, information will be readily available to my students in the workplace, I perceive minimal value in having them memorize material for exams. Better, in my opinion, to have them focus on analyzing, synthesizing, and applying information as they will on the job. By not having to recall material in the context of a timed exam, which is usually a stressful exercise, students can dwell on critical thinking, a skill employers seek when hiring. I typically provide take-home exam questions one to two weeks before the due date. Given the format, I have higher expectations in terms of quality of work, something I communicate when I discuss the questions with the students and how they can/should proceed with their answers.

Although I tend to formulate my questions conventionally (i.e., as one would expect in an IR course), I have experimented with heterodox ones. For example, in my upper-level War & Peace course, I have used John

Lennon's iconic "Imagine" song to ask a synthetic question. Because students may struggle with such a formulation, I provide a straightforward alternative question. Students appreciate having a choice.

While some students may balk at answering a question drawn from popular culture, they usually welcome creative assignments, especially "real-world" ones. In my Introduction to Politics & Government course, my students write a semester blog, using articles retweeted to @BergPOL, my department's Twitter account. They have to include international sources, usually foreign newspapers and magazines. In my upper-level Human Rights & Social Justice class, students write a memo to the CEO of an NGO that evaluates the organization's mission, administrative modus operandi, communication strategy (e.g., web page and social media), and overall effectiveness. In my upper-level US Foreign Policy course, with trepidation I added a Trump tweets blog in spring 2017. Fortunately, the president regularly tweeted on matters of foreign policy, which allowed my students to analyze a semester's worth of material.

Although I was proud (and relieved) that the Trump Twitter blog worked, I cannot take credit for the most creative assignment in any of my courses. In the second half of the spring 2017 semester, one of my human-rights students asked if I would consider an alternative assignment to the semester research paper. As someone most interested in activism, she proposed an advocacy event. After some discussion, the class and I came to an agreement. While a few students opted to do the paper, most students in this small seminar would research, organize, publicize, and host a campus advocacy event that would highlight several important human-rights issues, such as human trafficking, access to health care, and global climate change. They even secured various sponsorships, so that attendees would have food and drink—always an incentive for undergraduates reluctant to attend an educational event. Ale & Advocacy occurred at the end of the semester and proved a rousing success. Booths provided useful information and allowed attendees to sign petitions, which were then submitted to local, state, and federal representatives. By substituting a more practical assignment for the paper, the students were able to serve as campus activists, which very much pleased them. Instead of proceeding drearily with the usual drafting, presenting, and revising of a paper, students were enthused and energized by the advocacy project. As I ponder the next iteration of that course, I intend to reprise that assignment. Instead of making it optional, however, I will likely require every student to participate.

Creative in-class debates and simulations also draw students' attention. In my Introduction to Global Politics course, I have women make the case, Oxford Union-style, that the world would be as, or more, conflictual if women governed, while men argue that global society would be more peaceful in this alternative, matriarchal scenario. In my Introduction to Politics & Government, students simulate Question Time in the British Parliament—or a QT involving Heidelberg University's president, provost, dean of students, and other senior campus administrators. In my US Foreign Policy class, each student presents her/his draft memo, on a particular policy matter, to the National Security Council (NSC). Rather delightfully, I play the American president, while students represent the various other NSC members. Often, pointed questions make a student presenter significantly or fundamentally rethink her/his memo, which she/he then revises. The final version is thus typically much improved.

Political satire is another technique I have used, both as written assignment and classroom pedagogy. As a youth, I enjoyed political cartoons in the various newspapers and magazines I read. As a professor, I have supplemented cartoons with clips from satirical programs, such as The Daily Show, The Colbert Report, Last Week Tonight, and The Opposition. Given that satirists can say and show what reporters and hosts cannot, Trevor Noah can compare, for example, candidate Donald Trump to various African dictators via a hilarious video mashup that brilliantly juxtaposes Trump's bombast and hubris with Idi Amin's. I could have shown Fareed Zakaria discussing, on his GPS show, Trump's authoritarian and dictatorial ways, but many students would have been bored. But the Noah clip is so memorable that I continue to use it, two and a half years after it originally aired. I have found that political satire is a most effective way to convey all manner of theory and practice, with one caveat. Most satirical shows skew liberal, which can be offensive to conservative students. To remedy that, I ask them to submit clips, which I then show in class.

One way I know more than ever how my class is performing involves a pedagogical innovation I instituted some five years ago. After attending a Heidelberg faculty workshop, where a School of Education colleague explained how she used "think-pair-share" in her classrooms, I started using that technique. I ask my students to reflect on the reading(s) for the first 10 minutes of class, discuss for 10–15 minutes what they have written (I typically join a group or two), and, finally, have a class discussion wherein each group summarizes its conversation. Although I regularly proceed in this manner, and have been mostly pleased with the results, I have not abandoned lecturing, especially in introductory courses. In most classes, a mixed pedagogy works best for me.

After 17 years of teaching undergraduates about global politics and other political subjects, I have thus concluded the following: (1) Observe good teaching on your campus, no matter the discipline. (2) You can never have too many mentors. (3) Team teach. (4) The more experiential learning, the better. (5) Varied, creative assignments will prove more engaging and yield better work. (6) Student learning can and will occur in many different formats and contexts, both inside and outside the classroom. (7) Know when to lead and when to follow. (8) Teaching, advising, and mentoring form an academic trinity—attend to all three.

CHAPTER 23

"Love's Labor's Lost": Teaching IR in Germany

Axel Heck

Current institution: large public research university
Typical classroom setting: seminars of 10–30 students
Typical pedagogical approach: PowerPoint-based presentation and Q&A, regularly followed by group discussions
Disciplinary identity: Peace and Conflict, International Security

"Career Killer" or "Educating Professionals for Democracy"—What Is Teaching Good for?

In my contribution to this volume, I want to share my experiences teaching IR at political science departments at German universities. I will argue that due to structural constraints, incentives to invest time and effort in quality teaching are limited. In fact, under the "publish or perish" mentality that has occupied the academic system, teaching is often considered a "career killer." We have to be reminded of what teaching is good for and that it is not just another "annoying task" that distracts attention from more career-relevant issues. In Germany, universities are funded by the

A. Heck (✉)
University of Kiel, Kiel, Germany
e-mail: aheck@politik.uni-kiel.de

© The Author(s) 2020
J. Frueh (ed.), *Pedagogical Journeys through World Politics*,
Political Pedagogies, https://doi.org/10.1007/978-3-030-20305-4_23

public hand, that is, the taxpayer. Hence, teaching and educating students is our raison d'etre, the reason for our salary and the main justification for our jobs. Teaching IR is not only about theories of International Relations, methods, or case studies. It is also about conveying democratic norms, intellectual empowerment, and encouraging critical thinking in times of "fake news" and "alternative facts." Teaching provides us the opportunity to educate students how to cope with political complexity. It is for creating an environment where students can develop and progress into professionals for democracy, so they can separate the "sense" from the "nonsense," embrace diversity, and beware of simplicity. Regarding the variety of different theoretical approaches and scientific traditions, teaching IR courses, especially to undergraduates, is a perfect opportunity to practice intellectual openness, critical thinking and, last but not least, to develop fact-based arguments.

But before I come to my narrative, some words on German higher education are necessary because our system works slightly differently than Anglo-American universities. I will refer to structural constraints that might sound familiar to nearly all readers who are working in academia, but some are unique to the German system, and they have tremendous consequences for our ways of teaching. I will address critical aspects of a system that takes advantage of precarious job situations and is built on the self-exploitation of the academic staff. Just to be clear, this essay is not about complaining or self-pity. I have decided to pursue a university career intentionally. I had options to leave that would have been financially lucrative, as I started my professional career as a consultant in a small start-up company where I learned a lot about running a business. I wrote my Ph.D. thesis partly while I was working outside academia and I did this not to earn another degree. I applied for fellowships and jobs at the university because I wanted to—against all the odds, advice, and rational considerations. I knew the risks. I was aware of the financial hardships and limited chances to get a permanent position. But I was also sure that this was the only job in which I could entirely live out my passion for intellectual freedom, creativity, writing, thinking, and last but certainly not least, teaching.

From my very first teaching engagement in Mainz until today, I have always enjoyed and learned a lot from discussions with my students, and I am trying to turn the classroom into a lively space where thinking is allowed and encouraged. Of course, it doesn't work with every class, and it's easier in M.A. than in B.A courses where the curriculum is more or less set due to module structures. But even under the constraints of the

Bologna reform (which brought module structures, credit points and school-like teaching requirements to universities in Europe), it is so worth the effort and I love it. I don't want to do anything else—despite the degrading treatment of academics.

Max Weber had already written in the 1920s that pursuing a career in academia is a hazardous game (Weber 2014 [1919]: 15). But the fact that teaching has lost significance is not only the result of career-hungry junior scholars or post-docs going "all in" as they desperately try to get a professorship. Students' ignorance about the job situation of their teachers is part of the story as well. When I talk to students about the structures of the university system and whether they know about the conditions under which we are working, it's always the same. Most of them don't know, and many just don't care. They are not interested to know whether lecturers are permanent or not. A few years ago, we started a petition campaign to remind the public of the precarious situation of young scholars and proposed structural reforms. Of course, we asked our students for support as they are the largest and most powerful status group in our system, but solidarity was limited. But if things are to become better concerning the appreciation of teaching, it's not only on us—it also depends on students who care and are alert of the difficult circumstances under which we are working. We do not want pity, but we need solidarity and a reform of the German academic system. Occasionally, advanced M.A. students come to my office and ask for advice about starting a Ph.D. And then, I tell them what it means and takes.

A Career in Academia Sounds Like a Dream…

There are various career options for Ph.D. students—and getting a chance to work in academia always feels like a dream. The first and by far best option is the position as a research associate working with and for a professor. There is no equivalent in the Anglo-American system, as the German University fosters its "feudal legacy" where the professor remains the sovereign and the associates serve as entourage. Such posts are rare and poorly paid, as most predoctoral associates get a 50% contract for a fulltime job. Nevertheless, all Ph.D. students seeking a career at the university will apply for associate positions sooner or later. The most significant asset is that you will develop a close working relationship with the professor, so you are directly involved in the day-to-day business—with all benefits and duties: research, teaching, and administration. Depending on the skills and character of the professor, you will have—in the best case—an additional education and conversation partner in new theories, methods, and how to develop a research design for larger projects, or how to write a grant proposal. If you are lucky, the professor will give you advice about how to get papers published and you might be introduced to important academic networks. Regarding teaching skills, you have to educate yourself, or you can acquire certificates in higher education teaching by attending workshops and seminars offered by the university—which takes time, and time is a crucial factor.

The flipside of these associate positions is that the professor is not only your boss, but in most cases also the supervisor of your Ph.D. and he/she grades the thesis—not a committee like in other systems. So, you often depend on his/her personality, mood, and the opinion about the quality of your work and attitude. If you screw it up, your academic career might be over before it begins.

The second best option is a position within a larger research project funded by the German Research Foundation (DFG) or other funding institutions. These jobs are rare as well, but offer excellent opportunities to get a foot in the academic business. Your primary duty is to work on a case study, but you must also find time to pursue your Ph.D. project. The third option is to apply for a graduate school program. In this case, you can fully concentrate on your Ph.D. project, despite the classes you have to take, so you are a student again. But you have to find a way to enter the professional academic business, because you need a reliable network and have to prove your working experience if you want to move on in the system once you have finished your Ph.D. The fourth possibility is to apply for a graduate fellowship offered by lots of public and private institutions. In this case, you are highly dependent on your own resources as an external Ph.D. student at the chair of your supervisor. For some professors, being an outsider will not make a difference, but in most cases, you don't belong to the team—you are external. I started on a graduate fellowship and managed to get pre- and postdoctoral associate positions. I'm sure that without my experience as pre- and post-doc associate, I wouldn't have received my current job.

As stated above, time is a crucial factor. As soon as you pick up a Ph.D. project in Germany and you work on a contract at the university, the clock is ticking. According to German higher education law, you have six years to finish your Ph.D. and another six years as a post-doc researcher to qualify for a professorship. Although six years for a Ph.D. might sound like heaven for some readers, you finally have to face a very harsh reality. After you complete the twelve, you can only apply for extremely rare permanent positions, but keep in mind that only about 10% of the academic staff is permanent, and most of them are professors. Once you have completed the Ph.D., you have to make a fundamental decision: stay in academia and take the risk or leave for good—due to the extreme competition, a come-back is rather unlikely once you are out.

...AND MIGHT END UP IN A NIGHTMARE

So, if you decide to move on the academic path, it is time to pursue the so-called "Habilitation," the formal qualification for a professorship. If you want to become a professor, you need a position as a postdoctoral researcher at a chair. The best alternative for such a post-doc position is to get one of the rare so-called junior professorships (Assistant Professor equivalent) or Akademischer Rat (tenured, comparable to Associate Professor, nearly extinguished since junior professorships were created). The majority of post-docs are hired on contracts without tenure, and as soon as they expire and you have reached your maximum for twelve years (6 + 6), you are done. You cannot turn a post-doc contract into a perma-nent position by performance.

To be fair, I have to say that, theoretically, the university could offer employees a tenured position after the contract expires, but then the chair-holder and the faculty won't be able to hire someone else—the position is occupied until the post-doc retires or leaves for another job. Accordingly, the bitter reality for most colleagues working as untenured post-doc researchers is that they get a warm goodbye handshake once their contract expires and someone else, preferably younger, and, of course, much cheaper fills in the position. That is extremely good for universities as they have full flexibility regarding 90% of the academic staff because professors are public servants (Beamte) and therefore off limits (unless they do very, very stupid things). The situation is excellent for Ph.D. students or early career post-docs as well because they get a chance to enter an associate position whenever senior post-docs have to leave. For them, it might turn out quite badly as they are mostly in their late 30s or early 40s. Suddenly they are highly specialized academic dropouts bustling on the job mar-ket—no fun, especially for those who have a family to take care of. I have not even mentioned the gender inequality here. Many skilled women leave academia after the Ph.D. because of all these uncertainties.

Given the enormous pressure, especially on post-doc scholars, to get papers and books published in prestigious journals and with major publishing houses, as well as the need to acquire large amounts of external funding, "teaching experience" is just another box to be ticked on your scorecard. And even the best teaching record ever doesn't save you from losing your job when your post-doc contract expires and your 12 years are over.

When we talk about teaching IR in Germany, these structural constraints for post-docs have to be taken into account. They are the reason why teaching has lost its attraction. Yes, I have to admit that sometimes when I am disappointed because a grant proposal was turned down or a paper was rejected, I catch myself thinking about teaching as a pestering and time-consuming obligation that kills my career. Instead of teaching my nine courses per academic year, reading and grading about 90 term papers each semester, I would have been better off investing that time into my proposal that was just rejected, right? And the whole thing is existential because I can easily imagine myself as just another academic dropout whose dream of winning the lottery has turned into a nightmare.

But is a rejected grant proposal a sound excuse for poor teaching? Does that mean that we shouldn't care and think about education at all? Shouldn't we seek to become better teachers, to improve our skills despite all that? Have we forgotten about the reason for the existence of our publicly funded jobs? Are we distracted by teaching? Or, isn't it true that the run for publications in highly ranked journals and for grant money has distracted our focus from our primary task, which is teaching?

Most German universities do not charge tuition fees—this must sound like heaven for many students and families in Anglo-American countries and elsewhere in the world. As higher education is expensive, the taxpayer covers the costs. But taxpayers who send their kids to universities do not care about my "h-factor" or the amount of external funding I have acquired. The whole society that pays our salary expects us to provide students with the best education possible. Teaching is not only an essential part of our job and should not be considered just another "pestering obligation," as I do when the job gets me down. Education, in general, is one of the most important resources of our society, fostering and celebrating democratic values. But maybe we (and I include myself here) have lost the sense of it. Teaching IR is not only about IR theories—even if they are the main subject of the course. Teaching is a social responsibility and a duty to our society—especially in times when everything seems so complicated and in flux.

MY JOURNEY THROUGH THE SYSTEM—LEARNING IT THE HARD WAY

When I studied law at the University of Trier in 1998, nothing pointed toward a career in academia. Intimidated by all these people on the campus who looked so much older than me, I didn't feel very comfortable— probably like most other first semester students. Over time, social life at the university became more natural, and I successfully passed some exams, but everything was so annoying that after three semesters it occurred to me that I ended up on the wrong track. I knew the problem wasn't university as such, but the specifics of law studies. I was just unsatisfied and bored.

One day, my roommate told me that I really should think about changing my subject and consider political science instead of law. Good point, I thought, and so, I went to the study program office and asked for help. After a short interview, it was clear, that I should sign up for political science, which I did for summer term 2000. My first course in political science was an International Relations (IR) seminar on multilateralism in South East Asia offered by a young post-doc researcher named Dirk Nabers. I stepped in more or less by accident, but this course changed everything. I immediately knew that IR was going to be my occupation. Dirk later became professor and today we are colleagues at the University of Kiel—his office is right across the hallway.

In summer 2001, I decided to change to the Johann Wolfgang Goethe University in Frankfurt to continue the studies of political science and to focus on IR. I also started an internship at the Peace Research Institute Frankfurt on Monday the 10th of September in 2001. The happenings of the next day changed the world. I was not personally affected by 9/11, but the events dominated my research agenda for many years. My time in Frankfurt was extraordinarily inspiring and essential for my later career decisions. The spirit of the Frankfurt School was still present at the faculty of the social sciences, especially the Institute of Political Science (located in the unembellished and rotten AfE tower, which was finally blown up in 2014) became a hub for critical IR research in Germany, and the library on the 17th floor my "second home" for many years. I took courses offered by Gunther Hellmann, Harald Müller, Lothar Brock, Gert Krell, and some others. Gunther Hellmann was a key figure in these years, as he offered thought-provoking, critical seminars and introduced us to completely new approaches in IR scholarship. His teaching practice was rather unconventional, as he established an atmosphere where students were considered equal partners in intellectually challenging discussions. He truly encouraged critical thinking and offered alternative perspectives on IR. Soon, we formed a group of ambitious IR students who participated in Gunther's Wednesday colloquium to discuss our papers. Afterward, we regularly moved to the student bar called "Volkswirtschaft" to continue our discussions—now fueled by beer and the notorious local drink called "Apfelwein." Many colleagues from that time are still in academia; some even made international careers in IR.

Another key figure who inspired me was Lothar Brock. Lothar is a peace researcher by conviction, and due to his open-mindedness and curiosity, he keeps up with contemporary IR debates, although he retired many years ago. He still attends conferences and publishes frequently, and he showed me that teaching is not just another task in academic life. Lothar performs seminars with so much passion that he still attracts many, many students to take his courses. As a lecturer, he combines intellectuality and humanity in an unparalleled way, and he will always serve as the role model I will never reach. Lothar is an inspiration for attitude.

How did all this affect my style of teaching? To say it clearly: urging students to think critically is more important to me than teaching them to know where and why Waltz differs from Morgenthau—although they will learn about that (and a lot more) if and when they attend my classes. Gunther's postparadigmatic approach has particularly left traces in so far as my IR syllabi for undergraduate classes refer to classical theories but also include post-structuralist, gender studies, and feminist approaches, as well as texts on practice theory or the visual turn in IR. In M.A. courses on IR, for example, in one of my favorites titled "Media, Culture, and War," I go even far beyond that. Here, we leave the beaten track of IR, and I include texts from various disciplines such as sociology, communication, media, gaming, film, and theater studies to broaden the scope and intellectual horizon of my students. I hate the disciplinary narrow-mindedness anyway, and as interdisciplinary research has become the buzzword in IR, this course is my contribution for interdisciplinary teaching.

I started teaching at the University of Mainz, where I enrolled as a Ph.D. student, on an unpaid (!) teaching contract. I invested much time in course preparation and the supervision of term papers, and I wanted to do a good job. The feedback I got from students was overwhelming. I made the same mistake most do at the beginning: overpreparation and procrastination. Even years later some students told me, that it was the best course they had. Nice compliment, no question, but I neglected my Ph.D. project. Honestly, I think teaching preparation and seminars became the perfect excuse not to write my thesis. I could do that for a while, but procrastination is not a strategy I can recommend here. Despite all the freedoms we have, academia doesn't differ from other jobs in one respect: the time comes when all of us have to deliver. Once I had to present my progress in the colloquium of my supervisor, and it was a total mess. A more senior colleague later came to me and said, always remember: "you can't buy anything with the bright eyes of your students." I never forgot that lesson. Teaching is dangerous in the sense that it is quite easy to receive positive feedback from students and so you feel kindly rewarded for all your efforts. But if you forget the other obligations, there is a danger that all your love's labor is lost, because you'll be out of academia.

I had to learn it the hard way, but over time it becomes easier to find a balance. The funny thing is that since I have been teaching nine courses per academic year, I have published more papers and handed in more grant proposals than ever before. The difference is that as Senior Lecturer I am no longer working for a professor. For the first time, I am an independent researcher.

Teaching IR for Undergraduates: Catching, Keeping, and Educating Students

How do I organize my IR undergraduate teaching today? The most important precondition for teaching is student attendance and participation. If students don't come to class, not only love's labor but everything else is lost. At our political science department, student attendance in courses is voluntary. Students might sign up for courses and take exams, but it's up to them whether they come to class or stay away. I have no measures at my disposal to control for or even sanction nonattendance. So, the million dollar question is: how can we attract students, so they come to class every week (not to mention preparing the assigned reading)?

Being an idealist, I support abandoning the former rule of obligatory attendance because I believe in the freedom of choice. I assume students have chosen their subject due to intrinsic motivation and so I expect them to come to class anyway. I don't need attendance rules, and many students don't either. But reality shows me frequently, that not all student can handle academic freedom or just have a different approach to studying at a university. So, the first task in educating "professionals for democracy" is to catch and keep them in class because they don't have to come. Sometimes I think, that after so many years in teaching, I shouldn't care anymore whether they come or not. The truth is, I am still trying to get all students into the classroom who signed up for my courses by showing them that there is so much to learn they don't get from the articles and books (even, if they would read them). I have learned to accept that the vast majority of my students are neither interested in the "great debates" of IR in the twentieth century nor do they care about the difference between conventional and critical constructivism. The most important question for them is how to pass the exam, which is writing a theoretically informed research paper based on a case study—certainly not the easiest task. Regarding these term papers, I have three standard models: deductive, explanatory research designs for hypothesis testing; postpositivist research designs drawing on discourse analysis and other postmodern concepts; explorative studies to generate theories. My strategy to keep attendance rather high throughout the semester is simple. I explain and demonstrate in detail how students might use theories, concepts, and approaches, so they fit into the term paper models. Students are always keen on practical knowledge that is relevant for passing exams and if that's what it takes to keep them in class—they'll be served.

Sessions of my introductory courses on IR theories are mostly divided into two parts. The first part, I know it sounds old-school, is more of a teacher-centered learning situation. Based on the seminar reading, I address the audience, raising text-related questions, and encourage prepared students to engage in a discussion, and sometimes it works quite well. But basically, it is my turn to explain how theories work, how they are empirically applied or tested or what is at stake in all these debates and "turns" we have in IR. As a researcher I am part of it, I have the knowledge, and I try my best to share it with them.

Didactically, I am a traditionalist. I am using a mixture of PowerPoint presentation and Q&A elements, especially in the first part of a session. In the second part of each session, I invite all students (specifically those who came unprepared) to think about puzzles, problems, questions, and examples taken from contemporary global politics, so we can discuss the applicability of a theory or concept, its strengths, weaknesses, and how it relates to other theories concepts and how they might be used in term papers. We always have open and controversial discussions, where critical thinking is fostered and appreciated and, most important of all, every student can join in—given he or she was at least listening to the first part of the session.

The in-class discussion is sometimes very challenging but necessary, especially when it comes to highly controversial issues in international politics such as the use of military force, human rights protection, or the responsibility to protect. Students should not only learn how to apply theories to explain or better understand conflicts or foreign policy. For me even more important is that they learn to think about an issue from different perspectives. I am, therefore, keen on offering courses that cover a wide range of scientific approaches from hard-core positivism to post-structuralism and postmodern thinking in IR. In my understanding, courses on IR theories are perfect occasions to practice fundamental principles of democracy. Empowering students to critical thinking and self-reflection, forcing them to change perspectives, and approaching a problem from different theoretical angles are, for me, core tasks in IR teaching. Only in our class discussions can I encourage students to develop fact-based arguments instead of merely proclaiming, to criticize a position without insulting others, and to respect different opinions without getting upset.

Convincing students to come to class requires incentives for all of them and not only for those who have read the texts. Once I have them there, academic education begins, and any controversial group discussion is better than indifference, ignorance, and isolation.

Critics might object that my style of teaching fosters a race to the bottom as standards might be lowered to catch all instead of being elevated in favor of the well-prepared students. I have often thought about that because there have been times when I have become personally offended when students come to class unprepared, and once I threatened out of frustration that I would end the session immediately if this happened again. But this is not how it works. In times, when more and more students enroll to study programs and jobs such as mine depend on the number of students, a different teaching approach is required. Keeping the best students on the radar and providing encouraging structures does not necessarily mean abandoning all others.

CONCLUSION

Teaching is an essential part of our job, although the structures offer hardly any incentives for investing time into it. I am convinced that as an employee in the German public service, dependent on taxpayer money, it's more important than anything else. I consider teaching a privilege, and I try to make the best out of it—educating "professionals for democracy." But as a matter of fact, when we apply for professorships, publications and grants are often valued much higher than teaching experience.

Even worse are the structural constraints and shameful circumstances for academics in Germany, and we must do something about that. Theodor W. Adorno writes in his masterpiece Minima Moralia that "there is no right life in the wrong one," referring to the general inability to accommodate moral principles assumed to be right if the structural patterns that have brought them about are wrong (Adorno 1951: 41, my translation). Although I might have the best intentions in my teaching, I know that I am perpetuating a system that is wrong in many respects because I have adopted and comply with the functional "all in" logic of a hazardous game.

What can we do about that? We must change the patterns. This feudal system which fosters self-exploitation of young academics produces cohorts of highly qualified dropouts in their late 30s and unleashes a counterproductive competition among pre- and post-doc researchers must come to an end. At least post-doc researchers need independence, and I would prefer transparent incentive structures and target agreements regarding my teaching record, research output, and other duties, so my career would depend on performance and not on gambler's luck.

REFERENCES

Adorno, Theodor W. Minima Moralia. 1951. *Reflexionen aus dem beschädigten Leben*. Frankfurt am Main: Suhrkamp.
Weber, Max. 2014. *Wissenschaft als Beruf*. Berlin: Europäischer Literaturverlag, (1919).

CHAPTER 24

Journey to the Unknown: Survival, Re-awakening, Renewal, and Reformation

Brent J. Steele

Current institution: large state research I university
Typical classroom setting: seminars and large class lectures
Typical pedagogical approach: some lecture, but usually collaborative learning and readings discussions
Disciplinary identity: International Ethics, Foreign Policy, International Security, International Relations Theory

This chapter unfolds in four modes that correspond to my own journey in higher education. 'Survivalist mode' reviews my initiation as an instructor of International Relations, disclosing my own insecurity at that time over being 'capable' enough, both as an instructor *and* as a research-intensive junior scholar, to be hired into this vocation. '(Re-)awakening' engages a pivotal moment for me as a scholar and instructor following tenure. I learned the transformational potential that *administrative* positions can have in the lives of especially undergraduate scholars, and focus on a program that I had taught within, and then helped direct, at the University of Kansas (KU) during my last three years there (2010–2013).

B. J. Steele (✉)
University of Utah, Salt Lake City, UT, USA
e-mail: Brent.Steele@utah.edu

J. Frueh (ed.), *Pedagogical Journeys through World Politics*,
Political Pedagogies, https://doi.org/10.1007/978-3-030-20305-4_24

In my current role as the Director of Graduate Studies at the University of Utah, I have experienced a 'renewal' of sorts, discussed in the third section. Because of the positioning and status of our PhD program in the US political science academy, we've focused on making our graduate students exceptional instructors as well as scholars through pedagogical curriculum, experience, mentoring, and training. The fourth and concluding section looks forward to what a 'reformation' of PhD programs, centered around instructional and administrative training (first and foremost), might entail. Such a reformation would be in addition to the research purpose that current PhD programs in political science and international studies fulfill.

If there is one takeaway I hope to provide in my own journeys chapter it is this: we seem to have very little ability to confront, let alone transform, the seemingly hopeless neoliberal transmogrification of higher education and all it does and has done to our roles as scholars, instructors, and citizens. But there remains a great and often untapped potential in what many of us do. Yet we many times only realize this, as I have in writing this chapter, months and sometimes years after we've tapped into that potential. As my own journey is incomplete, I hope to appreciate those moments of pleasant surprise going forward, even if the anxieties that consume all four of my journey modes continue to be a part of my experiences in higher education going forward. That is where I conclude. For if there is one mode, then, that I want the rest of my journey as an instructor to enable, it is a mode of *appreciation*.

SURVIVALIST MODE

Two courses early in my career as an instructor made an impression on me. I taught my first college course right after I finished my MA at the University of Northern Iowa at the age of 23. I was not prepared intellectually, politically, or emotionally for this position, but I got lucky because it was the spring of 2000, the economy was humming, and US states (like Iowa in the late 1990s) were running budget surpluses.[1]

---

[1] The bursting of the tech bubble in late 2000, accelerated by the September 11 attacks in 2001, eliminated the surplus in Iowa and many states throughout the US, Todd Dorman, "Iowa's Surplus Slowly Fading," *Quad-City Times.* September 1, 2001. http://qctimes.com/news/iowa-s-surplus-slowly-fading/article_cbf89a6c-7652-5d50-8f0d-a80ec847f8ac.html

Smaller public universities were fiscally strong and this opened up an opportunity for me to teach my own course. I was lucky that my department chair, someone who became a good friend and research collaborator in the future (Rice and Steele 2001, 2004), hired me to do so. But being as overwhelmed as I was translated into a mixed set of experiences, largely stemming from two problems.

First, it was a course on 'Issues in Political Thought'. While I had taken a couple of courses in political philosophy and political theory in undergrad and graduate school, the areas of emphasis for my Master's thesis were International Relations and Comparative Politics (with a focus on the Middle East). The course topic was thus a bit afield of my own expertise. Second, and related, I tried both to project a seriousness and awkwardly to 'relate' to students in a way that simply didn't translate to generating respect.

I knew very early on that I was in over my head, perhaps even before the first class meeting, so how did I survive? There were two factors. First, I turned it into an 'Issues in *International* Political thought' course. International Political Theory in 2000 was not yet the field it is today, by which I mean it didn't yet have its own journals like the *Journal of International Political Theory*, *International Theory*, and or key outlining texts such as Tony Lang's (Lang 2015) study. But this pivot allowed me to draw from major thinkers (Hobbes, Locke, Marx, Machiavelli, and Thucydides) who were integral inspirations and resources for the IR 'paradigms' that, at the time, defined the field. And so I pivoted the course toward International Relations theory, somewhat indirectly, in order to have a bit more firm footing for my approach to the course. Second, I utilized a (then) recently published book by Michael Doyle (1997), *Ways of War and Peace: Realism, Liberalism and Socialism*, that provided me both an organizational method for the course and also a sort of 'instructor's textbook' to help translate the difficult primary sources (i.e. *Leviathan, Two Treatises, the Prince*, and *the History of the Peloponnesian War*, respectively) to an undergraduate audience and, to be honest, myself.[2]

My next independent course, International Ethics, was taught in the spring of 2004 while in my PhD program at the University of Iowa. I was in many ways much more prepared to teach it than the spring 2000 course.

---

[2] I met Professor Doyle in the fall of 2017, and told him how his book (which I brought with me and he signed for me), kept me afloat intellectually and structurally enough to teach the course.

I had been a teaching assistant (TA) for two courses the previous year, including winning an award for my work in the spring of 2003 as a TA for a US Foreign Policy course. Further, I had attended my first ISA meeting in 2003 in Portland, where I listened intently to a number of panels sponsored by the International Ethics section. I began developing my own course syllabus on the topic, and proposed it to my department to teach as a new course not yet offered to undergrads at the University of Iowa. I was more well-read and deeply connected to the topic I was teaching. Further, a number of students who I had previously advised as a TA took the course that spring.

It was indeed a better course experience than the first one, however there were still some problems. I found a format that worked early on—small group discussions for part of each meeting that unfolded into larger class discussions. But I relied on that too much, and the students by the end found my teaching approach stale. Further, while I was more prepared for the topic than my first course, I probably knew *too* much, and at a higher level, than I needed. I assigned my students too much and too difficult reading as a result. I recognized both these issues early on, but didn't change my approach or adjust the readings mid-semester for two reasons. First, I thought any changes would reek of weakness, and that students would transfer the observation that if I was willing to adjust readings then I was probably willing to adjust other things, like expectations for their work, or negotiate about their grades. Second, I was in the middle of my dissertation as well as preparing my portfolio for the upcoming year on the market, and adjustments required time I feared I could not sacrifice.

It's probably the second of these that was most important for the remaining years of my survivalist mode of teaching. Even as an ABD student, I was already being told what would define my approach to teaching for the first few years of a tenure-track position: 'Prioritize research first. If something has to give, it's your teaching. You won't be evaluated by employers, and/or your tenure committees, by how you teach'. Since I was targeting research universities and positions, I tried to focus more on publishing, attending conferences, shaping my research statement and CV. And yet, I did care about that spring 2004 course, and a few of the students seemed to enjoy it, although a number gave it less than stellar evaluations due to my noted mistakes. I nevertheless enjoyed the class and especially its urgency at the time. It was a presidential election year, I was writing a dissertation that intersected with the course's content, and, furthermore, the issues taught in the course were not abstract, but quite immediate. The ongoing war in Iraq, for instance, was in arguably its most important inflection point that spring.[3]

But survivalist mode isn't the worst mode to be in as a junior scholar. It 'teaches' you how to balance the different commitments we have in this vocation, perhaps through trial and error. Indeed, even though I taught my first few courses at the University of Kansas from 2005 onward with teaching taking a bit of a backseat to my research, I found that I could cautiously, experimentally, figure out how to improve my approach to teaching while still doing the main things I needed to do to have a chance at tenure and promotion (namely, publish, publish, publish). In fact, a non-zero-sum game emerged, for the more I focused on publishing, the sharper and more focused I found myself in the classroom setting as well. The mid-2000s were a turbulent time in international politics and especially for one teaching US foreign policy courses. Abstract theoretical texts and historical studies (I was really into Foucault, Fromm, Niebuhr, and Nietzsche back then), were somewhat therapeutic for me and became important influences not only for my research but also for conditioning me as an instructor. One skill I acquired (in fits and starts, of course), even in survivalist mode, was the ability to take abstract and complex philosophical ideas about politics, human nature, and violence, and translate those through the more tangible texts and discussions that shaped my undergraduate courses.

Now I just had to figure out how to have fun in the classroom again.

(Re-)Awakening

I recognize the problem with chronological narration. While it provides a decent way to contextualize our experiences and organize those for a reader or audience, it also doesn't really properly index how and why certain events unfolded in the manner that they did. Throughout most of the 2000s, I was in survivalist mode. But there were two experiences I had in the late 2000s that started to shift my perspective on teaching. First, in a

---

[3] That spring saw four key moments in 'Operation Iraqi Freedom': (1) the siege and then first battle of Fallujah which followed the Fallujah bridge incident (2) the emergence of the Mahdi army and the Shia resistance behind especially Cleric Moqtada al-Sadr, (3) the more pronounced presence of AQI, or Al Qaeda in Iraq, a forerunner to what would become known as the 'Islamic State' or ISIS, headed then by Abu Musab al-Zarqawi, and, perhaps most markedly, (4) the revelation of the Abu Ghraib torture photos on 60 minutes II and in a *New Yorker* (Hersh 2004) article.

series of courses from 2006 to 2009, I had a cohort of undergraduate students who kept taking my classes, bringing out all kinds of wonderful insights regarding the readings and topics, and who showed a genuine interest in ideas for their own sake. The students and the ideas they put forth in discussions had a wonderful woodwork effect upon their fellow students, as well as their instructor. Second, in the fall of 2009, the day after my department voted to give me tenure and promote me to Associate Professor, I gave what felt to me to be one of the best and most enthusiastic lectures that I had ever presented to my undergraduates taking the course I had developed back at Iowa—International Ethics. If I recall correctly, the lecture was on 'Just War and non-state actors'. The topic overlapped quite markedly with a book that Eric Heinze and I (Heinze and Steele 2009) had edited and published that same year, thus demonstrating the mutually enriching ways in which our research and teaching can intersect. That class was a particularly talented one. Many of the students went on to graduate programs the following year. One undergrad told me after my lecture that I seemed particularly motivated that day. I couldn't explain why this was the case at the time. But I now know that one of the benefits of tenure in higher education is not what it necessarily does for a research program, but rather, how it liberates instructors in the classroom. I felt *free* to engage my students, or perhaps, much freer than I had been before.[4]

In 2010 I agreed to both recruit students for, and then teach the first course in, KU's 'Global Scholars' program. Competition to get into this program is intense—all student files were reviewed before some students get invited for interviews, concluding in a final selection process where 15 students were ultimately selected. Selected scholars were then matched with faculty mentors, required to enroll in a spring semester (of their

---

[4] I don't wish to contextualize this too much, but the 2000s were a somewhat sensitive time to try and have open discussions about international politics in classrooms (Eakin 2001), especially in 'Red' states like Kansas where I was during this time. This was especially so after 9/11, as evidenced by a flurry of watchdog groups as well as the work of the 'American Council of Trustees and Alumni' (ACTA), who produced a report in November of 2001 titled 'Defending Civilization: How Our Universities Are Failing America and What Can Be Done About It' (ACTA 2001). Although a bit overblown in how they were characterized in Mearsheimer and Walt's infamous 'Israel Lobby' essay (2006), the 2000s included a number of pro-Israel interest groups who constructed 'watch' lists of professors for being anti-Israel. My only point was that tenure, an important milestone in a research professor's career, also had, for me, opened up more productive classroom discussions as an instructor as well.

sophomore year) seminar on an interdisciplinary topic, and finally had to present a research project at a symposium their senior year.

The topic of the sophomore seminar course I taught in the spring of 2011—'Truth in a Global Society'—was an interdisciplinary and intensely challenging one that I think stimulated, and even at times frustrated, this immensely talented group of undergraduates. The readings of the course were incredibly difficult and complex, with assigned works from Hannah Arendt, Michel Foucault, Ian Hacking, George Orwell, Richard Rorty, Allan Bloom, and many other philosophers and theorists. The students were required not only to read these works, but interpret them, engage them in a close-reading and discuss their own interpretations with the rest of the class. I also brought in KU faculty to lead discussions stemming from their own research on truth, and from a variety of disciplines (Britton 2010; Tell 2008, 2010). It was an incredibly difficult course, and yet the students all rose to the challenge, which was somewhat the opposite of the experience I had in the first course I taught a decade prior. In this case, I thought I once again had aimed too high with expectations, which would be met with student burnout or cynicism. It wasn't. In fact, the undergraduate scholars brought out aspects from the readings that I had never noticed before.

The program also provided $1000 of support for study abroad opportunities for each scholar, and the students went off in their subsequent years to study abroad programs throughout the world. I took over as Director of the Global Scholars program that summer (2011), so I was able to stay in contact with this cohort of scholars throughout the rest of their undergraduate years at KU. Right before I left KU in 2013, I helped organize the first Global Scholars research symposium, a culmination of the program for that first cohort of Scholars I had taught in the spring of 2011. They were finishing their undergraduate careers at KU, ready to go off to even bigger things in their lives. I was finishing my career at KU as well, ready to move on to a more research-intensive position at the University of Utah. In many ways, the symposium was a celebration.

As it should have been. The students presented their research projects, which in most cases were carried out during their study abroad programs, to a standing-room only audience that included their faculty mentors, their friends, and their families. Some were first-generation college students. Several were going off to Ivy League grad programs. A couple would head off to start their own companies. At one point during the closing roundtable Q and A session, a father of one of the scholars raised his hand, and asked them: 'Do you know how proud your parents are of each and every one of you?'

I call this period a re-awakening for several reasons. First, it demonstrated to me the two-way street of a classroom and a university—how we are impacted by students as much as they are impacted by us. Their interpretations, voices, concerns, and enjoyment regarding the materials we put in front of them are not only forces that are there to be 'evaluated'. They should be internalized, grappled with, and used to change our own perspectives on the subject. Second, it recalled the importance of a 'cohort effect' that one experiences in any social setting but most especially in college. It is an effect that instructors need to appreciate and open themselves up to being influenced by as well. Students are only in a university for a short time in their lives. It may not seem that way to them when they are going through their courses. It may not even seem that way to us when we have to work through a semester or two with a particularly difficult set of students. But college 'life' is but a short blip in the overall lifespan of a person. And yet, it has a profound impact on all of them. We should take advantage, as much as we can, of that short time we have with them, each of them, each cohort of them, that cross our paths.

Third, it brought home the importance of not only a classroom setting, but the impact of *interdisciplinary programs* upon a wider group of individuals. 'Inter-', 'Multi-', and 'trans-disciplinary' are all buzzwords that look good in grant applications and make higher ed administrators and consultants tingle with excitement. But behind all the buzz, there nevertheless is something substantively important about (especially) interdisciplinarity—beginning with its prefix, the etymology of which proves illustrative.[5] My sense, having been through a number of initiatives seeking out interdisciplinary research and program-building, is that the key obstacle for it is *not*, as we've long suspected, the sequestering of different disciplines and departments into their own 'silos'. Or, at least, not only that. Rather, it's a lack of *time* that would otherwise enable and incentivize interdisciplinary thinking and collaboration. More precisely, what made the Global Scholars version of interdisciplinarity successful was that it placed me, and the scholars, into a common space of a classroom, together. It liberated us to think outside of our own disciplinary routines and habits—without there necessarily being some firm set of 'outcomes' that we

---

[5] 'between', 'among', 'in the midst of', 'mutually', 'reciprocally', 'together', 'during. Dictionary.com' http://www.dictionary.com/browse/inter-

had to work toward. Most importantly, in a world that has become increasingly complex, chaotic, and unpredictable (or, at least, feels that way), *inter*disciplinarity is not only preferred, but required.

RENEWAL

At the University of Utah, I took over as the Director of Graduate Studies in the fall of 2014. I found out after accepting the position that it came with an agreement to also teach a one-credit hour course, titled 'Teaching Political Science'. The course is required of all funded PhD students (although the class is open to, and often enrolls, other students as well). While I at first approached the course as just another requirement of the position, I soon realized that it may be the most important work I do in my role as an administrator.

I reworked the course so that instead of meeting for an hour once a week (usually Friday mornings, when the PhD students did not have their own classes to attend or lead), we met once a month for 3 hours—making it more of a typical seminar. The course involves the students constructing a syllabus for a course that they plan to teach at some point in their careers as instructors. Along with building and refining a syllabus, students construct sample assignments and then do classroom observations and analyses of professors in our department. Across these components, the course includes three goals or purposes.

First and foremost, the class deals with issues that arise not only in a semester but in a career of teaching. These include assignment grading (rubrics, metrics, expectations), online teaching, problematic situations (including 'problem students'), and how to prepare undergraduate students for the post-college employment. Second, the course helps our emerging instructors get socialized into the broader landscape of higher education, a socialization that I never really had in my graduate program and one that I fear is more and more necessary in the coming years. While we talk about issues within the classroom, we also focus on broader issues. These include course evaluations and the gender biases that come through in those, employer/departmental expectations for service, preparing for tenure at a teaching institution, pursuing grants, interacting with the broader communities where their college or university is placed, and the likelihood that they will be approached to serve as administrators in those institutions at some point and how that dovetails (or not) with their own vocational goals and purposes.

A third purpose, one that seems to emerge informally even if it's not an explicit one, is for blowing off steam. This is usually the first semester in a PhD program for the enrolled students—and while the primary topic for each of the five meetings is pedagogically focused, they are also coming to grips with the workload and time management issues (work as a teaching assistant versus work as a graduate student, combined with familial and outside organizational commitments), that everyone faces as a PhD student. It also provides me a good opportunity, five times at least in their first semester in our program, to check in with them and see how they are doing handling all these expectations as well as managing the stress that it entails.

The course is, basically, a semester-long teaching workshop for junior scholars. But it is also a professionalization experience for them regarding how to better 'survive' (and here we are led back to my first mode) the world of higher education. And yet this environment that I'm teaching about is completely different than the one I entered almost 20 years ago. As a result, and as much as I draw on my own experiences as an instructor, scholar, administrator, not to mention as a parent who has imperfectly balanced all of this with those responsibilities, I suspect that the academy into which these new instructors will be employed presents a whole new set of challenges, and questions, for which I have no answers. Such challenges that have been brought up the past two times I have taught the course, and for which I have no answers, include:

- How should instructors handle the contemporary political environment, with particularly strong cross-streams regarding identity politics, re-emergent populisms and nationalism, corporatized media environments (including 'viral' social media platforms) making classroom discussions fraught with peril and dangers?
- How should instructors handle the above issues when tenure is becoming less and less secure and widespread?
- How should instructors handle all of the above, including class discussions on sensitive political topics, when an increasing number of states are not only allowing, but mandating, open and concealed-carry among students?
- Will anything reverse the post-global financial crisis trends where especially public universities and colleges have been subject to austerity-measures, tuition hikes, and cultural animosity by 'conservative' legislatures over education as a good in and of itself?

This was a 'renewal' in the sense that I have found a way to combine two seemingly 'secondary' practices of our vocation to research—teaching and administration—and discovered that training teachers was really a more important endeavor toward 'changing the world' than anything I could do in my research. As a result of my experiences during this renewal, it had occurred to me that something broader and more transformative might emerge. How might programs fulfill, through their PhD training, a *pedagogical* function that is otherwise secondary to the research-oriented purpose of such programs?

REFORMATION

My work as a director of graduate studies is ending. I will return to teach my own courses and focus more directly on my own research, purposes that I had imagined I would be pursuing when I originally accepted my position five years ago. And yet, in my capacity as a director of graduate studies in a program that places its Ph.D.'s in mainly teaching and/or administrative positions, I have wondered what a reorientation of vocational and institutional purpose would mean if our program (and perhaps others) did more to prepare our graduate students for these careers? What more could be done than just a one-credit-hour course in the first semester of a PhD program can provide? How might we reconfigure our PhD course and curriculum requirements so that we are creating not only effective, but elite and well-rounded instructors who also have the capacity to demonstrate scholarly and administrative acumen?

Such a reformation is not without its challenges and even if it worked, it would take that most rare resource nowadays, time. That said, four steps may prove useful to this end. First, instructors of graduate seminars could require a teaching component of their substantive courses. As a component of their seminars, graduate students might provide a lesson plan, a lecture, or even a draft syllabus, related to an undergraduate version of the course they are taking at the graduate level. They might, further, provide a draft teaching philosophy that reflects the student's experiences in the course and in their broader program. Second, but only if programs of study were (made to be) flexible enough to allow this, political science and international studies Ph.D. programs could require graduate students to take a course or two (or more?), and perhaps even a practicum, through their universities' schools or colleges of education, focused on teaching and/or higher education administration.

Third, the expectations for a dissertation could be expanded to include reflective and/or practice-based case studies of higher education teaching and administration—whether this was based on the PhD-candidate's first-hand experience over the course of several semesters performing these duties themselves, or as a set of field research experiences, or in a 'participant-observer' model, doing both. Such dissertations would still be focused on issues pertinent to the discipline of the PhD-candidate—in my case, International Relations. But they would pitch those issues (at least in one dissertation chapter), as ones that were road-tested or discussed within classroom and/or administrative settings. The purpose here would be to not only produce knowledge but also to see how it is (or is not) *executed* in the university environment. It would involve going into classrooms and observing knowledge as it unfolds as *an action* or, more precisely, *as an interaction*. Some of the questions I pose above—for which I have no answer—that nevertheless seem urgent for the PhD students I teach in the pedagogy course, could be the basis for some fascinating case-study intensive dissertations.

Fourth, and owing to the broader 'market-focused' and corporatist nature of higher education, such a reformation would entail a politics of higher education aesthetics—namely, practices centered around 'branding' such a Ph.D. program as a teaching and administratively focused one, distinguishing it from the conventional, traditional research-focused Ph.D. program. Would such a program prove attractive to would-be employers? I'm not sure. I suspect many small colleges will still pine for those shiny Ivy League PhD's, even if the latter when hired are unlikely to remain in such positions for very long. And internally, it will face a number of hurdles stemming from not only the attachments established academics have to institutional routines and the status quo, but also from a firm conviction regarding what a Ph.D., as an intellectual accomplishment, should reflect. But it might work, and it would be radically different than the status quo, homogenous approach to Ph.D. training that may be facing a critical juncture.

Conclusion

If I have one regret so far as an instructor that stands out more than most, it is that I failed to fully appreciate some of the more important, enjoyable, and transformative moments that emerged in all of the modes, *as they were happening*. I recognize now why that was. As a research-focused scholar—

or someone who wanted to act the part—as soon as a teaching or administrative-related accomplishment happened, I checked my own enthusiasm. I considered those moments 'extras' compared to the research accomplishments I needed to pile up. Of course, I now realize that no matter how much research I have produced, no matter how sound it may have been and appears to be, I am *never* going to impact the world, nor will it impact me, in as comprehensive a way as I have as an instructor. I now realize that those moments—from the ones I mention above to so many others that I continue to frequently recall and therefore rediscover—were ones where that impact was real, poignant, transformative, and hopeful.

Some of them, in hindsight, were predictable. Others were the outcome of surprise and contingency. But all were the result of something that I imagine my fellow constructivist scholars would appreciate—a combination of *structures* that shaped those moments (like the structure of the Global Scholars program), and the agency and *agents* that enacted and enabled them (like that of the scholars themselves). So the importance of sketching out the concluding 'reformation' proposal above remains its structural potential. Such potential would hopefully enable the surprise, creativity, and wonder that we often don't, but could more often, appreciate in our classrooms and institutions, *as they are happening*.

One possible drawback to such a proposal is that it could reinforce the hierarchical differences already in place between 'research' versus 'teaching'-focused academics. Many of us in academia see this hierarchy at work in a number of professional settings and practices, not least of which at conferences. It happens when attendees scan each other's nametags for institutional affiliations, but I've also seen it on display in the somewhat defensive manner in which some participants on roundtables discuss their experiences at teaching institutions, as if they should apologize for not pursuing a research-focused career.

However, we reorient our approach to not only teaching but mentoring future teachers, we need to push back against this hierarchical thinking. If we are looking to not only study the world but impact it as well, the largest number of journeys we've put into motion have been the ones we've helped set our students on via our courses and mentoring. A young adult's years in college are highly impactful, and our job is to prepare them to engage that world—make a place for themselves within it, and perhaps even transform it in their own, circumscribed capacities throughout their lives. We are a huge part of that process. So we may as well own up to it and enjoy that role ourselves.

REFERENCES

American Council of Trustees and Alumni. 2001. *Defending Civilization: How Our Universities Are Failing American and What Can Be Done About it.* http://2004.georgewbush.org/news/traitor_academics.pdf

Britton, Hannah. 2010. *Women in the South African Parliament: From Resistance to Governance.* Champaign: University of Illinois Press.

Dictionary.com. Inter-. http://www.dictionary.com/browse/inter-

Doyle, Michael. 1997. *Ways of War and Peace: Realism, Liberalism and Socialism.* New York: Norton.

Eakin, Emily. 2001. On the Lookout for Patriotic Incorrectness. *New York Times,* November 24. https://www.nytimes.com/2001/11/24/arts/on-the-look-out-for-patriotic-incorrectness.html

Heinze, Eric, and Brent J. Steele, eds. 2009. *Ethics, Authority, and War: Non-State Actors and the Just War Tradition.* 1st ed. New York: Palgrave Macmillan.

Hersh, Sy. 2004. Torture at Abu Ghraib American Soldiers Brutalized Iraqi Detainees. How Far Up Does the Blame Go? *New Yorker,* May 10. https://www.newyorker.com/magazine/2004/05/10/torture-at-abu-ghraib

Lang, Anthony F. 2015. *International Political Theory: An Introduction.* London/New York: Palgrave/Macmillan Education.

Mearsheimer, John J., and Stephen M. Walt. 2006. The Israel Lobby and U.S. Foreign Policy. *Middle East Policy* 13 (3): 29–87. https://doi.org/10.1111/j.1475-4967.2006.00260.x.

Rice, Tom W., and Brent Steele. 2001. White Ethnic Diversity and Community Attachment in Small Iowa Towns. *Social Science Quarterly* 82 (2): 397–407. https://doi.org/10.1111/0038-4941.00031.

Rice, Tom W., and Brent J. Steele. 2004. Subjective Well-Being and Culture Across Time and Space. *Journal of Cross-Cultural Psychology* 35 (6): 633–647. https://doi.org/10.1177/0022022104270107.

Tell, Dave. 2008. The 'Shocking Story' of Emmett Till and the Politics of Public Confession. *Quarterly Journal of Speech* 94 (2): 156–178. https://doi.org/10.1080/00335630801975426.

———. 2010. Rhetoric and Power: An Inquiry into Foucault's Critique of Confession. *Philosophy and Rhetoric* 43 (2): 95–117. https://doi.org/10.1353/par.0.0056.

Todd Dorman. 2001. Iowa's Surplus Slowly Fading. *Quad-City Times,* September 1. http://qctimes.com/news/iowa-s-surplus-slowly-fading/article_cbf89a6c-7652-5d50-8f0d-a80ec847f8ac.html

INDEX[1]

---

[1] Note: Page numbers followed by 'n' refer to notes.

© The Author(s) 2020   293
J. Frueh (ed.), *Pedagogical Journeys through World Politics,*
Political Pedagogies, https://doi.org/10.1007/978-3-030-20305-4

Printed by Printforce, United Kingdom